(handwritten inscription across top left) Jane, Thanks for your Support!

ARI'EL RISING
"EMPOWERED WOMEN IN THE 21ST CENTURY"

S. Denice Newton

Foreword by: Thandi Lujabe Rankoe

Pink Kiss Publishing Company
Gautier, Mississippi

Cover art by: Stephanie Tkach

Cover art and design by: CreationbyDonna.com

Interior design and typesetting by: InteriorBookDesigns.com

ISBN 978-0-9904442-3-7

Library of Congress Control Number: 2014913664

Published by:

Pink Kiss Publishing Company

P.O. Box 744

Gautier, Mississippi 39553

(228) 366-6829

www.pinkkisspublishing.com

Dr. Maya Angelou

Sunrise: April 4, 1928 Sunset: May 28, 2014

In loving memory of the lioness that roared on behalf of humanity through the written word, Dr. Maya Angelou. Thank you for taking up causes beyond your own and making a lasting impact on men, women, boys, and girls all over the world. You leave a legacy that although impossible to imitate, will forever remain a standard of living by which many will strive to achieve. You will be painfully missed, but God saw that your body was growing tired and your eyes were beginning to dim. You've finished your course and flown away into paradise. Rest peacefully, Mother Lioness, we'll see you in the morning…

-S. Denice Newton

Dedication

I dedicate this labor of love to women past, present, and future, because without us, there would be no world to impact. A special dedication to every strong, determined, and courageous woman in my life that taught me the power of love, prayer, and faith.

In Memoriam

I honor the memories of the following "lionesses" that impacted my life and left a legacy of love, kindness, and encouragement:

Anniebell Scarbrough, who counseled and mentored me during some of the most troubling days of my life.
Florence Segers Fuller, who taught me many valuable life lessons
Dorothy Shilo, whose smile was as warm as the noonday sun
Katrina (Kay) Atkinson, my very own Earth Angel.

I also honor the memory of a few "lions" that stood in support of my ministry and work…

Herman L. Brown, my stepfather and amazing singer
Edison Payne: For his powerful words of encouragement
Dr. Chirevo Victor Kwenda: For the phenomenal conversations and teachings when I visited the beautiful country of Zimbabwe.

Acknowledgments

I owe a debt of gratitude to the following people for believing in me and helping put me on the path of destiny…

My mother Dorothy and sisters Deanna, Karen, and Lillie, my two children, Tierra and Torey, my pastor, Dr. Dameion and wife, Lady Melessha Royal, Skyler and Cecily Jett, Thaddeus Howze, Reggie Bullock, Marcedes Fuller, Robert X. Golphin, Apostles Calvin and Judy Ellison, Jacque Howard, Sheila Fowler-Davis, and everyone that supported and prayed for me. I honestly love you all for your unselfish acts of kindness!

Rise, Ari'el Rise!

Looking into the mirror, a lioness she sees
A symbol of hope and courage, grace and bravery
She strives for perfection daily, walking strongly in her call
Making a difference in the world, helping others stand up tall
She is woman, she has a roar, watch Ari'el rise!

Ari'el is courageous, secure in her own skin
Wrapped in grace and confidence, her talents without end
She doesn't need a clique, a gang, a group, or crew
She follows after good things, begin each day anew
She is woman, she has a roar, watch Ari'el rise!

Looks are important, but Ari'el they don't define
She's more than skin and hair, she has a made up mind
Impacting the lives of others, with passion and much drive
She's focused and determined, beyond the nine to five
She is woman, she has a roar, watch Ari'el Rise!

Her roar is very powerful, a call to humanity
That help is available, to set the bonded free
She unites where there is division, turns chaos into peace
With love, compassion, and kindness, doubts and fears will cease
She is woman, she has a roar, watch Ari'el Rise!

©2014 S. Denice Newton

Contents

From the desk of Melessha Royal, First Lady of Contending For The Faith Church Ministries

So many people waste their lives trapped in vicious cycles of shame, depression, sadness, despair, hopelessness, and even mediocrity. However, it is not the will of God for us to live defeated lives, but to live "abundant lives" overflowing with joy, peace, and contentment (John 10:10). Also, God has not called us to mediocrity, but to do great works that will impact the world (John 14:12). So don't squander your lives in pitiable conditions. You only have one life to live. Live it to the fullest! Get up, and walk in your God-given destiny! Make your mark on the world! Fulfill your purpose in life, and enjoy every minute of it! This is the will of God concerning you (1 Thessalonians 5:16-18)! God bless…

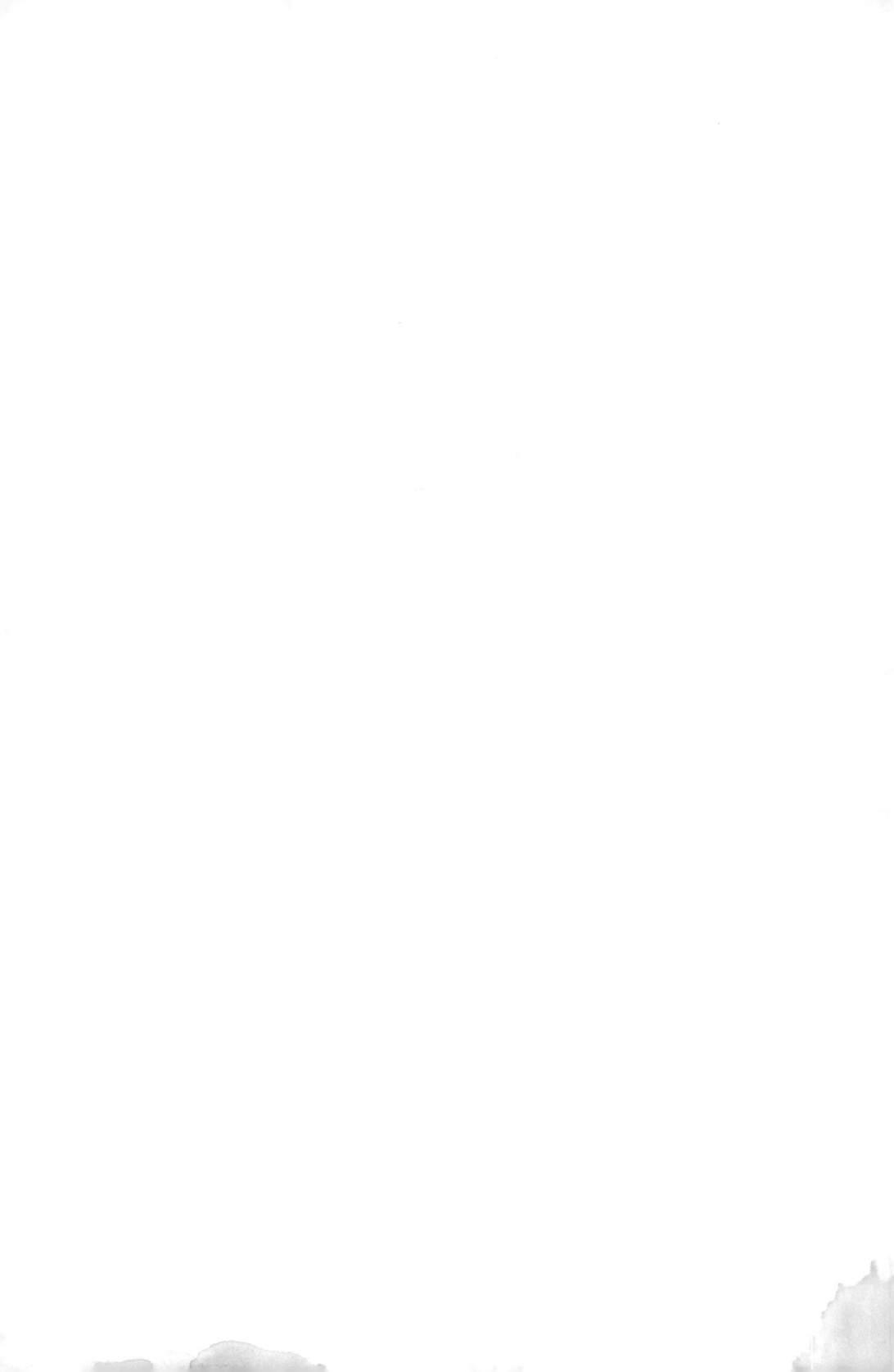

Love and gratitude for the "Son of Thunder" and the Elect Lady...

I'd like to dedicate this page to my pastor, Dameion L. Royal and his wife, Lady Melessha Royal. I thank them both for the encouragement, support, and prayers as I go about the Father's business. Lady Melessha, I truly thank you for the encouraging words. You never cease to make me feel empowered and inspired when we speak. As leader of our church women's ministry, you have certainly helped some of our ladies and girls not only recognize their calling, but walk powerfully in it. Your smile and warmth is very refreshing.

Pastor Dameion, I am so proud to have you as a spiritual leader. In this day of greed, corruption, and deception, particularly as it pertains to church leadership, it is comforting to have you at the helm of Contending for the Faith Church ministries. You teach your congregation to be authentic—to be real followers of Christ, live holy, and discern the times. Your testimony alone is a giant-killer! The word of God that you preach weekly is delivered with tremendous power and authority. You are the perfect example of a church leader and carry out the will of God Almighty without compromise. I'm learning to endure and stay in the fight! Thank you for all that you've done for me and spoken into my life. I see the promises of God manifesting each and every day, which gives me the strength to forge ahead. My trials have been many and my tribulations great. But the God of creation has made me the 'Super Conqueror" that compels me to shout "Hupernikao!" I pray that God allows you both to have a long, blessed life. I love you much!
~S. Denice Newton
Founder, Ari'el Rising Network

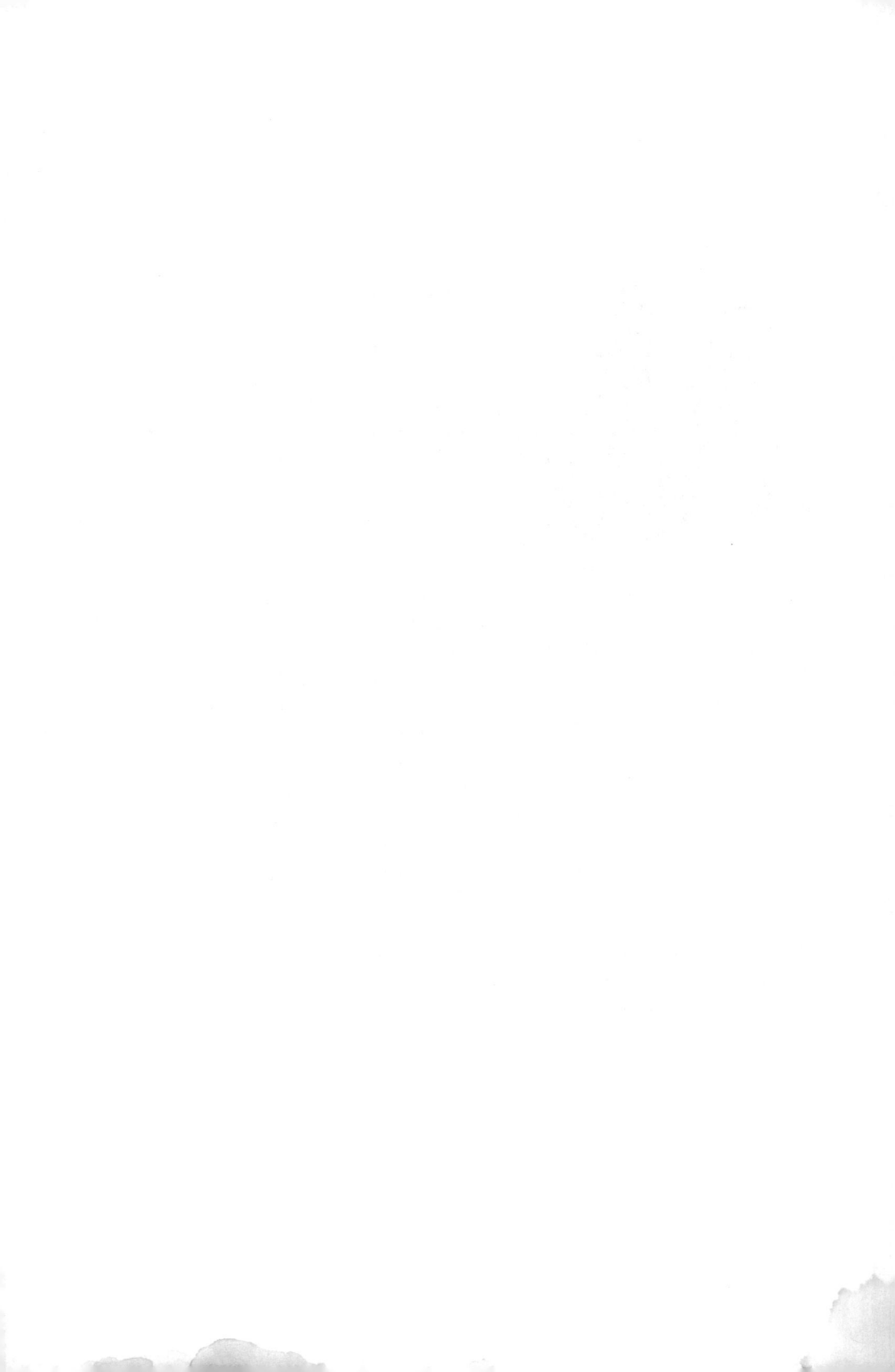

FOREWORD

~

I am a lioness. I was born on the 11th of August 1936. My parents named me Noluthando (meaning the one who is loved), but everyone calls me Thandi. Parents think hard before they give you a name and you are expected to keep to those values at school as you grow up and as an adult. One of my strongest memories of childhood was of a very loving father and a hard working mum who did the best she could to raise four children. I have always known if you want a better life or a good life you must work hard for it and it will pay off. I was pivotal in the struggle against apartheid. I left my parents when I was twenty-five years old and was away from my country and my family for thirty-three years of my life. I have no regret. My trials and tribulations, my separation from my loved ones, and my coming together with people have impacted and shaped my career.

Tanzania

My first visit to Tanzania was in 1961 as a freedom fighter. In 1995 I went back, having been elected as the first South African Ambassador by the newly elected government. I was the first woman to open a new embassy for South Africa in Tanzania. This was not easy, but I had to talk to myself and I told myself that I was not going to be a failure. When a woman decides or makes up her mind, she does well, even under difficult circumstances. Tanzania took care of all the liberation movements in Southern Africa until they were all free. We shared camps in Kongwa with FRELIMO, MPLA, ZAPU and SWAPO. Tanzania gave us land in Morogoro, Mazimbu where the ANC built houses, hospitals, farms, schools from kindergarten, theatres, etc. This is how we wanted the new South Africa to look. The freedom charter that was adopted at Kliptown on June 26, 1955, at the Congress of the People says: the doors of learning and of culture shall be opened, the land shall be shared among those who work it, all shall be equal before the law, and there shall be work and security.

At the time of my appointment there was no South African embassy, and so I had to start from scratch. I was very upset when I was appointed to Tanzania because my colleagues were sent back to countries where they were chief representatives. However, I think that was the best thing that ever happened to me, because as hard as it was, I gained a lot of experience, and today, diplomacy is in my blood.

Botswana

In 1961 I passed through Botswana en route to Tanzania. We already had an underground route that would take us via Francistown to Zambia helped by Kaunda's party (UNIP) and finally to Tanzania. I went back to Botswana in 1979 to do ANC work. Unfortunately, on 14 June 1985, we were raided by the South African Defence Force and thirteen comrades were slaughtered in cold blood. After burying the comrades, I had to leave Botswana for Zimbabwe. In September 1999, I was assigned to Botswana as the South African High Commissioner. Fortunately for me, I had the opportunity of living in Botswana before my appointment, and I was extremely happy to be appointed to a country where I knew the people, from whom I had learned many things which I would not have acquired if I had not lived in Botswana. I am very grateful, and thank the government and people in general for their warmth and acceptance. On the other hand, coming to Botswana was very emotional for me because it brought back memories of the 14 June 1985 raid. For me to settle down, I felt that a Reconciliation Day was very important in order to heal the wounds of that fatal day, to talk about what happened so that we could put it all behind us and get on with our lives.

A second reconciliation day was held in Francistown on 7 December 2001. This is where the refugees were confined, and the people of Francistown supported our struggle to the fullest. Reverend Canon Trevor Mwamba officiated (as he then was, and is now Bishop of Canterbury) at the Reconciliation Day in Francistown. His opening prayer was; "God of all nations, we pray for all the peoples of the world; for those who are consumed in mutual hatred and bitterness; for those who make war on their neighbours; for those who tyrannously oppress; for those who groan under cruelty and subjection."

Mozambique

In 2002, President Mbeki thought it good to post me to Mozambique as the South African High Commissioner. My perception of Mozambique was that of a comrade in the struggle. Coming to Mozambique brought back memories of our fallen freedom fighters, and especially the ones who were killed by the apartheid forces here in Mozambique. I, therefore, decided that the memory of these fallen heroes and heroines should not be forgotten. It is my opinion that the younger generation, those ones that were born free after 1994, should not take this freedom for granted. They should know that many people paid with their lives for this precious freedom that we now enjoy.

Norway

I arrived in Norway on October 2, 1988, to a warm reception by the Norwegian anti-apartheid group. Norway and her people were very enthusiastic supporters of our liberation movement. My party received enormous support in cash and in kind from the government, as well as from numerous Norwegian anti-apartheid associations. The government and the people of South Africa continue to enjoy good relations.

Egypt

I arrived in Cairo towards the end of 1967. The ANC offices were situated in a place called the African Association in Ahmed Hismat Street in Zamalek, a building donated by the Egyptian government among its numerous expressions of support for all African liberation movements. This was a most convenient location because it enabled all African political activists to converge in one place, and all of us spoke with one voice: telling our oppressive governments that it was time to relinquish power and restore democratic governance. My life and career was not limited to the countries that I have written about, but further included the countries of Zimbabwe, Zambia and Nigeria. My experience of these countries showed them to be true comrades in our struggle and from whom we received the utmost support.

The Strength of Women

I remember that on the 9th of August 1956 the women of South Africa marched to Union Buildings in Pretoria in protest against the Pass Laws. They came from all over South Africa in buses and others with children on their backs. They did not even tell their husbands (women can keep a secret). They do well even in war situations. That day they composed a song "Wathinta bafazi wathindi mbokodo uzakufa" meaning "you touch the women you have struck a rock you will be crushed." Even today, August 9th is celebrated all over South Africa.

I am a retired diplomat. To be a diplomat requires Integrity, Passion, Patriotism and Humility. You are representing the President of your country, and therefore, you need to not just follow the rules and regulations of your own state, but that of the nation you are posted to, and you need to know how to behave accordingly. I was fortunate to have had the experience of being part of a government in exile and received training in international relations in some of the best institutions around the world. I have published a few books about my experiences. I think this is important so we don't forget where we came from, especially the younger generation. All that is left now, aside from the joy I take in my daily life, is to celebrate the first female South African President. I do not know when—it may be that such a woman is already in the making. I have been blessed with one daughter, Matsheliso Lujabe, and a grandson, Jemelle Vuyani Chitepo, and hope they will now pick up the pieces and continue to write. Forward with the women!

I will end this with a foreword written by the late former President Nelson Mandela about my first publication "A dream fulfilled". He writes: "As we celebrate 50 years of the Freedom Charter, 50 years since the historic march by women on Pretoria, not forgetting the 30 years since the shameful massacre of unarmed school children in 1976, it is fitting that we remember and acknowledge the formations and individuals that made all of this possible. One of these is, of course, Thandi Lujabe- Rankoe, the subject of this fine and authoritative autobiography, which outlines for us, in sometimes uncompromising terms, the journey taken by herself – and by extension a whole swathe of humanity – from the cauldron of apartheid, through various postings in exile to a triumphant though demanding return to the native land."

—Thandi Lujabe Rankoe

INTRODUCTION

Women have been impacting the world since its inception. Take a look at Sister Eve. The Bible teaches in its Genesis account that Eve was formed from the side of man (Adam) to be his lifelong partner and help. The two enjoyed a state of paradise in the Garden of Eden, frolicking around unashamedly in the nude, enjoying exotic fruits and vegetables, and having not a care in the world. God allowed his first humans to eat from any tree that he had placed in the garden, except, the *Tree of the Knowledge of Good and Evil.* The first couple was strictly forbidden to touch that particular tree or they would face expulsion from the garden and eventual death. But the slick, conniving serpent convinced our dear sister to go against the Creator's wishes and enjoy the forbidden fruit, telling her that there would be no consequences for defiance and disobedience. The temptation was too great and Eve not only committed a mortal sin, but convinced her husband to do so as well. God was angered and issued punishment to all three individuals that affect us all today. The serpent would forever crawl on his belly in the dust and be a sworn enemy of mankind. Man would bruise his head, and he would bruise man's heel. Adam would have to work, sweat, and struggle for existence. And then there's Eve. For her part in the garden travesty, women would bring forth children in great pain and submit to the authority of their husbands. If you've ever had a baby, then you already know that childbirth is excruciatingly painful. Personally, I was given an epidural during both my deliveries for pain management. I can't imagine what it was like for poor Eve, no doctor, nurse, not even a Tylenol to help her through the trauma of childbirth. But she managed many more times after that.

Now, you don't have to be religious, a professing Christian, or a biblical believer to appreciate Eve's story. She was faithful to her man, became distracted, lost focus, made a poor decision, and had to live with its consequences. It is her historical role that brings me to this book. A woman caused change in the Garden of Eden, albeit negative, and set humanity on a course outside of its intended paradise. Now that's powerful. God's presence in the Garden of Eden is why I'm issuing this call to you, my sister (or brother, if you're reading this book). No matter your race, ethnicity, complexion, or beliefs, we are sisters in the struggle. Struggle for what? Survival! I'm sure you can agree that the world is in utter chaos. From widespread violence to political mayhem, declining immorality to incurable diseases, humanity is crying out for help, and with the dawn of each new day comes a whole new set of troubles. Broadcast news as I once knew it, is no more. Gone are the days of watching credible journalists give unbiased news reports and being entertained by an unforgettable, catchy jingle at the commercial break. I was born in the sixties, raised up in the seventies and came into adulthood in the eighties. Although there were reports of homicides, racial animosity, corruption, war, and disease back then too, it was not at the level that we currently see. The average news broadcast today is filled with the worst that humanity has to offer, and most is grossly sensation-alized. While I understand and agree that news and information needs to be disseminated to the public, I have a hard time understanding why we can't find viable solutions to the devastating issues crippling our lives and communities. No disrespect intended to the men of the world, but when it comes to leadership, there is a lot to be desired. The current political atmosphere in Washington, DC, is beyond dysfunctional. It is downright sickening in my opinion. Politics, a mostly male-led profession, is destroying the very fabric of our society. They can't get along, sabotage each other's efforts, and engage in selfish pursuits as the country suffers. The national debt continues to soar, unemployment is rising, food costs are exorbitant, healthcare is in shambles, world peace is shattered, morality is a thing of the past, and the family unit is nearly destroyed. All of this with men in charge. We must find new, better, or different ways of dealing with these issues. For most of mankind's history, women have held a subservient, second class role in society. Yes, even in the model of freedom, equality, and democracy, in the United States of America. Those of us that are Christians have held fast to the belief that men are to be leaders in the home, community, and every part of society. But how long can we stand on the sidelines and watch when our children's futures are in jeopardy, especially when we possess the talents and abilities to make a difference? I'm not suggesting that we rule over the men in our lives. Not at all. I am suggesting that we take what God has already placed in us to help answer the distress call that is being sent out all over the world. Using your gift, no matter what it is, can help save a life, realize a dream, feed the hungry, cure disease, curb violence, and more. But you must be willing. We must allow the spirit of the lioness to rise up within us. A lion's roar can be heard up to five miles away. The roar can be a sign of distress, a call for lost cubs, or a signal that all is well. In Hebrew the name Ari'el means, "Lion of God." If there is going to be significant changes implemented for the good of the next generation, then the lionesses of the world will have to take center stage. God has turned an attentive ear to the cries of the people. He has summoned the Ari'els and when they rise in unity, good things will start to unfold…

S. Denice Newton, Founder/Author

Ari'el Rising Network

ROAR: *Empowerment through the written and spoken word.*

Ari'el Rising was birthed from a combination of my struggle with clinical depression, a life-changing vision, and a call to reach out to humanity. I grieve in my heart and soul for this current generation. There are many deadly and evil influences claiming lives daily and without intervention, it will only worsen. I am convinced, beyond all doubt, that the solution to every problem in the world is already in our hands. But we must be willing to use our talents and abilities for the good of others. The world groans in pain and women are nurturers by nature. It is time for a collective movement of women to rise up for such a time as this—those strong, powerful, mourning and lamenting women that the Prophet Jeremiah talks about in the Bible.

As a child, I used to wonder why my thoughts, actions, beliefs, reactions, and behavior was so different from many around me. I was able to see, hear, and feel things that others couldn't. I could walk into an empty room and instantly sense a presence, good or bad. Within thirty seconds of meeting someone, I would feel their spirit—instantly knowing if they were who they appeared to be. Having this ability caused me to have many disappointing days throughout my life. I wanted to believe the best about people, but my own spirit was often in disagreement. Instead of embracing my "uniqueness," I tried to mold myself into someone more "normal." It didn't work out very well. Once I started to reject who I really was, my life took a series of twists and turns that left me confused and unhappy. Poor choices and decisions in relationships, careers, and money matters caused me to withdraw from all that I loved. Yes, I went through the daily motions of going to work and taking care of my children, but emotionally, I was detached. I was hollow. Failed romantic relationships made things much worse. I experienced a thirty pound weight gain over a short period, and being slender all my life, I couldn't stand to look at myself in the mirror. The double chin, muffin top, and increasing numbers on the scale suggested that I was no longer the same person. Fine lines, crow's feet, and blood pressure problems were constant reminders that I was aging with a ton of unfulfilled dreams. I managed to keep things up for appearances' sake. However, I continued to deny that part of me that was screaming to be released.

My unhappiness continued until I finally decided to seek medical help. I was eventually diagnosed with clinical depression and placed on the antidepressant Celexa. The medication helped. I no longer felt the need to keep the blinds closed and lights off. I started to get out of the house and do more with my children. I repaired relationships with people that I had cut out of my life. I re-dedicated myself to God and working in ministry. With my strength and confidence slowly returning, I prayed to God for revelation of His will for my life. He showed it to me in a vision one day as I sat on the couch watching television. It went like this: I was having a party in my house. There were all kinds of people there doing all kinds of immoral and illegal things. I was walking around with a tray filled with drugs, alcohol, and other things, serving the loud and boisterous guests. Let me clarify, I have NEVER done drugs or alcohol. It's never been my thing. But in this vision, I was giving them whatever they wanted. Someone knocked on the door and a friend said, "Sandra, there's a man at the door and he wants to talk to you."

"Who is it?" I asked, annoyed by the interruption.

"I don't know," she said. "He won't tell me anything. He only wants to talk to you."

I put the tray down and went to the door. A man dressed in white "Jesus" garb from head to foot stood there with his head bowed. *Who is this weirdo?* I said to myself. "You looking for me?" I asked him. The man never said a word. He gently pushed me back and entered the house. Without saying one word, he took me by the hand and led me into the dining room where my guests were partying. They all suddenly disappeared into thin air! He pulled a chair from the table, put his hand on my head, had me kneel in front of the chair, and put my hands in a "praying position." He began to speak in a language that I didn't understand. His hand was still on my head and I tried to look up at him, to understand what he was saying. At that point, he was no longer a person, but a blinding beam of light that went from the floor straight through the ceiling and into the sky! He continued to speak in the unknown language, but strangely, I understood each word! He empowered me to reach out to others near and far, with compassion and humility. I was to warn people of impending dangers and devastation. He placed a global ministry within me as evidenced by the beautiful unfamiliar language that I was able to understand. After that, I fully embraced my "uniqueness" and started to walk powerfully in my purpose. I began to write, speak, and teach others about rising above circumstances to find their own purpose. I was renewed and looked at life from a whole new set of lens, seeing no need to continue the antidepressants. With everything coming together, I just knew that support and appreciation for the new me would be through the roof! Sadly, it wasn't. In fact, I was more rejected than ever. But I vowed to continue on the illuminated path before me.

A few years later, it all made perfect sense. It was all in the name. Sandra, my first name, means "Helper of Mankind" in Greek. And that's pretty cool. But it is the English meaning that really defines me: "unheeded prophetess." That profound revelation empowered me to do even more! I can still see, hear, and feel things that many others can't, but the difference is that now I have no fear of it. As a child, my favorite thing to do was read books and write stories about castles and palaces. I had a fascination with royalty. In the stories that I wrote, I would be the Princess that met the handsome Prince and rode off into the sunset to live happily ever after. It was my way of escaping a life that I didn't find to be very happy at times. Additionally, I had a fascination with words. I loved pronouncing, reading, and writing them. I would read dictionaries and encyclopedias for fun. I would also watch news broadcasts and imitate my favorite anchors. That is when I got the thirst for public speaking. After placing first in an oratory contest in high school, I became a bit more encouraged about my path. However, I didn't pursue anything until after serving in the U.S. Army for a number of years.

Being exposed to other cultures, languages, and ways of living through my military travels, I started to journal my experiences. Many of these experiences gave me an even greater appreciation of life in America. It was then that I returned to college to get the necessary training to become a polished public speaker. My journey started in church. Standing before the congregation weekly to give announcements, teaching

Sunday school and Bible study occasionally, I became more confident of my skills and abilities. I prayed earnestly for God to prepare me to encourage, inspire and uplift others. He didn't waste any time in granting that request. Whether encouraging children to stay in school, inspiring the single parent to return to school, helping the victim of depression to find tomorrow, helping the racist release the evil troll within, or simply empowering black Americans to stand strong and pursue avenues of change and personal self-development, I have been called and groomed to stand before the masses. Working with at-risk, disadvantaged, minority children has given me a sobering insight into their world and I work tirelessly to find ways to help. It is painful to watch children without goals, aspirations, or dreams because society says that they are destined to go from the cradle to prison with nothing but pain and turmoil in between. I love helping them find their passion. They deserve at least that much.

For much of my life I struggled with esteem issues and a lack of confidence. It would be many years and a lot of hurt and rejection before that changed. I certainly think that being a soldier in the United States Army gave me the confidence boost that I seriously needed to realize my self-worth. Perhaps walking around armed with a semi-automatic rifle played a part as well. When I made myself available to the will of God, every gift and talent that lay dormant inside of me was activated. It wasn't long before I was writing for newspapers, news magazines, and becoming actively involved in my community. God would not allow the dark days of my past to dictate the bright future that he had in store for me. Today, I am unapologetically a follower of Jesus Christ and faithful Christian. I was literally saved from a life of mediocrity and failures. In 2010 I founded and started Generation BEFY Network, an acronym for black, educated, focused, and yielded. This movement is designed to encourage the pursuit of higher education and personal self-development as a counter and deterrent to destructive lifestyle choices in youth such as gangs, drugs, and violence. I am forever grateful to Marcedes Fuller, Robert X. Golphin, Jacque Howard, Sheila Fowler-Davis, Reggie Bullock and my church family for helping me get on this current path of kingdom work. My first conference to introduce the GBN was a great success! I've also been blessed to start the following: The ROAR Network (reach out and recover), a hub for other lions and lionesses to connect, network, and impact. Ari'el Rising: the women's empowerment movement. The Black Future Project: Keeping pride and progress relevant in the black community.

"The fastest way to change society is to mobilize the women of the world."

- Charles Malik

Roar

1

Youth | Family | Education

Education is the best friend. An educated person is respected everywhere. Education beats the beauty and the youth.

-Chanakya

Nadine Lee, Founder/CEO

Speak The Dream Foundation

ROAR: *Empowering foster and underserved youth*

As a very young child, I experienced feelings of fear, disappointment, anger, and abandonment after my mother gave me to strangers on a NYC street. Every day, I pressed my face and hands against the window looking for her, but she never came back to get me. From the window I would see her walk past, but she would never look at me. I knew that she saw me even though she acted as if she didn't. Two years later, my grandmother begrudgingly retrieved me from the strangers I lived with. In between violent beatings, she would say things to me like, "I hate you, you black cow! I hate you, you dumb ass!" Sleeping at night was unsettling as she would wait until I fell asleep and beat me without warning. The feeling of terror and fear of being awakened by the lash of a whip, belt, or extension cord affected my sleeping pattern for many years. Every day, I cried, prayed, and waited for my mother, but she never came back to get me. She eventually gave birth to my younger brother who was born with Fetal Alcohol Syndrome due to her alcoholism. She tried to kill him as an infant by attempting to drop him out of a third story window. He was later adopted. After years of physical and sexual abuse, foster care became my life until I turned eighteen. I was frightened and confused…still waiting for my mother…but she never came back to get me. I became a teen mother, had no guidance, support, or family. I had no idea of how to raise a child, and I still waited for my mother…but she never came back to get me.

While in foster care, I watched the other children who were left behind or thrown away and wondered if those children felt abandoned like I did. For many years, I wondered why no one ever came back to get me and the anger consumed me. I took a vested interest in and was impacted by the children that were in the foster homes where I was placed and to this day, I still remember each child and wonder where he/she must be. My heart and spirit still loves these children. For many years, I was angry and hurt that my mother, father or anyone else never came back to get me. I felt unwanted, unworthy and disregarded. Every time I experienced those feelings, it adversely affected my life as I made emotionally unhealthy decisions in an effort to muffle the pain. My childhood experiences, passion for children, and determination to do something to help children, guided me from thirty successful years in the corporate world to begin living my own ROAR! I started Speak the Dream Foundation in 2008, to help foster and other at-risk children feel wanted, worthy and supported. The organization exists to ensure that children understand that the circumstances under which they are living are temporary, and with love, support, focus, and education, they are not victims, but victors. After establishing the organization, I was informed that my mother, whom I had not seen in a few years, was suffering from dementia and other health issues. I was still angry with her and wanted no part in her life, but there was no one to care for her. She lived on the East Coast at that time and I felt very strongly that someone had to go back and get her. By process of elimination, it was going to be me. It was a difficult decision to make, but at the same time, it was the right decision. I traveled to the East Coast to convince her to return to California with me. Eventually, she agreed and the two of us began a long, cross country drive from Connecticut to California. I learned a lot about my mother during this cross country journey. Much about her life now makes more sense and even though it's not always easy, I realize now that I had to go back and get her. I had to love her, to help her heal, so I could heal and be able to ROAR for other children that have been left behind! Many people, young and old, are still waiting for someone to care enough to come back and get them. My ROAR (passion) is that every child I come in contact with, or that is a part of my organization, will know that someone came back and got him or her because EVERYONE deserves and is entitled to ROAR!!

Colleen Adams

Founder/Executive Director

Empowered Youth USA

ROAR: *Redirecting Youth*

I am sure I am one of the forty-nine other women in this book who are blessed to be swimming in their destiny. I am sure that is the common denominator for us all. I am not swimming in financial wealth, I am not swimming in fame, but I am exactly where I was born to be, doing exactly what I was born to do. The journey has been fascinating and I would not trade one second of it, the perceived good and 'bad.' I have come to understand that there is no such thing as a 'bad' event in your life, just another lesson that—if carefully attended to and learned from— is a vital part of the journey that leads to your destiny.

During a crisis in my life (there have been a few, more on that later!) a friend once advised me to take 'The Tombstone Test,' a curious, but life-altering request. He told me to figure out what I wanted my legacy in life to be, and then work backwards to achieve it. I determined that I wanted my tombstone to say "Light Worker...she left her corner of the world better than she found it." I have been working on achieving that since that very day. I have been asked many times at point-blank range why I do the work I do. I work with young inner-city boys between the ages of twelve and nineteen, most of whom have been court-referred to the program by the Department of Juvenile Justice. I have often been asked that question by members of the inner-city community, some of whom have taken offense that I do the work I do. My response is always the same: I do what I do because for me, it is about JUSTICE, not race. It is about man's inhumanity to man. I want no part of that and am candidly – often embarrassed – by the inhumanity and ignorance my race often imposes on those they do not know, understand; nor make any effort to know or understand. That to me is the genesis of true injustice: intolerance and lack of empathy and compassion for others who may not look like you. It is just fundamentally wrong and unacceptable to me. The only thing that makes any sense to me is to work to change it. Everything in my life has prepared me to do the work I do today, and I use every shred of experience and information I have ever had.

I was born to middle/upper-middle class parents in Chattanooga, TN. My young life was interestingly and essentially not unlike that of my young inner-city students, despite the alleged difference in our 'backgrounds.' I learned to understand that pain is pain, no matter from which neighborhood you come or which color you are. My dad was an alcoholic and my mom was addicted to diet pills. Behind closed doors, my family was massively dysfunctional and wrought with addiction and abuse that ranged from physical to emotional to sexual. It was hell to grow up in my house, but it gave me the capacity to understand pain firsthand, and to be able to sense that in others despite brave facades. I know, I had one. That and a very thick wall to protect myself. Sounds more like an 'inner-city youth' than a girl from Tennessee, right? But as I look back on it all, I realize that it was the best possible classroom for the work I now do. There is not one emotion, one feeling of sadness, hopelessness, rejection, low self-esteem or betrayal that I have not experienced, and all that now allows me to provide comfort and guidance to young people whose pain is truly my own. I also learned firsthand that it only takes one person to believe in you, for you to make it. Mine was Mrs. Green, the mom of one of my older sister's friends. Mrs. Green ran the local community center and just discovered me one day. I was completely shutdown, shy, with no self-confidence or self-esteem. I was doing my best to be invisible (you learn to be invisible when you grow up with abuse, because if someone discovers you are there, bad things will happen). Mrs. Green slowly coaxed me out of my shell and encouraged me to begin to see my gifts and value. Without her I would have become another statistic of my family.

Three out of the five children in my family became drug and alcohol addicted, and I only escaped because of the kindness of a stranger, who taught me to believe in myself and the limitless possibilities that lay ahead of me. I have spent my lifetime trying to repay Mrs. Green by being that lifeline for other emotionally lost and abandoned young people like me. I hope she would have been proud of me. That would mean a lot to me.

Today, my achievements are measured in young lives saved and transformed. But, as I am sure all in this book will tell you — YOURS is the life saved and transformed. The young men in my program are my heroes. They have taught me more about love, courage, and resilience in the face of adversity. How to keep hope alive in an environment and under circumstances so often deprived of the oxygen of the human spirit: love. Back to the Tombstone Test.

I would like my legacy to be that I left inner-city youth all over this country with the tools they need to build the future they so truly deserve to have. That is why there are 2 phases to my intervention program. The first phase is a community-based program called Empowered Youth Neighborhood, which focuses on life skills and character development. The second phase is a job development program called Empowered Youth Entrepreneurs, where our students and graduates are taught the fundamentals of social entrepreneurism and to create and run their own companies (such as EY StreetWear, an urban apparel line that the students and graduates design and sell; and The Empowered Youth Food Truck Incubator Program, where students are trained to become small business owners and chefs). My goal is to build a national network of community-based Empowered Youth programs that include both our Phase 1 intervention model (Empowered Youth Neighborhood) and our Phase 2 business models (Empowered Youth Entrepreneurs); and that national program will be run and managed by the young men themselves. Empowered youth empowering youth.

Change must come from within, by building new layers of leader-ship. My goal is to make YOUTH TRANSFORMATION THROUGH OPPORTUNITY a national call to arms that will rally a nation asleep to the torment that our inner-city youth call their childhoods and lives. If we provide our young inner-city men training and jobs, they will not have to resort to crime to support themselves and their families; they will not be vulnerable to gang recruitment because they will have HOPE for a better future, and we can break the cycle of the cradle to prison pipeline. I feel compelled to cite a *study that was conducted in 2003; a comparison of twin psychological studies by the Lancet and Rand corporations, which indicated that the average child in South Los Angeles is exhibiting greater levels of post-traumatic stress disorder than children of a similar age in Baghdad, the war-torn capital of Iraq. Our inner-city youth are living in war zones nationally and internationally. In my experience, born out of poverty, broken families, with absent fathers and/or positive male role models. Social change is NOT 'someone else's job,'...it is our job as a community. We are failing our children, they are not failing us. As Mahatma Gandhi so wisely demonstrated through his life, "You must be the change you wish to see in the world." I am working on that.

*Marlene Wong, PhD, Sheryl Kataoka, MSHS, Lisa Jaycox, PhD, University of California Los Angeles Center for Research in Managed Care, Cognitive Behavior Intervention for Trauma in Schools, (CBITS) [1]

*Jump up^ Stein, B., Jaycox, L., Kataoka, S., Wong, M., Tu, W., Elliot, M., & Fink, A. (2003). A mental health intervention for schoolchildren exposed to violence: A randomized control trial. The Journal of American Medical Association, 290, 603-611.[2]

Marguerite Benjamin Parker

Author, Publisher, Educator, Gift Designer

ROAR: *Fulfillment of Purpose*

Although I identify myself as an entrepreneur, having successfully run a multifaceted home-based enterprise for over a decade, my primary profession thus far has been as an educator. My experiences in higher education have allowed me to teach and advise others as well as to personally recognize and benefit from life's teachable moments.

Over the years, the most valuable lessons I have learned and been most committed to sharing are the following. These lessons are universal and can benefit every demographic regardless of age, gender, or any other category society constructs to limit divine potential. However, I believe if women embrace these lessons, the world at large will flourish. Refuse to exist in perpetual crisis mode. Live with the ability to contribute. The driving mechanism that is your body, is pre-programmed for survival at all cost. Consider the phenomenon of frost-bite. When the body is subjected to extreme cold, it automatically begins to protect what is most vital to survival—the heart and surrounding internal organs. At that point, your body decides that you can afford to lose fingers, toes, ears, nose and anything else not immediately necessary to keep you alive. Compared to the heart, your outer extremities are mere ornaments, dispensable, and are the first to be sacrificed. Likewise, when we function from day to day in crisis mode, whether it be a financial crisis, emotional crisis, physical crisis, or spiritual crisis, we do so at the expense of our higher functioning selves. As long as all of your vital energy is diverted to merely keeping one foot moving in front of the other, or keeping you from slipping off the edge of sanity, that energy will never be free to allow you to assist, sustain or enlighten others.

When we commit to making the adjustments that allow us to maintain healthy balance in all areas of our lives (managing our finances, avoiding dysfunctional relationships, etc.), we become capable of higher pursuits. Our creative energies abound and we make lasting contributions to society. Currently, our society is in dire need of a Renaissance. Instability delays the movement. Stop thinking it is noble to dim your light. There is no glory in lurking in the shade. There is a difference in being humble and being self-deprecating. Honest humility prevents you from belittling others. False humility belittles and limits your own potential. Humility should not prevent you from celebrating yourself. Acknowledging your own strengths and accomplishments should be done in a way that inspires hope in others, so that they, too, feel free to shine. No one benefits when we refuse to acknowledge, nurture, develop and display the gifts we have been given. Give yourself permission to be powerful, and empower others to step out of the shade. I believe it is an insult to the Creator when we minimize the gifts we have been given. Refuse to hide the spark; dare to fan the flame. Understand and accept your responsibility for fulfilling your purpose on earth. Trust that God is not in the business of wasting energy. Every spark of life exists for a purpose.

My personal philosophy is that every person has been gifted with a unique set of qualities and abilities that we each are to use to make our way prosperous and leave a lasting impression in the earth. I credit God with the ability to transform a blank page into a story or begin with a few seemingly unrelated products and create a beautiful gift that makes someone's day. The gift of creation is indeed divine and everyone, in some form, has a touch of divinity within. It is our responsibility while we reside on earth to discover, cultivate and use that spark of divinity in our lives to leave the world a better place than when we arrived. One's gifting and destiny can be in science, medicine, fine art, or even gift design. No matter the industry, we should love the work we do and use the work of our hands to benefit others. Inspiration is everywhere, but creativity/artistry is drawn from that God-given spark from within.

"A gift opens the way for the giver and ushers him into the presence of the great."
— *Proverbs 18:16, New International Version*

Andrieka J. Austin, Founder/Facilitator

Journey Girl, LLC

ROAR: *Building Self-Esteem*

Andrieka J. Austin ("AJ") is Founder/Facilitator of Journey Girl, LLC (www.JourneyGirl.org) where she empowers mothers and daughters seeking to have better relationships with themselves and each other through her organization's workshops and special events. She also encourages women social entrepreneurs by sharing her professional success and business sustainability practices, helping them make a bigger global impact and increase social change with customizable training and development programs for Socialprenistas™". She can be found speaking, encouraging, empowering, and engaging with diverse audiences of girls and women across the globe.
Connect on twitter:
@journeygirlatl.
Facebook: /journeygirlatlanta, or /missjourneygirl.

Favorite Quote: "I do what I love. I LOVE what I do!" -Andrieka J. Austin, Journey Girl, LLC.

As a result of surviving an extremely toxic relationship with her mother for most of her life, AJ has always kept the words of one of her beloved pastor's sermon in mind, "Your pain will always lead to your passion, and you have everything you need [within you] to succeed." This is the drive and the motivation to keep moving forward with the mission, to positively impact the lives of girls and women around the world, just like her. Her workshops, seminars, and special appearances at conferences and events are only the beginning of her journey. She also authors inspirational works and positive magazine contributions for girls and women, empowering them to live their best lives. The road to this type of work is never easy, but one thing she knows for sure...she is definitely on the right track to living her dreams, while teaching others to follow theirs! So, the journey continues.

How she got started/ what motivated her/ experiences.

Looking back on the past decade-and-a-half of working with youth, I now see how God was preparing me throughout my life. From one of my first encounters of working with a pre-teen girl who was contemplating suicide (and had included me in on the letter), to sharing the harsh realities of severely tainted relationships between mothers and daughters, I am reassured daily that I am living and walking in my true calling. Every success story and every tragedy has been the inspiration behind Journey Girl, LLC, where I help bridge the communication gap and serve as "the bond between girls and moms." I facilitate workshops for mothers and daughters on how to build better relationships with themselves and each other. One must truly and unconditionally know, understand, and give love to herself before she can do the same for others. This holds true for girls and women of all ages.

My message and what makes me roar: Mothers and daughters need to talk; face-to-face and side-by-side in the same room about sensitive, personal issues and dilemmas that may one day cause them to "lose each other" forever. If they don't speak about and address these issues now, tomorrow may very well be too late. Mothers and daughters everywhere share one wish; that their daughters would talk, and that their mothers would listen. Not having a relationship with my mother most of my life is what pulls on my heart that there is a need for what I do, and that this is truly my calling. It is my goal to help mothers and daughters across the nation to start a dialogue that will empower them to be (and stay) better for themselves, each other, and future generations of girls and moms to come. So, the journey continues.

My endeavors with this company have led me on many interesting journeys of growth and self-acceptance (for me, and the girls and moms I encounter). This includes meeting a shy teenage girl who is at the 'make or break' point of her life, working with girls who have survived domestic violence, sharing with young women living in shelters with children, and getting calls from mothers who personally request me to counsel, work with, and mentor their daughters to get them to break out of her shell and open up and share her feelings and her perspective on a potentially stressful living situation. This list expands daily. I also get to share the important, life-altering experiences of a mother and daughter and see the impact of my work. From attending college fairs and college campuses, discussing scholarships, and which courses to take, boyfriends and "beaux" [pronounced "boo"], to all of the other high school and family 'drama', plus, after school clubs and events. I have had conversations with and about teachers. I have lost touch and been reunited on the field of a graduation ceremony. I have helped girls and moms meet their (our) strategic goal of 'just getting her across that graduation stage!', and helped her survive those college days of living on her own and dorm room supply shopping. I have shared in conversations about how to 'survive' the college life, make friends, and connect with college-level professors. Landing that first corporate job, receiving that first check, and making that first deposit into her very first (and very own) savings account. I have also structured visits to local pregnancy resource centers with the intent of educating the next generation of decision makers with what her options are pertaining to making educated decisions about her future, as it relates to sexual education, resources, and information, no matter what she decides to do in the end. Conversations and life experiences like this are priceless. They would definitely mean so much more if we could empower mothers and daughters who are at a "sticking point" in their relationships, and are consistently bumping heads that 'journeys' like this are desperately needed. Together. "My mom won't listen." "My parents just don't understand." I've heard these statements countless times over the past decade from girls all around the world. Feeling as if no one is in the same "world" with them, and so, no one could possibly understand what they are going through. I decided to really sit, listen, and focus in on where these feelings come from and why so many girls feel this way when trying to communicate with their parents. My "journey" into this world gave me insight that I share with parents and leaders worldwide, as we all seek to solve this mystical riddle of communicating with today's girl. No, I'm not a mom (yet), however, the self-empowerment services I have been blessed to provide to teen girls and their moms, over the last decade and a half, has allowed me the privilege of entering the sacred world of teen and pre-teen girls (and boys). Young people open up to me about a vast array of private conversations and things that they would never consider telling their parents. Things like sex, drug overdosing, suicide attempts, and things they believe that their parents "just don't understand" is only a glimpse of the conversations I encounter with youth on an ongoing basis.

My role in the lives of our youth has given me the advantage and the confidence level of being a stranger, meaning that I'm not directly "blood-related" to them (and it is often easier to discuss anything with a stranger), the leverage of only a few years age differentiation (I'm not quite old enough to be their mom, yet I'm young enough to listen and understand their challenges. I have the privilege to be "on the outside looking in" and the ability to give an "unbiased" opinion and/or feedback on any given situation.) I am the one teens and pre-teen youth tend to confide in and share with. I have the coveted role in a teen's life that any mom (or dad) would envy and love to have. I stand in a position and a calling to serve as a mediator between the parent and the child. I am Journey Girl.

I am proud of Journey Girl's contributions to society and our many success stories, past, present, and those to come. I will always remember the sweet words of a reassuring mother to me that, "You brought me and my daughter closer together. Thank you." I can certainly identify with having a desire to bond and connect with mom. I experienced a traumatic childhood relationship with my mom, but now, this is what connects me to the girls and moms I serve. It wasn't until later in my teenage years that I met a wonderful lady who mentored me and guided me on my journey to self-discovery. She was actually my high school guidance counselor. Although she and I were not blood related, she was a mother-type figure in my life. What I learned from working with her as a teenage girl is what I want to share with you. I believe that there are five steps that are guaranteed to change the way girls and moms connect with each other. You can make each other's day by learning how to understand each other better. Simply ask yourself these simple questions to see how you can make things better:

1) Do you feel like you're losing your connection with each other?
2) Do you find it difficult to communicate (even the smallest things) with each other?
3) Is it sometimes difficult for you to understand each other's point-of-view on things?

4) Do you think it would be awesome to have a third-party's opinion (from a professional) to help "break things down" when discussing sensitive issues with each other?
5) How cool would it be to finally bring a sense of peace and settlement to your mother-daughter relationship challenges?

If you answered "yes" to even one of these questions, you are one of the many mother-daughter teams who know what you want to do, but it's just not happening, working, or getting the job done for you. No worries. Learning (and using) the following five techniques are important to help better (1) understand (2) communicate (3) translate (4) mediate (5) mend and bring peace to the "situations" between you two, both now and in the future, thus, impacting future daughters for generations to come. Introduce these steps to create a genuine, positive bonding relationship.

Step one is Communication.

Moms want their daughters to be able to open up to them more (and daughters want the same thing in return). Moms and daughters have the need to talk more about what's going on in their individual lives. This starts with active listening.

Step two is Understanding.

Moms want to get a small sense of understanding what their daughter is going through. This means processing what's being said, and seeing it from the other person's perspective.

Step three is Mediation.

Sometimes, certain mother-daughter discussions require an outside person (like a professional) to help mediate differences. Moms and daughters alike enjoy having a neutral, unbiased third party to help them through it all. Having someone there to facilitate the discussion means hearing the problem/obstacle at-hand, and bringing that challenge to the surface to ultimately find solutions. Step four Translation.

Mothers and daughters desire a full translation of the meaning of it all. Many times this requires a deeper understanding of communication issues and challenges from a mother's perspective, and from a daughter's perspective to help it all make sense. Sometimes it takes the mom admitting that she doesn't know it all, and daughters admitting that they actually do need the help and advice of a mom. Try to consider each other's view on things and help it make sense to you and her.

Step five is to Mend and Bring Peace.

It's always good to find a compromise on things. And, yes, it is possible for children and parents to compromise. Both moms and daughters want a "walk-through", a plan-of-action as to how to keep this open and honest dialogue going. Create an action plan to implement the agreed upon solutions. Come up with appropriate ways to evaluate your results together. Implementing an action plan shows you how to help the communication stay better between you and your mom.

The ultimate goal of each of these exercises is to help surface the challenges as well as the opportunities of positively communicating with each other. Try to reach some level of agreement about the nature of the challenge, the causes of the challenge, and all appropriate solutions to help meet and beat the challenges and to keep them from arising in the future. Open communication and the start of a positive, ongoing dialogue between mom and daughter is the key, and there are great ways to do this.

If you need help (from a professional, as suggested above), Journey Girl, LLC is here to help. Visit www.JourneyGirl.org for workshops with tips and ideas on how to help save and salvage the lifelong mother-daughter relationship you wish to create together. I am grateful that my life's story has led to the creation of a personal and professional development method and success strategy. Even my hobbies and personal interests show that I enjoy speaking to groups of girls and moms about building better relationships with themselves and each other. Having immediate access to a professional Teen Life Consultant, and inspirational resources and materials to help facilitate discussions, can help the healing and mending process. Have the benefit of knowing that someone else cares as much as you do about your own mother-daughter relationship. My future plans are to remain on this journey to positively impact the lives of girls and women around the world, for as long as I have been called to do so. I will also strive to share with other women business owners how they, too, can make a bigger impact and influence change through their own organizations as well.

Blair Brown

President at International Women Achievers' Awards and Principal at The Destiny Group

ROAR: *Making connections.*

Blair Brown was born on November 25, 1964, the youngest of four children and the second of twin girls. Born into a busy household, she was raised in Edmonton Alberta Canada, where she learned to multi-task at a young age, juggling piano, organ, sports, work, volunteerism, church and school. She has always had a desire to "help" and during her high school years, she received an award for Outstanding Contribution to Student Services from Jasper Place Composite High School. The multi-faceted Blair Brown was a young student that had a heart for people and always saw the best in everyone with whom she made contact. During her years in junior high or middle school, Blair was known as "Dear Abby," a title bestowed on her because of her ability to "connect" with people. It was that connection that had many willing to work with her and to learn from her. From her teenage years, she was already "helping people, and changing lives," a motto that she attached to her current company, The Destiny Group.

Blair loved to write as a child, and in 7th grade, her Language Arts teacher recognized her ability to communicate not only in writing, but also in her ability to deliver a message verbally. She still remembers her first short story, "The Highest Dream", a story that was reflective of where she wanted to be in life, and her desire to excel. She decided that she would study broadcast journalism from the moment she wrote that story in 7th grade. So, it was not a surprise to anyone that after graduating from high school, she would set her goal on entrance to the Northern Alberta Institute of Technology's Radio and Television Arts' program.

In 1987, Blair graduated from the Northern Alberta Institute of Technology, specializing in On Air Reporting. Two years later, she would leave Edmonton to pursue her career in the "big city" Toronto. Shortly after arriving in Toronto, Blair was offered a position with Royal LePage and the Trilon organization. Her TV career was put on hold and another chapter in her life was taking shape. In September 1996, Write Well Communications was created with the intentions of providing editorial assistance to small business owners and writers. The company's principal, Blair Brown, worked on a part-time basis to build her clientele and to create exposure. However, after years of volunteering her services with non-profit organizations, a new direction and many changes had taken place. In September 2007 The Destiny Group was created. The company added to the services provided including proposals, transcriptions and other administrative assistance. Combining professional acumen and philanthropic passion, The Destiny Group has re-branded itself to reflect its new mission of "helping people… changing lives!"

Through her years at Royal LePage, Blair developed an extensive background in communications and executive level administrative support, and also in working with start-up businesses in the private and corporate sector. After eighteen years with the Trilon/Brascan organization, she now works tirelessly with small existing and start-up businesses and with The International Women Achievers' Awards. Along with patience and dedication, Blair also possesses a great passion for helping people to realize their potential, and takes pleasure in the accomplishments of others. The importance of God, family and community is a natural way of life for her. Blair has been instrumental in consulting and assisting successful small businesses start-up in Ontario and the United Kingdom. She possesses a great ability to bring people, and their ideas/talents together and to find jobs for individuals; this has become a way of life for her. It's God, family and community for Blair.

THE INTERNATIONAL WOMEN ACHIEVERS' AWARDS

The International Women Achievers' Awards was founded in 2009, by Princess Boucher, who was a client of The Destiny Group. The

Awards were created to recognize and honour women from around the world; women who have excelled in their various fields of endeavours, and women who have made a difference in their respective communities. In 2012, Blair received an award from IWAA for the "Most Likely to Succeed" and immediately after, she returned to the organization as an alumni and quickly worked in the area of Business Development, and assisted in transforming the awards from an 'event' to a recognized business. Impressing the founder, Blair was offered a partnership and the presidency in the International Women Achievers' Award in 2013.

Using collaboration and inclusion, Blair has crossed borders, and has created a genuine global collaboration through the Global Ambassador Program, and with the addition of team members from the United States, India and Europe. She continues to develop IWAA as an international powerhouse in the movement of women empowerment. Her desire is to help in making IWAA a globally recognized and respected business, attracting world leaders, entertainment superstars and corporate businesses to invest, sponsor and promote the goal of IWAA to recognize many women who are unrecognized for who they are and what they do. Blair continues to wear many hats, including the role of wife and mother. In 2012, at the age of forty-seven, and against medical odds, Blair gave birth to beautiful and active baby boy. She lives for her family, her business, her clients, her companies and her God. She takes nothing for granted, but believes fully, the scripture "The Lord's lovingkindness indeed never cease, For His compassion never fail. They are new every morning; Great is Your faithfulness." Lamentation 3:22-24 NASB.

Dr. Maxine Bryant

Educator, Author, Activist, Entrepreneur

ROAR: *Getting the groove back.*

Maxine L. Bryant, Ph.D: Author, Motivational Speaker, Award Winning Poet, Spoken Word Artist, Teacher, Minister, Social Activist, Entrepreneur, Advocate for Persons With Criminal Histories.

"I have been called dynamic, motivational, thought-provoking, engaging, entertaining, intellectual, sharp, advocate for persons with criminal histories, etc. However, at my core, I am passionate for Christ! My name is Maxine L. Bryant and I have been on my God-given path for fifty-five years. I was born with severe asthma and later developed a speech impediment. Doctors told my mom that I would be asthmatic all of my life and that I would be unable to speak clearly without an operation, and that even with an operation, there was no guarantee that the speech impediment could be corrected. In high school, my counselor told my mom not to waste her money sending me to college because I wasn't college material.

"My journey began with a praying mother. I was adopted by my parents and was their only child, so she focused all of her praying energy on me. I'm no longer asthmatic. I never had the operation. I talk for a living. And, I have a Bachelor of Science degree, a Master of Arts degree, and a Ph.D. As a youngster, I wanted to be a heart surgeon. After discovering how many years of schooling I needed to complete, that desire dissipated and I decided to become a secretary. In my last year of high school, I took a secretarial science class. Our final project was to write a paper on a career we were not interested in. I chose to write about being a social worker in a prison. That paper changed my life – I knew I wanted to work with prisoners and set my sights on doing just that.

"After earning my bachelor's and master's degree in criminal justice, I opened a federal halfway house for non-violent offenders in Saginaw, MI. The weekend we officially opened, my dad died of cancer. One and a half years after opening the halfway house, my mom took ill and I moved to Indianapolis with my two children to care for her. Ten months after I moved, my mom died. I found myself in Indianapolis, alone with two children: Mayosha, age eleven and Jonathan, age four. At that time I was thirty-two and had been married and divorced three times between the age of twenty-one through thirty-one. I was looking for love in all of the wrong places. My second husband was physically, emotionally, and verbally abusive. While my first and third husbands did not abuse me physically or verbally, each of my marriages left me emotionally bankrupt. Perhaps a contributing factor for my misaligned search for love was the fact that I was molested by the church deacon when I was around five. Perhaps a factor was my mother's codependent personality, which contributed to me having attributes similar to a child of an alcoholic parent. I don't know. But I did know that I needed to engage in a serious self-analysis if I wanted to survive and be successful. I needed to learn to love me as God loved me. An outcome of my self-analysis was to become driven towards excellence in all I did. I discovered I had two burning passions: helping ex-offenders in their efforts to successfully reintegrate into society and developing and facilitating workshops. God has allowed me to do both throughout my life.

"In 1998 I started my business: Bryant Educational Seminars & Training – Delivering the BEST in training design and dynamics. I became well known across the country for my interactive, 'edutaining' workshops. The same year I started my business, the movie *How Stella Got Her Groove Back*, was released. By this time I had discovered that I had a gift for writing poetry and wrote a poem, I Want My Groove Back! The poem quickly became a favorite, as I would open some of my workshops with certain lines and stanza's from it. The positive feedback I received about the poem motivated me to develop a workshop based on the poem. The workshop was a tremendous hit. Agencies around Indiana were requesting 'Groove Back'. I did 'The Social Worker's Grooveback', 'Grooveback' for state workers, 'Grooveback' for counselors, 'Grooveback' for educators – the list was seemingly endless. I remember at one workshop I shared the story about wanting to be a heart surgeon. A participant told me that I was indeed a heart surgeon because I was helping people mend their hearts! At one 'Grooveback' workshop in Marion, IN, a participant suggested that I write a book because the workshop was so rich. The workshop focused on 'groove stealers', 'groove imitators', and being centered and grounded in oneself which is the essence of having 'groove'. Writing a book was not my dream; however, I played around with the concept and after many conversations with the Lord, 'I want my groove back!...God's Way' was born. The first print was in 2008. It was re-printed in 2010 and is still going strong!

"The Lord gave me the concept of having 'Grooveback Parties' to promote both the book and healing for people who attend. Hundreds of persons – mostly women – have been blessed at 'grooveback parties' – from Indiana to Michigan to Kentucky to Tennessee to Georgia and other states. Both the book and the parties are cathartic for me – as I share stories of my journey and invite others to do the same as we navigate our way to true groove, which cannot be realized without a relationship with God. We learn how to deal face-to-face with groove stealers – those people, places, situations, and things that knock us off our square. We learn how to recognize the groove imitators – those people, places, and things that we grab on to so we can feel good (they are always temporal and don't last long). We learn to follow God's wisdom provided to us in Scripture to look within ourselves and upward to Him to find real groove. Also in 2010, I published my second book, The Truth Be Told, which is a collection of some of my finest poetry. Some of my poems were inspired during my trip to Egypt in 1995. Others were inspired by events in my life, and yet others were written as specific requests for special occasions.

"In addition to designing and facilitating workshops, promoting 'Grooveback', and publishing poetry, I remained true to my passion of helping people with criminal histories to be successful and became well known as an advocate for and friend of ex-offenders. This parlayed into several government contract positions with federal projects such as Weed & Seed, the U.S. Attorney's Office of Southern Indiana, and Project Safe Neighborhoods. Eventually I was hired as the Director of Re-Entry of the Mayor of Indianapolis. I developed several programs designed to assist newly released prisoners in their reintegration efforts and became a requested national speaker on the topic of offender reintegration.

"In November, 2011, I experienced the ultimate groove-stealer. My daughter, Mayosha, died in a drowning accident. She was thirty-one. This was the ultimate test that determined if my 'grooveback' talk was just talk or could I really get centered in the Word of God and keep my groove! I'm not going to lie and say it was easy. However, I had done enough self-work to know that I could truly do "all things through Him that strengthens me". Two weeks after my daughter's funeral, I packed up and moved to Savannah, GA. God had been calling me to this place that I'd never seen before 2011. I used my daughter's death to motivate me to move and to finish my dissertation (I'd started working on my Ph.D. in 2007.) In our last conversation, on the day she died, she told me she was proud of me. I strive daily to continuously live up to her praise. God has certainly blessed me here: I successfully defended my dissertation in June, 2013 and attended commencement in January, 2014.

"I have resumed Grooveback parties with some frequency – both in Atlanta and Savannah. I am active in the spoken word community and The Truth Be Told was recently selected as a required text for a reading class at the Savannah Technical Institute. I am a Professor of Criminal Justice at Armstrong State University, where I was recently awarded the 2013-14 Outstanding Faculty Award! Additionally, my passion, skills, and expertise around offender reintegration are being noticed and I have been asked to be a keynote speaker and/or panelist about justice, economics, and offender reentry on multiple occasions.

"My experiences motivate me to continue to live my God-given life like its golden! Future plans? I plan to continue teaching. I love having the opportunity to seed into young minds and challenge them to move beyond mediocrity. I plan to continue writing. I'm working on my next book: Living In The Press. It is based on Paul's words in Philippians 3:13 and is designed to encourage readers while they are yet 'in the press' – which is whatever life is pressing upon them. I want to help them to press through and press on to whatever God has for them – we can't afford to get stuck in the press! Additionally, I had the privilege and honor to travel to Ghana, Africa in 2013 where I presented a paper entitled, A Comparative Overview of the Response to Prisoner Reintegration By Islam and The Black Church. While visiting the 'slave river' and the 'slave castle', poetry poured out of me; thus I plan to publish another book of poetry within the next two years.

"In summary, I believe God created the first man to live in groove -- a state of perfect peace in a perfect Garden. Sin entered the world and that perpetual state of peace dissipated. Since then, mankind has been chasing the 'pursuit of peacefulness' – some call it happiness. I call it groove. The ultimate state of groove will occur when Christ returns and gathers his Church and creates the New Heaven and the New Earth (Revelation 21:1). Until then, God gives us snippets of peace/groove as we journey through life. When it seems that I'm off center and out of groove, I encourage myself with my own words from the poem: 'I want my groove back! And, I'm gonna get it!'"

Jacquie "Lady J" Jeffers

Educator, Motivational Speaker, Songwriter

ROAR: *Inspiration through the spoken word*

Lady J is an educator, motivational speaker, songwriter, videographer, director and actress. Her passion for spreading positive messages through rapping is amazing! Elevating the self-esteem of others is her specialty. She has won several awards on the local and state levels for her innovative teaching style. She has been heard on radio stations. Her educational raps engage the audience. Students in elementary to high school are able to participate with enthusiasm and relate to the inspirational messages in her unique deliverance! At the annual Women's Empowerment Symposium held in Raleigh, North Carolina, she was recognized by her mentor and owner of Radio One, Ms. Cathy Hughes for her songwriting talent. In front of 14,000 people, Ms. Hughes read the lyrics to the intro song that Lady J wrote for Patti LaBelle to the audience. Ms. Hughes described Lady J as a "great songwriter". Ms. LaBelle asked her to write a song for her. As a result, "Through the Storm" was created based on Ms. LaBelle's Women's Empowerment speech.

On national television, she won RoseAnne's "Take the Day Off Contest" as RoseAnne professed to the television audience "Jacquie's got a lot of talent out there!" Lady Js believes that when she can get the audience involved her concept to encourage and uplift are accomplished. Lady J was a participant on Brian Dawson of K97.5's EOG Tour perform-ing her original rap "Pass My EOG's". She emceed for Wake County's

EOG Celebration at the Walnut Creek Amphitheater in 2013. She is a former education chairperson for the State of North Carolina's Martin Luther King, Jr. Commission and has served on the Grant Committee. Lady J has performed the song that she wrote about Dr. Martin Luther King, Jr. in many venues in North Carolina and at the Rosa Parks Museum in Alabama. As a motivational speaker, she keeps the audience's attention with participation. Her mentoring program entitled "Share the Dream Project" was created to inspire the youth to excel in academics and have good attendance and behavior all year long. In 2013, she co-hosted the television show *It's All That* in Rocky Mount with Everett Silver which was seen in 300,000 Eastern North Carolina homes!

Lady J says, "It is my strong belief that students will take a different approach to learning if the instructional techniques are varied. Compassion for Academics with Responsibility in Education is a motto that I use to inspire students. Merely presenting a lesson following the 6 steps of a lesson plan is a basic foundation for what is required. However, adding compassion for what I teach is essential. Constantly locating tangible devices, speakers, and visuals to assist students with a clear understanding of what is being taught makes compassion a reality in the classroom. I use newspapers to locate the author's purpose or ask a celebrity to send inspirational words via DVD.

Teaching students that academics are the most important part of having more opportunities in life is crucial. Striving for high grade point averages allows the student to join school clubs, apply for scholarships and have positive self-esteem. Incentives for good behavior and maintaining high averages involve obtaining support from community sponsors. I often like to incorporate a quote by actor Denzel Washington: "Do what you have to do, so you can do what you want to do." Academics can move you above and beyond with high expectations. Building character by being responsible for his or her actions and being active in community service makes a student a more productive individual. It is the assurance that the student "can" and remove the concept of I"cannot". Being responsible creates a no fault spirit to nurture analytical and critical thinking skills. The student's character has room for maturity and dependability. Education is the key to knowledge which never stops. Incorporating life skills to help students understand the significance of what they are learning is essential. Making the connections by using the proper grammar with a mock job interview is an example of a hands-on activity. Bringing in a banker to explain how to balance a checkbook or a journalist to discuss writing an editorial makes the lesson more interesting. Summarizing magazine articles from Newsweek expands the students' knowledge with global topics. Teaching students by connecting the content with life skills and building self-esteem makes learning more interesting. The attention span and participation increases! Students understand why their part in the educational process helps them to become productive independent learners. These are some of my methods of showing them that I C.A.R.E."

Nyellka C. Denham

Founder, Diamonds of Wholeness

Educator/Entrepreneur

ROAR: *Equipping Women and Girls for Success*
"You can't defeat what you don't have knowledge of"

Growing up in an undeveloped home with a father who did not love himself and a mother left to pick up all the pieces at a young age, is one of the main reasons why the non-profit organization "Diamond of Wholeness" had to come to reality.

I lost my father at the age of seven, due to alcohol and drug addiction. This caused a lot of heartache, low self-esteem and uncertainties in life for me and my siblings. Through the journey of life, I and my sister and brothers struggled deeply with the importance of loving ourselves, healthy relationships, money management and the concept of positive decision making. One of the main areas that tried to destroy my life was fornication, because I had a great need to feel loved by someone. This caused me personally to look for love in all the wrong places. Although we lived in a poverty stricken area in Detroit, Michigan, my mom knew the importance of education, which was the driving force of positive mental change. Education gave us a better view of ourselves and our future outside of a poverty environment. However, for me, my true self-worth — and having a clear understanding of my purpose — came from me learning how much God loved me. Although my mother struggled with providing for us, we were fortunate enough to attend private schools and programs that implemented skills and resources that gave me and my siblings hope and opportunities for our future.

There were many traumatic events that happened in my life, which naturally gave me a heart for the hurt and wounded. This is how I discovered I was called to mentor and teach. My personal mission is to help others reach their destiny. But my number one purpose is to teach and show, that if you have a relationship with God, then you are guaranteed a mental change, which leads to a successful life. My assignment on this earth is to love myself, educate, coach and mentor others to do the same.

After completing high school, I was still challenged to figure out what career path I was born to do. I tried college, but I experienced challenges that made me believe I could not achieve in the academic world. Because I knew I had a passion for hair and beauty I decided to attend cosmetology school. I completed cosmetology school in 2003. I became a cosmetology educator in 2007 and received my Trichology (hair loss within health and wellness) certification in 2010 and my Trichology instructor license in 2012. From pursuing this career, I learned quickly that you may appear confident on the outside, but that does not give a true picture of who you are on the inside.

Although my journey had some losses, I experienced many wins. I truly live for the excitement of what God has for me every day. In February 2014, I opened my salon and continuing education business named Elegant Nation, "The World of Enhancement." They call me 'The Beauty Tutor'. Having an entrepreneurial spirit and a purpose for helping others, Diamond of Wholeness was birthed in 2011. Diamonds of Wholeness will provide preventive and intervention methods of teaching in areas such as, self-esteem, decision making, positive choices and conflict management. Being the visionary of Diamonds of Wholeness, I have a great desire and deep passion for girls and women to practice, learn and live by applications which will equip them for success. Our goal is to make sure they have the ability to use these methods as a road map in life. This will begin a new and solid foundation for future families. Sometimes I can't believe the little black girl with low self-esteem from the Jefferies projects was chosen by God to change a damaged world into an Elegant Nation. The best of me is yet to come!!!!!

"*A woman is the full circle. Within her is the power to create, nurture and transform.*"

-Diane Mariechild

Roar

2

Media | Film | Entertainment

Before machines the only form of entertainment people really had was relationships.

-Douglas Coupland

Sheila Raye Charles

Minister, Singer, Author

Daughter of Soul Legend Ray Charles

ROAR: *Spreading hope to the lost*

I never dreamed that my life would take the path that it did. As a child, I dreamed of being a doctor, a lawyer, a cheerleader, or a psychologist like my mother. Well, I thought of her as a psychologist because she counseled and solved everyone's problems. Except mine. Don't get me wrong, my mom did do some problem solving, but only on those problems that I would reluctantly share.

I grew up in a family of greatness. Silky Betts, my great, great, great grandmother, was the first freed Black slave in Ohio. My grandparents settled down in a town called Cambridge and became one of the most influential families there—the most prominent black family hands down! Talk about a recipe to ROAR! I was destined to do that! On top of my mother's family legacy, I was the daughter of the legendary Ray Charles. I should have been on top of the world. However, that's not quite how it worked for me. I experienced sexual abuse as a young girl and saw my mother, a great woman, become a victim of abusive relationships and alcoholism. Life was not safe. There was also the anticipation of the phone ringing with "Ray" on the other end. Mine was a life full of false hopes, fear for my mother's life, and a visit from the sexual perpetrators coming to my room in the dark of night. Did I have good moments? Of course, but trauma always seemed to be at the forefront of my mind, especially as a child.

The effort to find my true self, not just being the daughter of Ray Charles, but the real ME, was not an easy task. I had been taught to identify myself by who I was related to—I was Sheila, daughter of Ray Charles, or 'that Betts girl'. But who was I really? I was more like the real me when I was high on whatever was available, so that's what I did. I got high and made myself up. When all was said and done, a Sheila appeared that I didn't even like! My life had spiraled to a place of hell that didn't seem likely to change and it soon took a turn that would impact me forever. A twenty year crack addiction sent me to federal prison for the third time and put me in the depths of hell. A mother of five children with custody of none, I was completely lost and hopeless. I cried out to God while lying on the concrete floor in federal prison, devoid of hope. Incredibly, something supernatural happened! The voice of God spoke to me and revealed that everything about the old Sheila, the one lying on the concrete floor, was built on a lie. The thoughts I had of myself were built on abuse, false hope and addiction. If I truly wanted to "fly like an eagle or roar like a lion," I had to let go of the lies that I accepted as truths. It was not easy as those lies were very familiar to me. I had to learn to trust God. I began to study his word and came to see who God had created me to be. I took to heart, the things that were written in the scriptures. I was wonderfully and perfectly made! I was the light of the world, the salt of the earth and I, Sheila Jean Robinson, was made in the image of God! Wow, can you hear me roar now? The word of God inspired me and gave me the freedom to be myself! I gained a freedom I had never known and receive promises from God that he reveals daily. I am able to share those promises with the world through my testimony and music because God's promises are for us – all of us, not just me! From out of the dark and into the light, I stand in hope and love. I know that my future is bright because I no longer orchestrate it. God is in control! My desire is to travel the globe sharing this message of love, grace and hope to a world that is so very lost. If I could say one thing to anyone who might listen it is 'Love never gives up!' I love you, God loves you, and you do have a hope and a future. Keep on believing. God is able!

Deborah Hayter

Publicist, Deborah Hayter Public Relations

ROAR: *Maximizing Exposure*

Deborah Hayter grew up in the Lincoln Park area of Chicago during the civil rights movement. Her role models were her parents, who worked tirelessly for better housing, health care and quality education in underserved communities. After graduating with a degree from DePaul University with a BA in Art History, Deborah was accepted into the Loyola University Art Master's Program in Florence, Italy, studying 17th Century tapestries. Deborah obtained her master's degree, but continued her academic career in Art and Communication at Kings College in the United Kingdom. While on a school holiday, she traveled with her parents to West Africa, where she witnessed first-hand the devastation brought on by extreme poverty. It had a profound impact on her, and as a result, she returned to the United States (Chicago) and recruited volunteers for Catholic Charities' Homeless Shelter Program. During this period she attended school and worked for Curtom Records. Under the tutelage of Curtis Mayfield, Deborah gained considerable knowledge and insight about the business side of the music industry at the company that represented artists such as Etta James and Tyrone Davis.

"In those days, I would answer the phone, get coffee, pose for album covers and find backup singers," said Deborah. When the company was sold, Deborah accepted a brand marketing position with Barton Distributors, traveling all over the world branding their product (Corona, Cervesa Modelo Beer) promoted by the rock Group Chicago. Several years later, Deborah married and lived in Europe before returning to the United States. During this time she was recruited by her former college roommate, Samantha Grier, to assist in the development of a program that would provide Teddy Bears to ease the suffering and deprivation experienced by children living under debilitating circumstances. Thus, Caring for Children and the Teddy Bear Program was founded. At this point Deborah discovered her talent for bringing together celebrities to assist in causes that made a difference in other's lives.

After the National Campaign launch of Caring for Children, Deborah accepted a position as the Director of Marketing for the Presidio Trust. She traveled to Moscow with the Curator and other administrators to oversee a special exhibition called the Unseen Treasures of Imperial Russia. The exhibition became one of the most popular Smithsonian Exhibits for three years running with high visibility in print, TV and radio media. The exhibit was eventually viewed by more than 20,000 visitors. In addition, over $500,000 was raised to promote multi-cultural activities throughout California. At the end of the exhibition, Deborah accepted a position at the University of California/San Francisco as a Faculty Research Assistant to Cardiologist and Mechanical Circulatory Heart Specialist, Dr. Stan Glantz. Dr Glantz, the author of several books, most notably, "The Cigarette Papers", is recognized as a tireless advocate for anti-smoking legislation. Working with Dr. Glantz was a pivotal time for Deborah, learning about publishing and how to promote first-time authors. Dr. Glantz eventually became a much sought after speaker and his book sales were impressive. "The Cigarette Papers" was also made into an HBO Special. On Dr. Glantz's recommendation, Deborah was promoted to Marketing Director of the UCSF Cardiology Fellowship Program, working with pharmaceutical companies that provided grants and sponsorship to research heart related diseases. A chance encounter with a former professor and screenwriter/author Serita Stevens altered Deborah's career path, changing her focus to working in public relations for film and television projects. Stevens, who wrote a total of thirty-two books and is also a forensic nurse and consultant to several television drama series, introduced Deborah to many of her colleagues in film and television.

To date, Deborah has provided PR for a total of eleven Film Festivals, nine independent films, three upcoming television shows, several screenwriters and has placed her clients in a number of celebrity charities including The Halle Barry Celebrity Golf Tournament, The Lupus Foundation Orange Ball, Celebrity Poker Tournaments, The Danny Thomas St. Jude Foundation, Save the Wild Mustangs, Save the Music Foundation, Step Up Women's Foundation, The Voice (Celebrities Making a Difference), Mo's Kitchen (With Robin Williams, Danny Glover, Sharon Stone), The Diabetes Foundation, Compton Jr. Posse, Healthy Smile, the Melanoma Foundation, Save The Music, MusicCares, and a number of cause related foundations.

Deborah continues to work tirelessly for her clients: authors promoting their books; entertainers; record producers; filmmakers and foundations maximizing their exposure and publicity in print, television, radio, and internet media. Deborah enjoys reading mystery novels and riding her horse, Sandy.

Memberships: National Association of Publicists; Film Industry Network (Los Angeles); Film Network (Las Vegas); Las Vegas Music & Entertainment Assn; National Association of Black Female Executives in Music and Entertainment, Former Board Member of the Chicago Art Institute; Public Relations Society of America; Media Bistro, American Society of Journalists and Authors, The Beverly Hills Chapter of the NAACP.

Lynnette Taylor

Award-Winning Journalist/Anchor

WITN

ROAR: *Advocacy for the homeless and less fortunate.*

A professor once told me, and our entire Communications class, to just forget about becoming journalists upon graduation. *Excuse me?* I thought. *I'm a junior and two years into my major. This is not the time to turn around, now!* "You might as well get your degree and then turn around and get a master's in something else, because you will not get a job in your major," she said. This went on for more than an hour. I learned nothing in class that day, only that I needed to prove her and everyone else wrong.

Two years later, I did. I graduated from East Carolina University and one week later I started my part-time job at WITN as an associate producer. God is Good! This was the bottom of the barrel job. I made minimum wage and worked the graveyard shift; 3am until 10am. Then it became 3am until 1pm. I did this on the weekends, but my primary job: Blockbuster Video, Monday thru Friday, paid my rent, electric bill, food and other necessities to survive. If I had to tell one more person to rewind their videos before returning them, I didn't know what to do! Oh! The days of video tapes! I digress! I was very poor! Sometimes running out of funds for personal products just so I could pay my rent. As an associate producer, I took advantage of being inside the newsroom. I went to the news director's office on a regular basis, letting him know I wanted a chance to get out into the field. I went out with reporters after my regular shift, just so I could learn more about gathering the news. I put together my own stories, so I could sharpen my skills. I even drove more than forty-five minutes away from home, to work with one of our photographers who normally worked, solo, gathering the news. This opportunity allowed me to work on this story from start to finish. This opportunity turned into my first story, this opportunity turned into my first reporting position and my start in front of the camera, instead of behind the scenes. That was just eleven months into starting at WITN. Goal number one achieved: To be a reporter! NEXT GOAL: Become an anchor!

There is more money in sitting behind that desk. The news desk is like a throne for anchors. It took about three years to get a weekend morning anchoring position. I still reported during the week for three days and reported after my morning show anchoring gig. I carried my own equipment. I didn't have a team of people, helping me investigate stories, shoot my video or even do my makeup. I did it all. Every day was an eye-opening experience. On occasion, I encountered those who couldn't believe black women were on TV, even in early 2000. Some just kept their thoughts to themselves, others were more vocal.

During a story about dead fish washing ashore in Beaufort County, I discovered a person who had a large parcel of land with an old home and a trailer near the shore. He seemed close to 100 years old. I walked up to him, with my camera in tow, to get his personal account of living off the shore, where dead fish washed ashore to rot. He wasn't interested in being on TV, but he had a lot to say. He, at first, told me about his family that owned this land who also owned slaves. He spoke of the cemetery nearby where his family was buried, while the Blacks were buried in unmarked graves on the land...even in the dirt I stood on. After a long conversation, I listened out of respect for my elders. He proceeds to ask me what I do at the TV station. He said, "I've never seen you before." I told him I mainly work weekends anchoring the morning show. He said, "What do you do? Make biscuits?" I was shocked! He thought I was the help. I had no response for him. NEXT GOAL: Leave and join another news station.

I wanted a new adventure in my career. I was coming up on five years at the station and felt it was my time to make a move. I wasn't going to make it to prime time staying at WITN. So I sent my resume reel to stations, north and south of North Carolina. I didn't get one bite! I realized my contract was coming up and I didn't have an option, but to re-sign for multiple years, again. A former reporter who moved to

Florida three years prior, kept in contact with me. He said I should send my reel to him for his news director to view. I needed a second opinion, maybe some pointers to make my reel better, so I agreed. I didn't want to move to Florida because of the heat. But wouldn't you know, the news director liked my reel enough, that he offered me a job. They didn't have a need for a reporter, but would make room for me until someone at their station left. I couldn't believe it. God's Hands were moving for me and I didn't understand why until I made the move. It was there I met a woman who spent her life helping the homeless. In the heat of the summer, there she was and her white, fifteen passenger van filled with bags and bags of clothes. At sixty-seven years old, she was still very agile. But she sat on a folding lawn chair and spread out her free clothes on a blanket placed on the ground. She sat and watched as people picked through her free items. I went there to do a story on her. She was the Mother Teresa of Gainesville, Florida.

As she spoke to me, I understood why I ended up in Florida. Sister Hazel Williams spoke to me prophetically about my life. As a believer of Christ, she knew things about me, only God could tell her. I was searching for something greater in my life and she became my teacher. From that moment on, I found the greater calling in my life. I joined her church, I got baptized, and I rededicated my life to helping others. I became a missionary for God and would help her clothe those who needed it and eventually we started a nighttime feeding table for the homeless three nights a week. This was one of the greatest times of my life. It was fulfilling to do something for strangers. But those strangers became my greatest joy. I spent four years in Gainesville, Florida, serving God and working in TV. I thank my godmother, Sister Hazel, for showing me the way. She also helped me realize the man I left in North Carolina four years ago, was the man I loved unconditionally. After reuniting, Frederic and I married in Florida, but his work was in North Carolina. He drew me back to my home state and eventually back to WITN.

I quickly joined my old crew of co-workers at WITN and quickly worked on stories that garnered awards from the Associated Press and the Radio and Television News Directors Association of NC (RTNDANC) – one of my dreams! I was blessed to not only report and anchor, but to eventually make my debut on prime time TV as the 6pm anchor in 2009.

God is truly AMAZING! I now think about my future—my next goal! I'm leaving my options open. I'm dreaming of running my business. I'm dreaming of opening a place where every homeless person gets assistance in every city in the country! I'm dreaming of being successful, the way God has always blessed me.

Gemma Bulos

Award-winning singer, speaker, and Social Entrepreneur

ROAR: *To bring clean water to Africa and Asia*

How to Accidentally Change the World:

Can you believe the mission to bring 210,000 people clean water in Asia and Africa started with a song? I've almost died a few times, the first on my twentieth birthday. I was in Rosario, Mexico with friends and they bought me a parasailing ride as a gift. If you've never been parasailing, it's a big parachute that you're attached to via a harness, tightly bound around your hips and shoulders. The harness is then attached to a 500 foot rope, tied to a speedboat and when the boatman hits the gas you're up and airborne! Fun, right? It took about a minute for the blood to rush from my hands and pain to kick in on my arms to realize something might be wrong. Apparently, I wasn't hooked into the harness right. It was too loose and when I was whisked into the air, it locked around the middle of my upper arms, forcing my arms straight up and pressing against my ears. In a perfect ride, the straps are tucked snugly under your arms, so you have freedom of movement, be able to navigate the parachute and land safely on the beach, as instructed. But for me, because the straps were too loose and I couldn't pull my arms back down, I was quickly losing the strength and blood in my arms. When it came time to try and land myself on the beach, I could not muster up the strength to pull the parachute enough to get me on the beach, and I got yanked back up by a gust of wind. I had already been up there for fifteen minutes. With my arms in helpless surrender, I was in so much pain that I fainted.

When I awoke, I was disoriented and scared and had absolutely no idea what to do. All I could think was "stop the pain, stop the pain." I slowly and instinctually, but not thinking rationally, started to peel the straps off. When I took off the second one, I flipped upside down, hanging from my knees 300 feet in the air over the water. I was looking down thinking, *I'm going to die in the water*. After what felt like an eternity, my knees finally let go too, and I went free-falling head first into the water. From 300 feet, it's like hitting concrete. Luckily, I flipped and landed in the water in a sitting position. I later found out that I had broken my back in three places. As I look back, I realize it could have been worse. I could have landed on the beach. Water actually embraced me and broke my fall, allowing me to float up to the surface. Unfortunately, it floated me face down. So, I was unconscious again. But this time, it was beautiful. I started to feel my body dissolving in the water. I became part of the water. I was moving where it was leading me. I was ebbing, flowing, and it was one of the most beautiful feelings to be part of this vast and powerful ocean. I remember thinking, *I could live here, I want to live here, be part of this ocean*. It was so peaceful and blissful. Then I heard a voice. It said, "Haven't I always taken care of you?" That was just when I was ready to surrender and 'cross over.' But before I could figure out where the voice came from, I felt a hand grab me by the back of my life vest, yank me out of my watery bliss, stick me in a boat and bring me back to land. Now the second time I almost died…

I lived in New York City. By day, I was a pre-school teacher, and by night, I was a professional jazz singer. Every Tuesday and Thursday I would get out of the train in the basement of the World Trade Center to go teach my pre-school class at 8:50 in the morning. On Tuesday, September 11, 2001, I didn't want to go to work, so I called in sick. Whenever something tragic happens to me, I always try to find a piece of inspiration that is going to help me start my own personal healing and hopefully help others do the same. Being in NYC right after that tragedy was a totally different place. Only two weeks before, you were on the train, pressed up against five or six different strangers, their armpits in your face, and yet you knew nothing about these people. In all our intimacy, you didn't even acknowledge that they were there. Yet, after the tragedy, walking the streets, on the bus, or in line, people were looking at each other. They were connecting as if to say, "I know what you're feeling, I feel it too."

During this time, I had to change the way I saw the world. I had to look at it, not as a divisive community being totally separated by this tragedy, but as an opportunity for people to come together and connect, albeit through their sadness and their grief. I wanted to try to create that sense of connection again, that kind of unity, this time, not through tragedy and grief, but through celebration. I wanted us to celebrate that we are all the same, that we all want the same things for ourselves, family, and friends. To be connected, to have happiness, opportunity, security, and peace. So I wrote a song, called "We Rise" as my way of bringing people together. I had this crazy idea that I was going to build a million voice choir around the world to sing it. So, I left my job, life, and career, gave away all my belongings, left my relationship and apartment. I took my backpack and guitar, and with what little money I had, I started to travel around the world, inviting people to be part of this global peace movement. One of the major themes in the song when I wrote it was the notion that "it takes a single drop of water to start a wave." So that was my invitation to people, to see themselves as that drop. Every thought, every word, every action will ripple out and will impact those around them. So, I started to be known as the 'water lady', the 'lady singing for water'.

I started getting invited to conferences all over the world forenvironmental justice, women's empowerment, youth leadership, conflict resolution, and peace… And magical things started to happen. People heard about what I was doing and I was getting airline, train and bus tickets handed to me. One woman handed me $2,000 before I got on a plane to go to Russia, just to make sure I was taken care of. A woman in Barcelona, Spain came up to me and said, "You're that woman singing for water." I didn't have a place to stay that night, and she brought me to her home and I had a place to stay for ten days! I was taken care of everywhere I went! Everywhere!

In 2003, I got invited to bring the song to the Water for Life conference at the United Nations. Here I was, at this incredibly important global gathering, and the only reason I was there was because I happened to inadvertently use water as a metaphor in my song. That was it. But on that day, at that conference, I came to find out that there was an actual water crisis. Who knew? Who knew that 1 out of 7 people in the world did not have access to fresh water? Forget *clean* water, but just *fresh* water. Who knew that over half the hospital beds in the world on any given day are occupied by people with water-related illnesses? Who knew that women around the world in developing countries collectively spend forty billion hours fetching water and not having any other opportunity to do anything else? Who knew that 1 out of 10 girls drop out of school in 8th grade because there are no toilets and they start menstruating? Who knew that every fifteen seconds a child dies from water related disease? I certainly didn't. And that was a game changer. Here I was, thinking that this song was leading me everywhere I wanted to go, thinking this is where I needed to be or what I needed to do for my purpose. And, meanwhile, it actually transformed from being my metaphor to my cause and ultimately my destiny.

September 21, 2004 was the day that I invited everyone around the world to sing "We Rise" from all over the planet. After about two years of travel, I had been able to mobilize over 100 cities in 60 countries to sing "We Rise" from wherever they were. It was incredible because this was way before Facebook and Twitter. People found out through word of mouth because we didn't even have any press! And honestly, although it was incredibly inspirational, it was also very bittersweet, because I had to ask myself, "Six minutes of united song, what about minute seven? What's next? What does peace actually look like on the ground?" And the answer was clear: water. So I started to learn everything I possibly could about the water crisis. I found out that the first recorded peace treaty was in ancient Mesopotamia over 4500 years ago, a treaty over water. I learned about the grassroots movements happening in South America, Africa and Asia, where small villages were fighting back against corporations taking their water and privatizing, and selling it for profit. But the villages were winning. I found out about some of those kinds of grassroots movements happening in the US too, but not succeeding. I started to see this bigger picture about how water affects every single living being on this planet. Including the country of my heritage, the Philippines.

The Philippines is an island nation plagued by monsoons, typhoons, floods, and conflict year-round. And not one a year, but multiple a year. It is, in fact, the most disaster prone region in all of Southeast Asia. One of their biggest challenges is not that they don't have water, but that they have too much, but no local infrastructure to manage it, deliver it and make sure it's not contaminated. So, after my research, I learned how to build a really simple water treatment technology that anyone could build around the world if you had cement, sand, and gravel. It was a really efficient technology that had never been brought to the Philippines before. So, when we brought it there, we knew that we couldn't just focus on transferring a technology, teaching people how to make it and then walking away. This is something that international development has done for many years and it has been failing. We had to figure out an efficient way that the community itself could provide clean water and make it sustainable. So, I was lucky enough to win an award from Queen Latifah and Covergirl for Women Who are Changing the World Through Music. So now I had the seed capital to start this. We were told that people in various communities didn't like handouts. They didn't want people to come in and do things for them. They wanted to be able to provide the solutions themselves, generate some income so that they could manage it and take the profits to reinvest in their own community development. So that's what we did. We worked together with them to design a program to facilitate a process in which they were not looking at what they didn't have – they were identifying all the resources that they did have and figured out how to harness it. So all we did was support them with tools and skills to identify their issues; how they were going to solve it; the technology they were going to implement; and then we helped them create an organizational infrastructure that could manage taking in income so that they could pay their staff, maintain the system, and reinvest in their own development. Apparently, that was considered an innovative social entrepreneurial model according to Echoing Green, Schwab Foundation, Ernst & Young and The Tech Awards. We started winning many awards. It was insane! We couldn't believe it because all we did was listen to the wisdom of the community.

Our original plan was to only be there for three months, maybe six. It has now been six years, and although I'm no longer with that organization, they are still thriving! I'm working with women now in Africa as the Director of Global Women's Water Initiative, because they are the ones most burdened by the lack of water.

In just under eight years, the programs I started have provided over 210,000 people with clean water and sanitation in Asia and Africa. What?? Wait a minute! I was a jazz singer! I was a preschool teacher! How did I get here? If you had asked me eight years ago what I would be doing, I never in a million years would have imagined this. I know you're going to think this is corny, but honestly, I think water had plans for me from the beginning.

From the time I was floating half dead with a broken neck in Mexico on my twentieth birthday to this present time, I have been on a journey that I could have never dreamed of. And all it took was doing what my heart told me to do. It truly does take a single drop of water to start a wave. In my case it was a 300 foot drop! We may not know where we're going, but we do know that it just takes that one commitment to get there. What's your drop?

Tryneal Addison

Host, What Girls Think

ROAR: *Inspiring Young Girls and Women*

You know, I'd like to say that my journey of becoming a successful talk show host started back when I was five years old, but that certainly was not that case. When I was five years old I realized I wanted to be in the entertainment industry after seeing Raven Symone on *The Cosby Show*. I loved her wit, her energy and her charm. She was everything I wanted to be. Around that time, my mom began taking me to local auditions. I would get callbacks, but they would ask for thousands of dollars! Although my mom could afford it, she didn't feel that it should be so expensive or cost at all! I stopped going to auditions until I turned twelve years old. I went to modeling and acting auditions and was rejected each time.. It really hurt my feelings. I thought, "God, is this for me?" It really weighed on my self-esteem. I just felt that I should give up and try something else, but I didn't. I kept trying.

Fast forward to age fourteen, ninth grade. I was accepted into a prestigious art high school in my local town. The school rated very high in acting, singing, and dancing. If you got into this school, then you were somebody! I got in but only stayed one day! I hated it! It was not the place for me. I was uncomfortable and not in the element that I wanted to be in. I thought if I went to an art school I would finally be around people like me… but I was DEAD wrong. I left that school and went to another high school. I didn't like that school either. I chose to be homeschooled with a tutor which worked out well for me. I was able to focus on my studies and had time to work on things pertaining to my career. I began going to auditions again, landing a few petty jobs here and there. But I wanted more. I wanted greater! I joined a local talent agency and stayed with them for about six months. They never got me a job. My mother became very ill and I had to take care of her alone at the age of fourteen. I have two other siblings, but they were not much help. Taking care of mom was very challenging. I couldn't focus in school or hang out with my friends. I felt as if my youth was taken from me and I had to become a woman…a mother to my own mother. Play time was over. I was angry, gained tons of weight, and had no one to talk to. I couldn't talk to my mom because I didn't want to make her feel worse than she already felt. She had enough going on in her own life. I finally talked to the guidance counselor at school. Talking to her helped me to relieve some stress.

Once I was able to talk about how I felt, I began doing better in school and was finally at peace. With less stress in my life. I started losing the weight. However, I was still frustrated with my career. I was beginning to believe that maybe it wasn't what God had planned for my life. But I was so wrong! My mom told me that I had a great voice to be a talk show host. She said, "you have a voice that could inspire and you should use that. It is your gift. That is what you should be, a talk show host!"

My mother is my number one motivator! Once she said that, it was like something sparked inside of me. I felt like I was pregnant and that it was time to give birth to this new idea. It was amazing! God used my mom to help me discover my destiny. After that, I sat down and wrote proposals, sending them to production companies. I was inspired enough to send one to Ellen and Oprah! For two years I sent out proposals, but never got any callbacks. Although I was frustrated, I kept praying and refused to give up.

One night I was up pretty late, determined to keep looking until I found my answer. I finally found my blessing! A Web Television Network was looking for new independent producers and new show ideas! I was excited and happy! I couldn't wait to call them the next day! Although proposals were to be sent by email, I decided to call and talk to them personally. I actually called the owner while I was at school and spoke with him for about thirty minutes. He liked my voice and show idea and agreed to produce my show! This was done before I even submitted a proposal! I called my mom and she was through the roof with excitement. We began working on the show, which was called, *What Girls Think!* It was the teen version of *The View.*

I needed four girls for the show and began the search. I ended up finding four amazing girls to do the show with me. We were all from different cities and decided to connect through the use of Internet technology. The producer shipped out five cameras and Bluetooth devices for us to use for the show. Major doors were starting to open up for me. I received local and national press coverage, which was fascinating! I remember the first time my mom saw me in our local newspaper, she cried her eyes out because she was so proud of what I had accomplished! She knew that hosting a talk show and motivating young people was my calling. The show lasted about two and a half years. Graduation and college preparation complicated things. We had to get new girls, but things just didn't work out. My producer and I decided to end the show a year ago.

Ending the show was hurtful because of all the work that I had put into it. It was my baby that I had birthed. I was accepted into Radio College but had to take a leave of absence to care for my ill mother again. I desired to be a radio personality or talk show host and felt that my mom's illness would once again block my dreams. Being less active and social, I started to gain the weight back. I grew tired of feeling sorry for myself and decided to start sending out proposals again. One day I was on my LinkedIn account and this guy sent an email to me about his new television network that would be on Time Warner Cable. I was like "OMG!! Is this a sign, God?" He was looking for investors. I knew he must have sent this message to me by mistake because I didn't even know I was connected to him on this site. I felt in my spirit this might be my chance, but I did something bad. I told a little lie to get his attention. I told him I knew investors that might be interested. He told me to give him a call the next day, so I did. We talked and I told him I knew investors, but I really needed to ask him a question. I asked him if he was looking for show ideas for his network. He said, "YES!" I told him I have an idea for a talk show and he loved it! He said, "I guess God connected us because I'm going to make your dreams come true!" At first I was a little side-eyed because I don't know how many times I've heard that. But he was the real deal! He became my manager and I finally got my TV show! I put together my new show "*The Tryneal Addison Show*" that will be debuting later this year on his network! What's even better is that Time Warner Cable was bought out by Comcast, so the show will have a broader audience! I'm moving to Los Angeles to start my new life! Don't

EVER give up on your dreams. God is always watching you, and even when you hit bumpy roads, they are all a part of your journey! If it is meant to be, it will be. Just have patience and determination and trust God. My future is looking mighty bright and I can't wait to see where my journey will take me next!

Milliea Taylor McKinney

Conscious Music Entertainment, Founder/President

ROAR: *Positive lyrics and entertainment for youth.*

My journey started in education, touching lives of the young. I had always been around children. I am from a large family of twelve, six boys and six girls. Being third from the youngest, it was only natural that I would be surrounded by children in vocation and advocacy. My journey in education prepared me for writing and music. The loves of my life include my sons Joseph and Joshua, my grandchildren Matthew, Alexandria, and Emma Grace, my daughter-in-law Jennifer, and all my brothers and sisters, biological and in Christ.

I am the founder of Conscious Music Entertainment and share ownership with Kevin Lambert, Rhythm and Praise artist and founder of the H13 Project. He also shares in the operations of my other companies, Conscious Radio and Conscious Records that serve as platforms for positive music opportunities. Working in the country music business, I earned the love and respect of some of the greatest names in the industry. As a songwriter, I also earned credibility and many awards. I learned that the true journey to success was being humble and giving glory and gratitude to God, because with him, all things are made possible.

At CME Enterprise, we strive to plant the seeds of God's love in all of our projects. Our most recent one, Music For Aids, is a compilation of mainstream and independent artists benefiting the Dave Baker Foundation. Before taking on this project, I was blessed to have been given a song from my Lord and Savior that would plant hope in a world filled with pain. I was led to the amazing voice of Sheila Raye Charles, who blessed the song with beauty and grace. "We Are Hope" was named "Song of the Year" and is still among the top 10 on charts around the world. This song of hope is also the theme song for the MuZart World Foundation, an organization founded by former VP of MCA Records, Pat Melfi, that restores music legacy in public schools.

My greatest hope and message is to spread the love of Christ in the hearts of humanity through the universal language of music.

In this photo: Naomi Ackerman and daughters Ella, Hadar, and Zohar
Photo credit: Karee Maxson

Naomi Ackerman

The Advot Project, Founder/Executive Director

ROAR: *Surviving Abuse*

My late father was an amazing storyteller. He used to tell us about his life as a poor immigrant's son in Dorchester, Massachusetts, and as a student in Boys' Latin school. He told stories of justice, of marching with Dr. Martin Luther King, and of doing the right thing, not because it was a choice, but because it was a way of life. He told beautiful Jewish stories, making me fall in love again and again with my people and my heritage. He had a heavy Bostonian accent and a clear, strong moral compass. That distinctive voice told beautiful, meaningful stories that moved me and made me who I am today. My father never spoke of or told any stories about his experience as an American soldier in World War II, or what is was like to be a Jewish man liberating the Dachau concentration camp. That story made him eventually pick up our family and move from the United States to Israel, as he would say, the home of the Jews, a place where we would always be safe. I was nine years old, taken to a country where I didn't know the language very well. I had no friends and was immersed in a totally new culture, so, I, too, became a storyteller. I would sit and talk to my dolls and my Barbies telling them how hard it is and how I miss my old home. I then dared to tell my new Israeli friends about America and the life I had—adding fantastical facts no one could ever check since then there was no Internet or any way to know if what I was saying was real or not. These stories, some true, and some made up, helped me find my place and bridge the gap between old and new, familiar and unknown. After serving in the Israeli military, I went to college in Jerusalem. Jerusalem is the ultimate city of stories. Every stone you touch, every person you meet, the many sounds you hear, is a layered story filled with history, religion, conflict, pain, and beauty. I lived in Jerusalem for ten years. After graduating from acting school, I founded an Arab Jewish theater group, where we used the stage to tell stories. We tried to tell interesting, moving stories—stories that made a difference. In this theatre group I learned that we all have a story, and our stories are the refection of the people we meet, the places we have been, the laughter and the pain, our darkness and our light. So many times we think we are the only ones who have a story, or no one can possibly understand our story because they didn't live it. Worse than that, we close our ears and hearts to stories that are different or unfamiliar to us, because we are afraid. We may even shut their stories out because we were taught or told not to listen to them. These were very hard times in the region; bloody, hate-filled times. Our theatre group held on tight to each other through the violence and the rage. We stood on the stage in strong conviction, that together, our story would change the story around us. After a few productions with this theater group, I was commissioned to write a new theatre piece about a battered woman. I created *Flowers Aren't Enough*, a one-woman show that deals with the issue of domestic violence. It is an intense, deep, moving show woven from true stories of a remarkable woman who survived abuse and hardship.

After more than a decade of performing *Flowers Aren't Enough* over 1500 times globally, I realized that I have the power to be the voice of those who cannot stand up and tell their stories. Theatre has the power to give a voice to the silent; to be the voice of change. Change is slow, change is hard, change is painful, but change can happen. I have seen change first-hand. I have been changed. After moving back to the United States, to Los Angeles in 2006, my experiences performing and conducting workshops around the world, and the strong belief in the power of theatre to facilitate renovation, I founded The Advot Project, a nonprofit 501(c)3 corporation. Advot means ripples in the Hebrew language. Change, like a ripple, starts small but leads to overwhelmingly positive transformations. The Advot Project uses theater and storytelling as a communication tool to foster self-esteem, promote healthy relationships and prevent violence, primarily amongst the most vulnerable in society. Through a variety of unique programs, participants become better communicators, learn how to discover and then declare their own self-worth. They develop the capacity to exhibit greater kindness and compassion; first for themselves, and then with others. Advot believes that individuals have a right to live free of fear, enjoy healthy relationships, and be respected for who they are. Most of The Advot Project's work today is with incarcerated girls. Once a week I go up to a juvenile incarceration facility and listen to stories of tough, rough, sweet, amazing, broken girls. These are girls that life has been incredibly unkind to, yet they still smile and laugh and have deep wisdom far beyond their years. I will end with a story from there.

Freedom:

I run a theatre program with incarcerated girls, when asking my girls in Juvie, what it means to be free this is what they said:

Clair: Freedom is not being locked up, and simply walking the street.

Valerie: Freedom means family and friends. Ennis: Freedom is to not be afraid of anything, to be open emotionally, physically, mentally, verbally.

Bianca: Freedom is…Fun, Rejoicing, Energy, Excitement, Dancing, and Outgoing.

Astrid: Freedom is happily ever after, oh, and ice cream.

Lexis: Freedom is being beautiful at any time of day.

I have worn the same perfume for the past twenty years and so I have a very distinctive scent. I transferred that scent to my babies when I held them in their snuggle carriers. People have remarked that my smell precedes my entrance into a room and lingers long after I leave. As I was standing in the recreation room one afternoon in the detention facility one of the young women I work with came up to me and said, "Ms. Nomi, you smell so good!" To which another girl chimed in, "Yeah, she always smells good. She has that good lady smell!" And, still, a third young woman looked at me with a big smile and asked rhetorically, "Ms., I love standing real close to you, know why? 'Cause you, you smell like freedom!"
Working with incarcerated youth has taught me a lot about freedom:

> ➢ Freedom is the smell of perfume just as much as it is the smell of trees in bloom.
> ➢ Freedom is hearing the laughter of your children playing at home, not just hoping for a smile through prison bars.
> ➢ Freedom is having someone look into your eyes, making you feel worthy.
> ➢ Freedom is someone saying, "I love you," and not wanting anything in return.
> ➢ Freedom is knowing that you matter.
> ➢ Freedom can be experienced in the simplest of moments, and yet we often deny others even the smallest taste of it.
> ➢ Freedom is believing in the possibility of change, knowing you can be better TODAY, and having some control over your destiny.

Can you smell freedom? People don't always like to hear my stories from juvenile hall. Today, I ask you to listen to stories you don't want to hear. Tell the stories you are afraid to tell. The more stories are told, the better and deeper we listen. The deeper we listen, truly listen, the world will, and can be a better place.

Naomi Ackerman
Wife, Mother, writer, performer, activist.
Founder Executive Director The Advot (ripples) Project
www.theadvotproject.org
www.naomiackerman.com
ackerman.naomi@gmail.com

Deanetta Thompson

CWL XPRESS Online Magazine, Founder

ROAR: *Confidence In God's Promises*

Growing up for me was a matter of mental survival, maneuvering my way around all the obstacles Satan placed in my path. Looking back on it, I did not know they were obstacles planted, I thought it was just a way of life. When you are not living your life for God, you do not recognize Satan's tactics. You are on the battlefield, but you don't understand the battle.

I was born and raised in Chicago. I dropped out of high school at the age of fourteen and traveled down some dangerous roads which lead me to a path of destruction for the next few years of my life. After many pleas from my mother, I left Chicago at the age of twenty-one and moved to Terry, Mississippi. There I continued my education and received my GED. After receiving my GED, I returned back to Chicago and enrolled in Olive Harvey Jr. College, earning my Associate Degree in Liberal Arts on May 2, 1986.

After graduating, I began to make some foolish decisions causing my life to spiral out of control; I was on my way to hell. Once again God came to my rescue! I knew then it was time for a change in my lifestyle and spiritual life. After numerous attempts, I tried to join the military. I was facing a six year prison sentence if found guilty for a crime I did not commit. However, I was there when it happened. I was in the wrong place at the wrong time. Once again God came to my rescue. God covered me from the enemy. I was able to clear my name to avoid a prison sentence and enlisted in the United States Army in 1987 and retired after twenty years of active duty in 2007. During my tenure in the Armed Forces, I received my B.A. in Biblical Studies from Amridge University (formally Regions University) in December of 2006. Three years later I obtained my Master of Science Degree from Liberty University graduating May 10, 2009. During the same year, I was diagnosed with a brain tumor. I underwent brain surgery at Michael E. DeBakey VA Hospital in Houston, Texas. Fast forward, I was diagnosed with Vascular Dementia in 2013.

In April 2011, I started an online magazine for Christian women called Christian Women Lifestyle xPress Online Magazine (cwlxpress.com). CWL xPress Online Magazine is a free, faith-based non-denominational magazine geared towards women. CWL xPress Online Magazine sheds a spotlight on women learning, sharing and growing from adversity, trials, and tribulations. CWL xPress is unique in its own way. It is used as a voice for those who have a testimony to share that can encourage or inspire someone else who is struggling with the same issues or dealing with other issues.

I am a living testimony when God has already designed the blueprint for your life, there is nothing on this earth or in the atmosphere that can stop his plans from being implemented. This truly makes me roar!

India Hines

No Junk Productions, Founder/President

ROAR: *Finding Your Passion*

HOW I GOT STARTED?

My first experience in media started in high school when I entered a school statewide "Extemporaneous Speaking Contest". Among the hundreds of young girls who competed, I came in second and felt a joy like I'd never felt before, even though I didn't win. That competition changed my life! I opened up in a way I never thought possible and embraced a gift I didn't know I had. Here's what happened! I was given a piece of paper and told to talk about what was on the paper for two to three minutes with only a few minutes of preparation before I spoke. I also had to be creative and make the judges believe what I was saying so they could judge me based on my overall presentation. I LOVED expressing myself for that short period of time and little did I know, but I was one step closer to finding my passion in life. When I think about it now, it amazes me that I took on such a challenge, but seeing now that my "yes, I can" attitude allowed me to know I could do well and how that experience gave me a glimpse into how powerful a POSITIVE mental attitude can be.

On that particular day so long ago, you would have thought I'd won first place, even though I took home the second place prize, because I embraced the positive, saw the glass half full instead of half empty and just knew somehow on that day that "I could do all things through Christ who strengthens me," even though I didn't really have a close relationship with him at that time in my life. Today, when I deal with a negative situation, I always look for the positive, even when things seem stacked against me because I know that what you think YOU CAN DO and what you SPEAK OUT LOUD will work for you in a positive way if you let it.

EXPERIENCES

For years I worked in corporate America, but I always knew that my purpose in life would reveal itself to me one day, but in the meantime, I was ready to find out what my purpose and passion was. As a result, I moved around a lot from job to job, but took pride in always doing my best work in every position while continuing my search for what I was meant to do and that is how I began my WONDERFUL JOURNEY. I stumbled into the world of modeling and found that instead of being on the stage, I wanted to run the show, and even though I knew nothing about running the show, I had no fear. I looked doubt in the eye, learned all I could, worked hard, stayed focused and began running the show and produced and directed many Fashion Entertainment Productions and they were all very successful. I was responsible for PR, media, booking talent, designing all of the marketing pieces, selling tickets, writing the entire show, commentating all of my productions. I did it all and embraced the world of fashion and entertainment, but found out quickly that unless God was at the head of my life, I would always be exhausted and close to being hospitalized when each production was over. I now know that my health suffered because I carried everything on my own shoulders instead of allowing my Lord and Savior Jesus Christ to carry everything I did on his.

My life has been filled with many people who encouraged me and fed life into me. One of my biggest supporters was my mother who always told me, "Honey, you can do anything you want." I thank God, I believed her. My father has also been one of my biggest supporters because of his unconditional love and I can't forget my friends, my children, my husband and family who have all been there for me. I can't thank them enough. You see, it takes a team to accomplish anything, and if you think you can do it alone, think again because it's impossible. My radio journey began when I applied for a job as an account executive at a major radio station in Memphis, Tennessee, even though I was still working for a job many people would have thought twice about leaving because I was making good money and the prestige of having this job was a reason to keep the job. However, at that time, money wasn't the key to my happiness and I needed more in my life. I'd never worked in radio before, but I quickly learned the radio language, sold radio commercials and used my voice for many radio commercials for my clients. I really enjoyed my radio job and for me, there was no turning back. After leaving the state of Tennessee, I took another job in radio at a station in Columbus, Ohio, and after that I produced a radio show with no idea of what was required, but again, God stepped in and guided me and my next radio experience lead me to my radio show "Food 4 Your Soul" at WIGO AM, a station in Ellenwood, Georgia.

I'VE FOUND MY PASSION! and today I am hosting my radio show "Food 4 Your Soul" in Atlanta, Georgia, and worldwide at Love 860 WAEC AM. I am also a voice talent and I produce and coordinate many events through my company No Junk Productions. I am an example of how even though my radio show and event journey started out with great adversity (two deaths, one of a friend and business partner and the death of my son's college basketball roommate, both at the same time and right in the midst of formulating my company) and at one of the lowest times in my life, I am thriving and didn't quit. My road hasn't been easy. It was tough, but I was determined. I smiled even when I wanted to cry and I stayed focused.

A couple of events coming up for No Junk Productions are "GOOD BROTHA", a salute to fathers who take care of their family and children and do so proudly and "A Family RAYunion", a celebration of the music, life and family of the late great Ray Charles. My future plans for "Food 4 Your Soul" The Radio Show with India Hines" and No Junk Productions are to keep airing and presenting positively POSITIVE radio and events and giving indie and mainstream artists with a positive message of love or a heart for Christ a voice. I am passionate about this because it's important to me to keep positive music and events alive in our communities.

Kings and Queens, I am honored to share some of my life's journey with you and humbled to have been chosen as an Ari'el woman. I am an Ari'el woman because I am committed to standing strong, even through adversity and will continue to help make a positive difference in other people's lives. I know that I may not make all the right decisions and sometimes I will fail, but even so, I will be okay because I have a father who is a King and because he made me in his image, I am a Queen and I will walk like the Queen I was born to be and allow my almighty father to guide me. Stay encouraged, beautiful people! Keep moving forward and always remember that my God and your God don't make NO JUNK. Keep it POSITIVELY positive!

Bio:

Born and raised in Columbus, Ohio, and residing in Georgia since 1995, India Hines has been involved in the fashion and entertainment industry for more than twenty-six years. During that time, she has worked with celebrity and independent artists in virtually every area of entertainment. In 2004, India realized her true calling of lifting people up and feeding their souls in a positive way through the arts. As President of No Junk Productions and host of "Food 4 Your Soul" The Radio Show (Love 860 AM WAEC) & Events with India Hines, India is committed to providing artists whose music or art reflect a positive message or a heart for Christ with an opportunity to present their talent to audiences who will support them through her radio show and the special events that she promotes and hosts on a regular basis.

India enjoys using her voice, which many describe as a true gift to host and promote positive projects, products and special events. She began her career as a moderator and as the "Voice of the Memphis Symphony." India has since received recognition and accolades from fellow radio and media who appreciate her ability to use her voice in effective ways as she hosts events and her own radio show for the past seven years and is a skilled voice talent having had the pleasure of introducing many celebrity and independent artists. India's love of people and passion for bringing life to an event is what fuels her excellence as a voice talent. India was nominated for "Best in Media" at Atlanta's 2009 Gospel Choice Awards, and in 2007 was brought on board to produce the SOLD-OUT and successful "Project Runway" style designer fashion competition & entertainment fundraiser "Designed for a Purpose" to benefit Dress for Success Atlanta. India also recently helped produce "True Dreams Business Showcase 2013".

To be a guest on "Food 4 Your Soul" The Radio Show with India Hines, appear at a "Food 4 Your Soul" event, have No Junk Productions plan your next event or want to advertise or book India Hines as Voice Talent for your event, call 678-371-6036 or email: info@nojunkproductions.com. Listen to "Food 4 Your Soul" The Radio Show with India Hines Monday through Friday at 6 a.m. and Tuesdays and Thursdays at 2 p.m. locally in metro Atlanta on Love 860 WAEC AM or worldwide on the web at www.NojunkProductions.com.

Josie Passantino
Singer, Songwriter, Radio Host
ROAR: *Chasing Dreams*

Josie Passantino, known as the Radio Sweetheart, is the founder and owner of The Josie Network. The Josie Network includes the Worldwide Award Nominated Josie Show, Josie Show Special Edition Episodes, Josie Show Concert Series, Josie Passantino Music, and the licensed radio station Country Blast Radio. Josie started her career at the age of fourteen years old when she started a web based radio show. It didn't take long for Josie to grow her listening base to a large worldwide audience who fell in love with her "real" talk and approach to bringing entertainment to audiences of all ages. Josie was noticed, hired, and signed by other shows on different networks to host radio shows and live events, be the voice of several PSA's, and also signed to a record label to share her sound and music with the world as a recording artist. Through all of Josie's work she has learned that the microphone is a very powerful tool that she can use to not only entertain listeners, but to also share important messages to help others and in turn help make the world a better place.

"You can follow your dreams, no matter what your age! I'm Josie Passantino and I started to follow my dreams at the age of fourteen years old. In large public schools with over-crowded classrooms, I did not have the experience where children were given the message that it was okay to have your voice heard. Thankfully, I have supportive parents who have always instilled in me the importance of loving what you do, never holding back, and making it count. I was taken out of the negative public school situation I was in, and placed in a remote learning environment at a fantastic school that encouraged me to continue to do well in school and follow my dreams. I was in a school with other children my age that were doing remarkable things, so from that point forward I never considered my age a hindrance and I just kept moving forward. This positive change was my turning point and I felt like I could do anything.

Being surrounded by positivity really motivates me by making me want to have others also feel what a positive experience is no matter what their dream. I found radio by accident actually, when a couple of friends and I started doing some Internet recordings. That first moment I sat behind a microphone with the record light on, I was hooked. My friends quickly left as things started becoming more demanding after a few weeks, but I wasn't ready to let go. So I was encouraged to keep going on my own, and thankfully, that is what I did. I started bringing in guests to speak with and then I found my niche. I loved speaking with people and asking questions to find out more about them and what they do. That first interview with a CMT host made me realize I loved conducting interviews. Now at the age of nineteen, I have conducted over 600 interviews to date. I started with an audience of eighteen listeners and today as my network (The Josie Network) continues to expand, I have hundreds of thousands of listeners worldwide that tune into the Live Josie Show.

About a year ago I also had the great honor of becoming a CMA (Country Music Association) member. Since I started my show, I have always had listeners in the United States as well as other countries. So I was determined to keep the work that I did on a worldwide level, which the Internet has allowed me to do. In this manner I am not limited by bandwidth, so I work hard to continue my worldwide approach in everything I set out to do. Now syndicated and heard in over forty-six countries weekly, I am so thankful that I have stayed true to my world-wide approach. I get the opportunity to spread the word about organizations throughout the world and speak with artists and guests from many countries. The connection and sharing of ideas between the dreams that so many also share across countries is priceless. I learned quickly how powerful of a tool the microphone could be and that I could do what I love and help people at the same time.

In my interviews of artists on the Josie Show, I loved being able to get their music heard worldwide on my show and getting their information out to help them in any way I could as they pursued their dreams. It was an amazing feeling! Then I felt another level of satisfaction when I had a guest on with a large amount of fans all of a much younger age group. I remember that show like it was just yesterday. I was able to give these young children an opportunity to call in to my show and speak with someone they enjoyed on television and looked up to who was a positive role model. I'll never forget their excitement and all the messages afterwards about how happy that moment made them and how inspired they were. So I added on the Josie Show Special Edition Episodes to continue to make audiences have that experience. I wanted to find a way to further make a difference with my voice. I was asked to create a couple PSA's (public service announcements) and I loved the idea of being able to use my voice and share with my audiences important messages. I did a message about saving our planet, water, and animals from plastic pollution. Then I did another message against bullying, which is still playing today on my station and others. My hope is that people who listen to my shows or station hear the message and become more aware to help those that might be in need or to give them advice if they are in the situation themselves.

In addition to PSA messages, spreading the word about a cause, I have always had a love for music and wanted to share positive experiences through song. I learned to play the cello, baritone, and tuba. I really loved the sound of large instruments. I also enjoyed singing in choirs, talent shows, and enjoyed vocal lessons over the years as well. I really wanted to record music. I was blessed to meet a songwriter through my show and she began to teach me the fine art of songwriting. I have written about seven songs to date and recorded my first single.

My first song was about what I really believe in and that is following your dreams, no matter what your age, and not letting anything hold you back while also realizing that the support a person has, is something to be so thankful for. Along with the help of a great songwriting mentor, I wrote "Teenage Girl" and shared with anyone who wanted to listen, the message of believing in you. My song did quite well, staying at number one on request charts for over twenty-five weeks and received airplay on Internet, AM, and FM stations. This made me happy to know that positive messages are still well received and I hope that someone heard the song and decided that they, too, can follow their dreams.

As the Josie Network continued to grow, we started receiving calls from organizations and individuals that needed to spread the word about a project they were working on or to help someone in need. This sparked the start up of the Josie Show Outreach Program that I am so proud of. We have been a part of helping raise funds for musical artist's medical expenses, children's medical expenses, promoting medical research hospitals and organizations for childhood cancer, and helping raise funds for tornado victims. We have had the opportunity to get the word out about organizations to help families stand up against violence, raised awareness of positive lyrics for our youth through radio-a-thons for organizations, raised awareness and money for programs to keep and put music programs back into schools.

I have also worked over the years as a mentor helping others with their passion and dreams in radio and music. I have enjoyed helping arrange for new young artists just starting out with their dream to speak with career artists in their genre. It is always a great experience for everyone involved. I have been blessed to be able to add a worldwide licensed country music radio station that plays the best mix of all that is country from signed and independent artists named Country Blast Radio www.countryblastradio.com. This will continue to get artists' music out 24/7 worldwide and to further that we have just started up the Josie Show Concert Series that will help continue to get artists in front of a live audience in venues around the nation while they are also being broad-casted worldwide on our show and station.

I will always seek ways to continue to follow my dreams while doing work that can assist others in following their dreams. This continues to remain my goal and ultimate dream. In closing, it is always important to find a way to give back and help others. Positivity goes a long way and even the smallest gesture can mean so much to someone. Lending your time, voice, and talents to someone can be the difference in their lives. I hope you enjoyed my story and get a chance to stop by and say hello www.josieshow.com. So remember to follow your passions, dream big, make good friends along the way, make what you do count, and enjoy the whole experience.

One of my favorite quotes is, "You are never too old to set another goal or to dream a new dream" by C.S. Lewis.

Demi Chanel

Filmmaker/Domestic Violence Survivor

ROAR: *Perseverance In Pain*

My name is Demi Chanel and I am the proud mother of three kids. I got pregnant at the tender age of seventeen with my first son. Being the daughter of a minister, it was one of the hardest pieces of news that I ever had to deliver to my parents. Although very upset, my parents quickly bounced back from the issue at hand and supported me 100% through the pregnancy. On March 6, 1994, I gave birth to a healthy baby boy name K'shaun. I went to college starting in May of that same year and never allowed that one mistake to bring me down. Soon after having K'shaun, I got married to someone that at the time, I thought I would spend the rest of my life with. We purchased a beautiful home together in North Carolina. I loved that home; the only thing I did not like was the fact that the wash area was outside under the carport, which actually worked in my favor because it would later help save my life. So after purchasing the new home and getting settled with my marriage, I found out that baby number two was on the way. I had my second baby boy Malik on June 15, 1999. You would have thought that this was another great milestone to add to our family, but it was just the opposite. My husband became very violent and abusive to me. He would always come back and say that he was sorry and would never do it again, but after several broken ribs, along with cuts on my body from the abuse, nothing changed. The only thing that did change was the fact that I was expecting baby number three. I had a lot of mixed emotions about being pregnant. I knew that I wanted my baby, but I just did not want to do this with him being the father. After all, I was making plans to leave him as soon as I was able to build up the courage.

I had my third child Mylove on July 13, 2000. I was so excited because she was my first girl. The happiness was soon taken away. After all, I wasn't pregnant anymore, so he could beat me without having to be careful because he didn't want to hurt the baby. The beatings resumed as expected. He would beat me in front of our kids so often that they actually got used to hearing the arguments and seeing the fights. They would no longer get frightened and continue to play as if nothing was happening. The only one that really understood what was going on was my oldest son K'shaun. He would come to my rescue and help me fight off the man he considered a monster. This went on for several years. I was scared to get help and had no faith in the judicial system. They would only hold him for 48 hours and then let him go. I knew for a fact that he was coming back for us as soon as he was released, and I was afraid that he would kill me. He got worse over the years and I had to leave or I would die. I was so desperate for help that I confided in my father, the man I loved most in my life. I was his jewel and knew that it would hurt him to know that someone was hurting his baby girl. But I had to tell him.

My dad lived in Anchorage, Alaska at the time. I remember calling him on the phone that night saying, "Daddy, he's been beating me for years and I can't do this anymore!" My dad went into a rage. He called the local police station immediately to notify them of what was going on with me. The police showed up at my house to take a report, and from that moment, I knew that it was on. I knew that if I didn't plan an escape route for my kids and me, that he would kill me in front of them and I could not allow that to happen.

For weeks I tried to plan the best way to leave. It had to be perfect. There could be no room for error. It had gotten so bad, that I was picturing my dead body lying on the floor while my kids played over me, not realizing that their mommy was dead. All the thoughts of what could have happened to me in front of my kids was taunting my mind! I had no peace anymore. I lived in constant fear and I was ready to leave the prison that I had formed in my mind.

One night he came home and I could smell alcohol on his breath. He started an argument. It was so petty that I don't remember what it was about. I remember my kids being on the floor playing. I had given them a bath already and was praying that they would fall asleep before their dad got home. I knew in my heart that something was going to happen. I could feel it. Unfortunately, he came home early and the arguing began. I remember K'shaun saying, "Daddy, leave my mommy alone!" He pushed my son out of the way to get to me and I lost it. He hit me, but this time, I hit him back. He started punching me and then he pushed me to the ground.

I fell beside my two youngest kids and my heart dropped. While I was on the floor, he started kicking and punching me. I covered my face to keep him from hitting me in my face. I was able to see my kids through the cracks of my fingers. My babies paid us no mind. The fighting continued off and on for hours. They continued to play as if nothing was happening.

They didn't care that mommy was screaming and that their older brother was helping mommy fight. That was normal to them now. I knew that I could no longer do this. Was this the life that I was going to choose for my kids and I? God reminded me that there are Kings walking in my babies. The more I thought about that, the more I fought. But the more I fought, the more he would fight. Actually, he kept fighting until he got tired. He sat down on the edge of the couch to catch his breath. I unfolded myself from the fetal position that I had formed to keep him from hurting me. I slowly got up off the floor, hesitant, because I didn't want to spark another fight, so I moved carefully. I slowly pulled myself up. I was holding my breath because I was so scared but he didn't move this time, he was too exhausted from beating me. All those weeks that I spent planning an escape route went straight out the window. I didn't remember anything I had planned, but I knew that I had to plan some-thing quick or he was going to kill me that night. I picked up my babies and I took them to the bathroom and started running water in the bathtub. All I could think about was that he knew that kids already had their baths and would catch on to what I was trying to do. He would kill me for sure. All the things that taunted my mind, all the dreams that I had was about to come true, he was about to kill me in front of my kids. But a quiet voice within said, "Do everything that I tell you to do." And I did. I started to run the water in the tub. I locked the door and also pulled the drawer behind it as a second barrier in case he caught on and tried to break in. I was pacing back and forth in the bathroom while K'shaun was trying to keep the babies calm. He was such a great helper to me during that time. As I was pacing, the spirit of God said to me,

"Open the bathroom window!" Now keep in mind, my bathroom window was about five feet off the ground and I was too wide to fit through it. I immediately doubted the spirit of God and said, "I can't fit through there. Only the babies can fit through that small space." The spirit of God spoke to me again and said, "Do as I asked you to do, open the window." So I started slowing pushing the window up. I was so paranoid that he would hear me that it seemed to take hours to get it opened.

I finally got the window open and I started pacing back and forth again asking God, "What now? What am I supposed to do now? It's one o'clock in the morning. I can't just drop my kids out the window without me!" All these things, I am saying to myself. I could still hear K'shaun in the background trying to keep the kids quiet. They were fighting sleep by that time, but I needed to keep them up because I didn't know what the next move would be. Then God spoke to me and said to drop the kids out the window and tell K'shaun to take them to their nana's house, a quarter of a mile away. By this time, I was about to lose my mind. I couldn't send my six-year-old son out at one in the morning to run down the street with two toddlers by himself. I had a strong urge to just take my chances and finally conjured up the nerve to do it. I was only in the bathroom a good ten minutes, but it felt like forever. I got on my knees so that I could be face-to-face with K'shaun. I grabbed him by the shoulders, looked in his big, pretty brown eyes, and said, "I am going to drop you out the window and then give your brother and sister to you!"

K'Shaun started to cry and said, "Mommy, are you coming with me?" I had to look my baby in the eyes as his tears began to flow. I didn't know if that was going to be my last time seeing him or not. I just knew in my heart, that once I got up the nerve to come out the bathroom—or he rested enough to come look for me to fight me again and found me without his kids, he was going to kill me. It was one of the hardest decisions I ever had to make as a parent, but I could not allow my children to witness me being killed by their father. I told K'shaun that I promised that I would come where they were, but he had to leave now. I dropped my baby out the window. When I dropped him, he fell on the ground and quickly jumped back up. I then took a deep breath and dropped Malik out, and luckily, he caught him. He put Malik down on the ground barefoot with only a T-shirt on. I then took another deep breath and dropped Mylove who had fallen asleep. It was harder to drop her because she had no control over her body. I finally dropped her. K'shaun caught her and held on to her tightly. He looked up at me and said, "Mommy, he's going to kill you." I promised my baby that I was coming to nana's house and for him to just run and don't look back regardless of who called him. I watched my six-year-old son struggle to run with an eleven-month-old baby, who had just learned to walk, and a nine-month-old baby that was not even walking yet. I looked out the window until he was out of sight. I then slid down the wall and fought to keep my tears in. I wanted to wait a little while to give my kids time to make it to my mom's house in case he went looking for them after realizing they were gone. I finally found the courage to walk out of the bathroom. Surprisingly, he was still sitting in the same place I left him.

He stared me up and down with a demonic look. He didn't even realize the kids were gone. At that point, I was planning an escape in my mind. I was terrified because I knew that he was coming back for more. I saw a basket of clothes that were already washed and neatly folded. The spirit of God spoke to me again and said, "Grab the basket of clothes and go outside." Again, doubting God, I said to myself, "He's going to know that I am not washing any clothes because those clothes are folded already!" But I gathered myself and was obedient to the spirit. After all, I had nothing to lose at that point. My kids were gone and sooner or later, he was going to fight me again. So I grabbed the basket of clothes. Now if you remember earlier on in the story, I mentioned that I purchased a new home that I loved, the only thing I hated was that my washroom was outside of the home. Well, if that washroom was not outside, I probably wouldn't be here today to tell this story. Once I got out the door, I dropped the basket and ran for my life. As I was running, I could see a figure running towards me in the dark and I started yelling, "Help! Please help me! He's going to kill me!" To my surprise, it was my mother coming towards me. She was out of breath from running.

She said, "When those kids were banging on my door and I saw them without you, I just knew he had killed you." I was lucky enough to get away. I beat the odds! I did it! I finally got the nerve to walk away from the devil that was in my life. That same devil that told me that I would never be anything. That same devil that would spit in my face and beat me in front of our kids. I made it when others didn't. I didn't allow that to break me down. I am now a filmmaker based in Atlanta Georgia. I have worked with some of the greatest people in the industry. I met a great man that accepted me with every one of my flaws and my past demons. He stood by my side and loved me unconditionally. It is like I never ever missed a beat when it comes to love. He has accepted my children as his own. God took care of me and gave me everything that the enemy thought he took from me and more. Now I walk with my head held high. I know that I have a purpose and I live daily to do what I've been called to do. I don't regret what I went through. The only thing I regret is doubting that God would bring me through it. I am a better woman because of that man. I am no longer a scorned, battered woman. I am a woman of God, I am a mother, I am a soon to be wife, I am a CEO.

Victoria Theodore

Keyboardist/Vocalist-Tours With Stevie Wonder
"Posse" Keyboardist/Vocalist-The Arsenio Hall Show
ROAR: *Impacting Through Music*

Victoria Theodore is a well-educated, talented musician from the San Francisco Bay area. A graduate of Oberlin College Conservatory of Music, she has two bachelor degrees: Bachelor of Music in Classical Piano Performance and Computer Music, and Bachelor of Arts in Music History. Additionally, she is a Stanford University graduate with a Masters of Arts Degree in Classical Piano Performance. As a teen, Victoria studied piano and voice in the UC Berkeley Young Musician's Program (YMP) and sang (and began her accompanying career) with the Oakland Youth Chorus (OYC), under the direction of Trente Morant. While studying for her MA, Victoria performed with several San Francisco Bay Area ensembles and bands, including The Peninsula Symphony, Theatreworks, Hayward Little Theater, Oakland Youth Chorus, and jazz bands Victoria Theodore Quintet, Time Will Tell Sextet, LMNOP and 10BassT.

Shortly after graduation from Stanford, Victoria toured nationally as a keyboardist for Capitol Records artists Oaktown 357 - produced by MC Hammer. In 2007, Victoria was hired to tour with the legendary Stevie Wonder, traveling around the world playing keyboards and singing background vocals in his band. Performing with Wonder gave her the opportunity to work with such incredible artists as Sting, Prince, John Mayer, Tony Bennett, John Legend, Esperanza Spalding, and many others. Victoria's musical genius landed her a coveted spot in the "new Posse," a hand-picked band performing for the Arsenio Hall show which made its debut in late summer 2013. Wide ranging musical versatility makes her a highly sought after performer for bands, choruses, churches, and artists of various music genres.

Women of the World

Musical Ensemble

ROAR: *Dreaming Big!*

Women of the World is an international ensemble of musicians focused on vocal music from all over the world. The four core vocalists, Ayumi Ueda (Japan), Giorgia Renosto (Italy), Annette Philip (India) and Deborah Pierre (Haiti), along with their eclectic band, explore and perform music in 23 languages, honoring global folk traditions. In many ways, the ensemble is a microcosm of the world, with members working closely together, not just to create and perform music, but also learning about each other's countries, cultures, languages, beliefs and practices.

Over the years, Women of the World has received accolades and collaborated with many renowned artists including Bobby McFerrin, Angelique Kidjo, Mario Frangoulis, and the Boston Pops Orchestra led by Maestro Keith Lockhart. With tours in Japan and North America, including performances at the Blue Note Jazz Club, Carnegie Hall, Boston Symphony Hall, BeanTown Jazz Festival, TEDxBoston, and United Nations events, Women of the World strives to engage in, and support peace building efforts, and other movements that help foster unity amidst the rich diversity that surrounds us.

To date, Women of the World has united over 200 international women artists in this richly diverse musical collective. Women of the World began as an idea. Japanese vocalist, Ayumi Ueda had a childhood dream to meet and perform with people from all over the world. When she began studying at Berklee College of Music, this vision was still strong in her heart. In 2008, she formed Women of the World, collaborating with the most unique musicians she could find at the college. In her journey she met the vocalists that are now the core essence of Women of the World, Giorgia Renosto from Italy, Annette Philip from India, and Deborah Pierre from United States. With six other instrumentalists, they form an ensemble of ten musicians representing nine countries, performing a vast repertoire of music spanning twenty-three languages. The ensemble has become a family of sorts, with each member focused on expanding the original idea.

"Music binds us together in many different ways. With nine cultures represented in the ensemble, we learn about different perspectives and ways of life. Each culture has its own traditions, practices, and beliefs. We may all be completely different, but we share the same sky. There is so much in common, and so much different. We try to celebrate both our similarities and our differences. As a microcosm of the world, we practice peace in our daily interactions inside and outside the band setting, and every day, we find new ways to bring about more understanding in the world through our music. In our travels since 2008, we found that learning music, studying lyrics and their meaning, as well as researching a specific genre is a great way to understand more about a country and its culture. Music has helped us make new friends, no matter where we are in the world.

"Our immediate plans include a brand new CD we will release in 2014 and a three-country Spring tour in 2015 spanning Japan, India and Italy. Our big dreams? A Grammy, tours throughout the world, collaborations with indigenous artists in smaller villages around the world, and a lifetime of learning and sharing. A message to all the readers of this wonderful book... Dream big! Don't be afraid of encountering differences, be they differences of mindset, of opinion, or of traditions. Meeting people who have ideas opposite to yours are experiences to be treasured! Respect, kindness and open hearts are the keys to honest communication. Life is truly beautiful, and gratitude makes it even more beautiful! We look forward to sharing our stories and our joy with you at one of our live shows!" 'If you want something said, ask a man; if you want something done, ask a woman.' -Margaret Thatcher

Jerri Lange

Journalist, Author, Educator

Jerri: A Black Woman's Life In The Media

ROAR: *Empowering Black Women*

Have you ever wondered why things never really change for the better no matter how hard you work to make the world a better place? Every time you seem to be getting somewhere, solving your problems, things are pulled out from beneath you and you have to start all over again. While all of this is going on, you're trying to find time for your family. Your husband is still looking for a job that he enjoys and is qualified to perform. He can't find one. You are concerned not only for your own children, but the other children wandering the streets, trying to find a place after school and stay out of trouble. Sound familiar? Welcome to the world of the Black Woman in America.

For many years, a lot of work has gone into creating a place where groups of people exist in a community created for them. Indians are on Reservations, Chinese are in Chinatown, Japanese are in Japantown and Black people are in Ghettos. Mexicans have their own Spanish-speaking communities. Any race considered people of color create their own neighborhoods when coming to America. Vietnamese, Asians from lesser known countries, Middle-Eastern people from Iraq, Iran, Russians, etc., are somehow accommodated. If they are very affluent or high level people from their countries, then they can live wherever they want.

When you think about it, it really is an open book. We all watch these communities spring up, but I don't think we know just how well it works. With cameras on street corners, we no longer complain because we know how dangerous some of our communities have become. We used to call that 'Catch-22.' It seems we have no place to go but inside — and perhaps that's where we should have gone a long time ago. I'm talking about the inner self, because believe it or not, that is still where the answers are. So the question is, how can we as Black Women empower ourselves? Start untying the knot? Get rid of the chains? We certainly can't do it if we don't know who we really are. I'm talking about going way back…learning our true history. Not only African History, but others rarely talked about. Who were the Amazon women? The Black Madonna? She is in almost every South American country, but most adored in Poland. Did anybody ever really check this out? During my trip to Brazil, I saw Black Jesus and the Black Virgin Mary and Child everywhere I went. Travel reveals many things. There are hundreds of Black Madonna or Black Virgin Mary statues and paintings in Europe. She has been there all this time and no one ever mentions her name. There are people out there who know who we really are and waiting for us to "wake up." The question is: who are we and why are we so important at this time? For one thing, we are carrying ancient DNA in our blood. We are catalysts for change…ancient people who still carry memories in our hearts and minds. We are "change agents" and it is OUR time. Our energy is immediately felt when we enter a room. We command attention and think it is racist because we have been programmed to feel inferior. We are kept down while others pass us by. But now the world is in trouble and we need to get back to our ancient memories to make things right again. We need a brand new Revolution — not with guns, but with new ideas. Bill and Melinda Gates have become the richest couple in the world by giving money away to heal the sick in Africa and other poor nations. But Wall Street still doesn't get it! Although America still has not fulfilled its destiny, everyone knows where it is headed. The forefathers of this country had a dream and all the naysayers in the world cannot match the power of a dream! As Shakespeare once told us, all the beautiful things of the world are the "stuff dreams are made of." Why should we doubt him? The poet Alfred Lord Tennyson said, "thoughts are things with airy wings." I believe him. Great writers have been leaving clues since the beginning of time, but most of us have been diverted to look to the 'outer' world as a means of change, when it all begins in the 'inner' world. It is that sixth sense that we must develop if we are to make a lasting change. And it all begins with a dream! What about Martin Luther King's dream? It changed an entire nation and spoke to our humanity. Now we have watched it begin to change back again. Somebody has been dreaming a terrible dream and we must come up with another one. But just what is a dream? Is it real? I'm not talking about the images you see when you're asleep. I'm talking about the images you can and must make while awake. It's like throwing a ball out into the universe and waiting for it to come back. To make the dream come true, you must be in the location and position to be able to catch it when it returns! In other words, don't be caught waiting at the airport when your ship comes in! This means hard work, perseverance, and determination. Once you catch the ball it belongs to you and no one can take it away.

You have to be careful about what you release into the atmosphere. If you want to be sick, you will be. If you want to be impoverished, then you'll be in poverty. If you want success, you can have it. Just knowing these things is powerful. However, the media uses terms like disadvantaged, welfare recipients, welfare queens, underclass, impoverished, ignorant, lazy, minorities and others to crush your dreams. Show me thirty million people who describe themselves with the use of those words and I'll show you thirty million people trapped in someone else's dream. Words are powerful because they send out messages. The Bible says, "In the beginning was the Word, and the Word was God." What more proof do you need? Before God could create this universe, He had to first start with the Word and the "Word was made flesh." That's you and me! We were created with words. We now need words to communicate with each other, paint images, and create new things. Words describe things—without them we cannot say what we believe in or what we mean. Words have been used to uplift, destroy, magnify, and diminish. Words are vehicles through which we can express sadness and joy. A well-turned word can either bring peace or start wars at the negotiating table. Words are also verbal manifestations of thoughts and carries a great deal of power. Your words and thoughts should not be destructive. Their purpose is to build, not destroy, give life, not take it away. There is power in positive thinking. Your responsibility is to find the connection and start your dream. It means being still and listening, then thinking gentle and beautiful thoughts.

In one of my published speeches, "Women, America's Greatest Untapped Natural Resource," I mention an interview with General Tang Zi Chang, a member of one of the oldest dynasties in China. General

Tang gave me great insight into Ancient China. In his book, "Principles of Conflict," General Chang states, "through the formation of ancient Chinese pictograms, they can trace and credit almost every important creation of culture to women and of war to men. I guess you're wondering how and why I have gathered the information I have shared with you that involves the inner rather than the outer world that is usually our goal. I can honestly tell you that it started when I was very young. I was fourteen years old and sitting on the porch with my friends after a meeting of our youth group at church. We all started asking each other what we wanted to do in life and who we wanted to become. I remember looking up at the stars and saying, "I just want to know what's out there." I am sure that's what caused me to become an avid reader. I loved books and discovering new things and ideas. When I eventually saw the sign, "Know ye the truth and the truth shall set you free," I was hooked. The best thing about this kind of thinking is that it keeps you free, always on the lookout for the unexpected. As I look back, this attitude kept me from soaking up the negative things that happen to black people in the Ghetto. My mind was always somewhere else, "looking up." So, my attitude towards life was well-established by the time I faced the pitfalls waiting for me.

I finally wrote my autobiography, *Jerri, A Black Woman's Life In The Media*. I married, had three children, divorced and was a single mother most of my life. I went back to school when I was thirty-six years old — Merritt College, and it changed my life. My counselor enrolled me in English Literature and I never looked back. My political career began in 1953 when I was appointed Legislative Secretary to Assemblyman W. Byron Rumford, 17th District. He was the first black Assemblyman elected to the California State Legislature. I assisted him in setting up the Assembly Interim Committee on Public Health for the State Legislature. Byron also passed the Fair Employment practices and Fair Housing laws, opening the way for black people to get better jobs and housing in the state of California. From politics, I was hired to become Public Affairs Director and Host on KBHK television I also worked at KGO and KQED, a PBS station. I moved to Honolulu to work on KHET where I wrote and produced television shows. That was my happiest time in televisions since I took issue with other stations entertaining rather than educating the public.

After publishing my book, I continued to write and lecture. I managed to teach in the Broadcast Communication Arts department at San Francisco State University for three years which was an absolute joy!

In 1975, I moderated the International Year of the Woman at the Sheraton Palace hotel in San Francisco. It was my first contact with women all over the world. We were given an earful about the use of natural resources by powerful countries, while the smaller ones struggled to survive. It was truly an eye-opener.

I later traveled with nine other women on a State Department of five South American countries and found out how resilient they are. We visited Columbia, Argentina, Brazil, Chile, and Peru. Women are literally carrying those countries on their backs—holding the families together. If you can forgive those that hurt you, no matter the circumstances, love those around you, no matter the faults, find peace within while everything around you is falling apart, then you will begin to truly live for the first time in your life. My wish for you is to dream as high as you can and don't let anyone interfere with your dream to become more than you could ever imagine. This is a wake up call. We must read books, write books, and understand the role of the media in its mission to control our destiny. Wake up! The King of Kings has a job for you to do and you are ready to do it! The whole world is in crisis and we have the answer inside our hearts. Start reading. Start writing. Let your voice be heard!

Kari Ruel

Publisher/Founder

Napa Valley Life Magazine

It amazes me how life often does become full-circle. Experiences and events that we might trivialize at the time can come back years later to take on a whole new meaning. I've been in the media business for thirty years and have been involved in television, radio, sports remotes, Associated Press, newspapers and magazines. Basically, I've dabbled in it all, but the one common denominator I've shared in whatever medium I was involved in was my ability to tell someone else's story. People fascinate me and their life's journey is unique. Being a journalist works for me because I never got past the "Why?" stage and I can certainly ask a lot of questions.

My father is a retired Army Colonel so my family moved around a lot in my earlier years. I was born in Germany and have lived in a number of states. My shy demeanor handicapped me at first, but eventually I learned to focus my attention on other kids and would find something interesting about them to talk to them about. We eventually settled in Michigan and I spent my high school years on a 60-acre horse farm. The farm taught me about hard work, dedication and caring for other living things. There weren't many girls in the immediate neighborhood so I spent a lot of time exploring, going on adventures and collecting water samples from nearby streams and ponds. Music was also a big part of our family. Every family member could play at least three instru-ments. I was on a path to become a biologist/music teacher.

I wasn't the most coordinated person growing up, but I could run so I was a member of the high school track team. My senior year, I got hurt and couldn't compete. I was still somewhat on the shy side. The coach asked if I would announce the track meets. I was devastated at the thought, but I didn't want to disappoint him so I took the microphone in my hand and magic happened. I was no longer shy and became the voice of the Lowell Red Arrows. Same thing happened in college. I was asked to announce the National Junior Collegiate Swim Meet. The coach knew my high school coach. A college English Professor took notice of my writing ability and suggested I intern with the Grand Rapids Press. I hesitantly accepted and caught the journalism bug. I changed my major from music/biology to broadcast journalism and I've been in the media business ever since.

There were two other major influencers in my life; my grandparents on my mom's side who taught me about living simply and being happy with what one has and to always reuse, recycle and repurpose and my dad's mom who lived with us once our family was stateside. She was always happy, optimistic and her message was simple; Love life long and bright, laugh, share a little bit of everything you have, be kind, be silly, enjoy the view, forgive, aim high and don't forget to play. My grandfa-ther also gave me my first camera at age seven or eight and I have been taking pictures ever since.

When asked about obstacles I've overcome it's hard to look back and reflect because I have learned to look adversity straight on and ask how can I get to YES. Struggles are mere bumps in the road and a teachable moment. I have never let other's define who I am nor did I go with the social norm. After being disenchanted with main stream media and their need to only report on those things that create fear or scarcity, my former business partner and I started a magazine in the Napa Valley that showcased intriguing people, celebrated goodness and embraced the beauty of the wine country. We were told that positive news doesn't sell and we would never survive. We had no money, no office and no equipment, but we found friends who believe in us and let us use their computer at their retail store in the evenings. After seven years, my business partner wanted to move his career path towards his other love of music and I carried on with the magazine on my own.

My choice in men always seemed to counter my optimistic positive demeanor and resulted in one failed marriage and one long-term live-in relationship that did not end well. The negativity in those relationships drove me further to never give up my dream and make the impossible happen. The one thing I never compromised was my kids and being there to raise them. For most of the sixteen years that I have owned my magazine I have worked out of the house and raised a healthy, well-adjusted daughter and son plus I help raise my ex-significant other's three daughters whom I am still close to.

Life can be a challenge on a continuous basis and sometimes, bad things happen to good people, but the key for success is how we choose to react to those situations.

Coming back full circle, I still ask a lot of questions and see goodness in people. My roar is my ability to be a muse for others by helping and encouraging them to do what it is they love. Sustainability is also important to me. Remembering what my grandparents taught me, I strive to lower my carbon footprint, I recycle, reuse and repurpose whenever I can and eat healthy organic natural food that I grow myself. I'm still not afraid of a microphone and have been doing a radio show off and on for twenty years. My most recent show is entitled "Sustainable Life." I believe in giving back to my community and that community has no borders. My kids and I have done mission work local and abroad. I'm adventurous and hike 1000 miles a year and I often host house concerts in my backyard for traveling professional musicians.

My 17-year old niece came to stay with me in the summer of 2014 and worked as an intern for me. She followed me on interview after interview. The one thing I wanted her to part with from her experience is everyone has a story and we can always learn something from each person we meet. We just have to listen with an open heart and no prejudgments.

Namaste.

"There is a growing strength in women, but
it's in the forehead, not the forearm."

-Beverly Sills

Roar

3

Philanthrophy | Ministry | Activism

"How far you go in life depends on your being tender with the young, compassionate with the aged, sympathetic with the striving, and tolerant of the weak and strong, because someday in your life, you will have been all of these."

-Unknown

Katie Hamilton Shaffer

Philanthropist, CCO/Founder, Feast It Forward

ROAR: *Philanthropy and Charitable Giving*

When I was a child, there was a myriad of things I wanted to be when I grew up. My dreams were to be a chef, a professional soccer player, a singer, or Martha Stewart (yes, you may insert a giggle here). My dad always said that as a child, I had more spitfire than the Energizer bunny. I didn't just play with the boys, I beat them. I could easily strap on my cleats and get dirty on the field, and then change hats quickly to "set up shop" on our living room floor with my crafts to produce handmade invitations for my birthday parties. When delivering them to my friends, they looked at me cockeyed and laughed, but nevertheless, I was proud. I taught myself to properly cook a filet mignon at age twelve, which was a big feat as my mother's seared meats were nothing less than perfect. I hosted countless bake sales on the street where I grew up, and soon discovered that these things I loved to do also made people happy. This childhood obsession with Martha Stewart morphed over the years into a true passion for food, wine and entertaining. But there was more.

My ROAR: What if I could combine my passions for food, wine, and making people happy for a GREATER cause? It's this thought that guided my unique career path all these years. I have never been afraid to try something new. After all, my favorite quote is, "The road to success is always under construction" (Lily Tomlin). I pursued everything that I cared about with that bunny's unrelenting drive. If I fell, I got up. This energy and perseverance made it easy to make friends and find fans.

Out of high school, I accepted a Division-1 college soccer scholarship, and afterwards played a brief time in the semi-pro circuit. Call me crazy, but I also pursued a country music recording contract after winning a statewide singing competition, gaining interest from Nashville labels. Eventually I decided to hang up my cleats and pass the mic. In 2004, I moved to the beautiful Napa Valley on a search to pursue my true passions: all things food, wine and philanthropy. Managing events and wine education at a local winery, I received my first chance to combine my passion for food and wine with a true desire to help individuals when my mentor Britt Van Giesen's daughter was diagnosed with a rare disease – Rett Syndrome. To support families whose children were suffering with this debilitating illness, we quickly founded the Erika Van Giesen Foundation in 2004. Through our foundation we created an annual fundraiser that kicked off in 2005, "Erika's Dream." This premier, high profile food and wine gala brought together all our friends to showcase their brands and culinary delights, as epicurean enthusiasts had the opportunity to enjoy an elite evening offering all that Napa Valley had to offer – it was the perfect combination and clout. Little did I know that at one of our events, five years later I would meet my future business partners – long time, dear friends of my mentor and his wife. After only two galas, the event raised enough money to help establish "Katie's Clinic" at Children's Hospital Oakland. This clinic is currently the only Rett-focused clinic on the West Coast dedicated to helping families and their afflicted daughters.

Feeling ready for something new, I left the wine business in mid-2007 to manage fundraising for the California Big Brothers Big Sisters of the North Bay to curate events, significantly increasing the chapter's donor base. Soon realizing I was actually missing what I had just left behind, I opted to incorporate the two by starting a small wine label, partnering with a friend's winery, Juslyn Vineyards, appropriately named "Guidance" to help raise additional funds for Big Brothers Big Sisters. The following year I was approached by Elaine Honig to help with her local fundraiser, "Wine, Women & Shoes," and expand it into a national fundraising format. I'm proud to say to this day that her company, a unique fashion-driven food and wine event, is now hosted in over thirty states and has raised over $12M dollars for women's and children's charities. The stars were aligning, and those coming into my life were teaching me lessons to help me find my true path, my "ROAR".

In 2009, after brainstorming over a glass of wine with girlfriends (isn't that how most business is done?!) I co-founded a wine company called "Toolbox Wine Co," whose mission "Serious Wines. Playful Marketing" concept donated a portion of all sales to Habitat for Humanity – "Building" hope and awareness, one bottle at a time – hence the name, Toolbox. It was all starting to come together. In 2011 I was proud to be named one of San Francisco's "Magnificent 7" leading entrepreneurs in Bay Area Food and Wine, followed by the honor of being named one of San Francisco's "40 under 40" by the San Francisco Business Times in 2012. This class included many names that today are considered emerging leaders in business. Where I was, where I am…and where I am going. All of my experience has led here, to Feast it Forward.

In late 2009 while building the Toolbox brand, I decided to take another idea and make it a reality. Throughout my career, I've been struck by what incredible things can be accomplished when you bring together amazing people over fantastic food and wine. With the acquisition of Toolbox in 2012, I was finally able to dedicate all of my time to Feast it Forward. Now in the midst of our official launch, we are ready to truly go "Beyond the Bottle." What is ironic is that my Producer is a brand expert who produced Martha Stewart's daily show, garnering ten Emmy nominations and winning four Emmy Awards. With my partners and co-founders who I met back in 2010 while planning "Erika's Dream" (Kevin and Rebecca Gouveia of Veia Productions) Feast it Forward showcases goodwill and charitable giving through culinary and wine related content and handcrafted products. This web based social networking community will play a key role in growing the lifestyle brand on a national and global level, serving as a backbone in building brand awareness. To enhance the brand and mission on a global level, this June we have the unique opportunity to travel to Malawi, Africa with Northern California couple, Rob Hampton, DDS and his wife Claudia Sansone to film their ongoing humanitarian efforts in several remote villages. I am honored to call them my friends, and they serve as yet another inspiration. We will be documenting the incredible, historical, social shifts that their work has directly facilitated over the last several years. This follows on the coattails of the Dalai Lama presenting Dr. Rob with the "Unsung Hero of Compassion" award for all his philanthropic endeavors. Traveling with Feast it Forward to Malawi is a world class team of doctors, educators, and an agronomist in addition to our renowned film crew, comprised of award winning filmmakers who have all adopted Feast it Forward's mission: to encourage people to live a philanthropic lifestyle. Rob and Claudia, while very special in their commitment, are also everyday people who serve as a prime example of how we can live beyond our own backyard and make a real global impact.

This year is especially monumental because, along with everything else, there will be groundbreaking on Dothi Village's first pre-school, paving the way for an early childhood education program. This celebrates more than another classroom; it signals a major social transformation in Malawi. Those of us who came up with our simple company motto, "Inspiring Stories. Philanthropic Living" wanted to be there to film this continuing act of cross-cultural generosity and engagement. Our plan is that Feast it Forward will be a community where philanthropic lifestyle fans, professionals, tastemakers and brand ambassadors from around the globe will have the opportunity to comment, communicate and network. Webisodes will act as a creative factory for members with inspirational stories, recipes, perfect pairings and philanthropic news on content, profiles and purchasing opportunities.

Feast it Forward website soft-launch is live, featuring initial informative and inspiring videos alongside our products and charitable events where you can join the mission and movement. There's something to be said for doing what you love and you won't work a day in your life. Believe in your "ROAR" and pursue your dreams. If you fall, get up. Beyond passion, generosity is infectious. So ask yourself, how do YOU Feast it Forward? We'd love to hear from you. Learn more at www.feastitforward.com.

Carletha Ward

Founder, Rehoboth Church With A Promise

Pastor/Author/Life Purpose Coach

ROAR: *The Pursuit of Purpose*

In Pursuit of Purpose

Everyone is afraid on some level. Even so, many are moving ahead and making great strides, pursuing purpose, realizing fulfillment, and glorifying God with their lives. So what is their secret? Perhaps the secret is anticipating the fear, but understanding that God has already ordained you to do a work and He will see you through to the end. Much of what we fear never happens anyway, so it is very likely that your fear is just a waste of time and energy. Take a step toward change and fulfillment of God's promise for your life.

But consider this: It requires work to pursue purpose. It requires work to be different, to reach higher heights. It requires effort and diligence. It requires commitment to go the distance. Too many people just are not willing to put forth the effort. They would rather take the crumbs, take the handout, accept the pity, accomplish as little as possible. But I believe that God has a few that feel the burden to step out from behind the shadows and pursue their God-inspired destiny. It's a step of faith. But once you start out on the journey, you find that each day provides rewards that make you want to see what tomorrow brings. It's exciting, challenging, inspiring and it builds your faith. The pursuit of purpose requires commitment.

Just as you are beginning to get serious about your purpose, and just as you are feeling motivated in your spirit, the enemy will begin to try to feed you negative impressions of yourself and of your circumstances. His job is to try to shut you down before your commitment is established. But don't forget that God has already determined that you will fulfill your purpose if you continue to pursue. It's not enough to have potential. You must pursue purpose. You must stoke the fire of success. Turn potential into destiny, in spite of the challenges, in spite of the tricks of the enemy. Believe that you have been created to do something unique and special. Every day you should watch for, and respond to, the many opportunities present themselves. Like Joseph, the favored son of Jacob, you have to continue to hold on to the dreams that God has placed inside us. Be committed to the end. Understand that some people won't understand or embrace what God is doing in your life. This may require some changes in relationships. Don't abandon people just because you are changing, but don't allow anyone to break your spirit. The road of purpose is full of twists and turns. As you pursue purpose, you will need the support and encouragement of other people who are like-minded to help you stay on track and who will not allow you to settle for less than what you can have. There is greatness inside of you. Dare to take a step in pursuit of that greatness. Pursue purpose and live!

Wendy "Quietstorm" Lee

Christian Comedienne, Minister

ROAR: *Healing and pain management through laughter*

Comedienne Quiestorm, born Wendy D. Lee was raised in rural Brunswick County (original home of Brunswick Stew) located in southern Virginia. She is second oldest of six children by her biological mother. However, she was raised along with her stepbrother by her father and stepmother.

Wendy received her primary and secondary education through Brunswick County Public Schools. Afterwards, she received a B.S. Degree from Chowan University in Murfreesboro, NC.

After the traumatic loss of her stepmother, Wendy accepted Christ while being only a junior in high school. Her pursuit of holiness unto the LORD caused her to discover a multitude of gifts such as drawing, writing, singing, dancing, hospitality and the ability to connect with people through laughter. In January 2001 Wendy was licensed as a minister by her father in the gospel. January 2006 Wendy was introduced to the Christian entertainment industry as comedienne "Quietstorm". Traveling the United States, bringing healing through laughter has been the joy of her life! Becoming a comedienne was certainly not in Wendy's plan, but she thanks God for such a beautiful surprise. Shared joy is double joy. Shared sorrow is half sorrow – Swedish Proverb

My Story:

The series of events that transformed timid Wendy Lee into Minister/Comedienne Quietstorm is a story fit for television. As with all people, I survived many traumatic experiences ranging from being given away by my birth mother, enduring physical abuse from my father, the painful loss of my stepmother and struggling to find my identity and find my voice. One of the biggest obstacles I am yet conquering is the spirit of fear. At one time during my childhood, I was a borderline pantophobic – had a fear of almost everything. Much of my life has been a lonely existence. However, it is in those alone times where my creative imagination blossoms.

In solitude God speaks loudest and His voice is heard with clarity. Comedy presented itself to me out of an act of spontaneity. While attending a church talent show I decided to tell some jokes. At that time I was still in extreme timidity, so I read the jokes from the paper on which I had written them. Afterwards, the pastor of that church prayed over me and gave me the offering that they had received that night. As a result, people from the audience began asking me to come to their church and tell jokes. For seven years (denying that I was a comedienne) I did comedy whenever I was called upon. It was November 2005 I received an email that would alter my path – an advertisement of a Christian Comedian Conference.

In January of 2006 I drove to Nashville, Tennessee for a weekend that would literally change my name. It was there that Quietstorm came out of her shell. One of things that blessed me tremendously was spending three days with silly people who loved Jesus as much as I did. Sadly, many Christians have this misconception that Christianity requires that one must be serious at all times. It is believed that jesting and joking has no place in the house of God. Oh, but on the contrary – laughter is healing! Medical science has confirmed what the scripture speaks, "A merry heart doeth good like a medicine." Laughter breaks barriers, transcends culture and transcends age gaps.

An experience that left an indelible mark was during my teens while working at McDonald's. My shift manager lost her mother, but she came to work the very next day. When asked why she didn't find a replacement for her shift, these were her words, "I looked at the schedule to see who I'd be working with and saw Wendy's name. I decided to come in because I knew she would say something to keep me laughing." A more recent experience embedded in my memory is of a family I visited several years ago. After passing their driveway twice, I decided to yield to the urge to stop by their home. I spent about six hours visiting with them - talking, laughing, watching television and sharing experiences. The father of this family went into the kitchen to prepare dinner. Afterwards he calls for his wife, two adult children and myself to come dine. We were so engrossed in conversation that we didn't heed the call. After about the third call I was the only one who accepted the invitation. When the father and I sat down to the table, he says, "Thank you for coming to visit us today." I replied, "You're welcome." He answers, "No. THANK YOU for coming. Laughter has not been in this house for months. We rarely see each other even when everyone is home. Usually everyone is off to themselves. It is good to see my family in the same room together. They came out to see you. So, thank you for coming."

It is expressions like these where I recognize that what I possess is a healing balm, it is restoration, it is the ability to bring different people together for the same purpose, it is the ability to tear down barriers just through laughter. The majority of strangers I encounter during my daily routine, the conversation begins with me saying something humorous.

Comedy for me is an evangelistic tool. The question and/or statement that many ask after learning I am a clean comedienne is, "How can you be funny without profanity? That must be hard." This usually leads to a conversation about my personal walk with Christ, my morals, standards and lifestyle of godliness. Ironically, my ministerial shoes walk a very serious path. My teaching style has evolved to incorporate less humor now than when I first started. The LORD has entrusted me with an extremely serious ministry dealing with issues of the heart as well as emotional and physical healing. These areas must be handled very delicately. I also have a strong gift of prophecy and the discernment of spirits.

Another area where I am seriously passionate is worship. Through worship my issues are dealt with, my pain vanishes away, my inadequacies are irrelevant, what people said and did to me does not matter. Through worship the reality of scripture is revealed – ". . . in thy presence is the fulness of joy; at thy right hand are pleasures for evermore."

My future goals are to grow first as an individual, then as a minister and a comedienne. To have good success, it is essential to be the best at what you do. Whatever you do, do it well and as unto the LORD. There are books, CDs, DVDs, stage plays, skits, songs and more inside of me that must come out immediately. It is imperative that I begin incorporating my personal life into my stand up routine. Now is the time to tell my story. Kevin Hart entitled his stand up movie project "Laugh at My Pain." It's time that I allow people to do just that. The good news is—my wounds have become scars. Scars are merely proof that I've been healed.

the poet **yolantha**

Yolantha Harrison-Pace

Author, Poet, Children's Advocate To Haiti and India

ROAR: *Underserved women and children.*

If God can use lil' ol' me...
then He can most certainly use big ol' you.
Love and "yes you can" from Yolantha Harrison-Pace

Today I am an award winning poet and author, a teaching artist and Children's Advocate to Haiti and India. My most recent book publications are through www.trubupress.com.
HAITI: The After Shocks of Hope
HERE'S TO HAITI: Kiss, America, Kiss!!!
SHOUT, MAMMY, SHOUT!!!
    I am a performing arts specialist and playwright. One of my plays, THE WHOLE SKY, had the honor of being premiered and produced at Berea College. I am a textile artist and make dolls and prayer journals to raise funds for my mission trips. I mention these few accolades only to encourage you. Because no one, especially not myself would ever have predicted that I would amount to anything. You see—I grew up a horrific stutterer on the wrong side of the tracks in Amarillo, Texas. I am old enough to remember segregation, Jim Crow laws and "FOR WHITES ONLY" signs. I am old enough to have been called gal, Nigra, Colored, Negro, Black and African American. My speech impediment was so embarrassing not just to me, but for my family. So I was told, "SHUT UP,

AND COME BACK WHEN YOU HAVE SOMETHING TO SAY."
Needless to say, I did "shut up" and did not say much until I left home
and graduated college. In this day and age, unfortunately, I would more
than likely have been branded as having some form of attention deficit
and possibly medicated. Back then, however; I was branded as "the quiet
type" and as a "thinker". But in reality I was an observer. And later in life
found my direction as an advocate for the underdog, and the voice of
under served women and children in America and beyond.

Having grown up with bullying and corporal punishment at home
and in school (not only could a parent legally beat us as children, but you
could even get a "whuppin" at school). I married into the same kind of
dysfunctional behaviors. I thought mental and physical abuse was the
norm. Until I saw my daughter abused by my husband, her father.
Something clicked in me and a fire inside of me roared, "NO, THIS ENDS
HERE," and I left. Walked out of my house without a plan. That's where
faith came in, and not faith as I knew it growing up. Because on my road
to healing I found that "religious folks" with all of their "religious
psycobable" in spite of their "good intentions" can send you to hell in a
hand basket. It was at this point that I learned to "study to show myself
approved" and not to depend on "mammy and pappy's salvation" to get
me through. I had to find God for myself and embrace the multitude of
promises available to me as His child.

I began advocating for us as women and how valuable we are. One of
my strategies out of the dungeon of abuse was to keep a journal. One
October during Domestic Violence month a woman at my church who
was over the Women's Shelter was putting on a city-wide event. She was
at her wits end because she could not find a speaker to represent those
who have been abused. No one would come forth and speak on
"our/my" behalf. I told her, "I'll speak". She was amazed, "You,
Yolantha?" I spoke for that event, pulling from my journals. These
journals turned into my first book called WING-PLUCKED BUTTERFLY:
one woman's war on hate crimes against women and children. I
published 2 "palmettes" that can be given to teenagers and women to
help them recognize when they are in trouble. (HINT...HINT...and GET
OUT!!!). I began speaking and hosting workshops encouraging women
and emphasizing how wonderful we are. As an inspiration-
al/motivational speaker and workshop facilitator, I teach that hope
without a strategy is just a Walt Disney wish upon a star. Thus, a woman
who has faith with works CAN ACCOMPLISH ANYTHING.

THE WORTH OF A WOMAN
(a love note from God)

You are forgiven
forgive yourselves.
Women, stop wallowing in original sin.
I have redeemed you as the chosen ones.
How do I forgive?
all debts to Eden's Garden were paid and forgiven
privately
at a well of water when my Son, Jesus, asked a
woman for a drink.
I forgave the fingers that picked forbidden fruit
purifying them when my son accepted a cup of water from
her apple stained hands.
Publicly
by stopping your stoning
reflecting the sins of the world back to man's soul.
My forgiveness reinforced your feminine value through just
the hem of your Lord's garment.
But
most of all
I forgave you through the depth of my
intimacy
with the birth of Jesus.
My grace does not look back.
You, too, as women must turn around
and reclaim the Eden of your hearts.
And the joy of your freedom
through the forgiving birth of Jesus from your blessed
and
sanctified wombs.

<><><><><><><><>

JESUS CAME FROM THE
WOMB OF A WOMAN...
HOW POWERFUL AND VICTORIOUS IS THAT?.
MOVE THAT MOUNTAIN: Dance, Mountain, Dance!!!
I've lived mustard seed faith.
I've said, "Move, mountain." and it moved.

I've said,
"MOOOOOOOOOVE, MOUNTAIN!!!" and it moved.
The mountain of gossip.
The mountain of deceit.
The mountain of cheating and lies.
The mountain of impatience and impertinence.
The mountain of being the right color at the wrong time.
The mountain of enemies, spousal abuse and negligence.
The mountain of birth, death, and abortions.
The mountain of all of my sins moved.
But after the mountain ranges moved,
there was nothing but empty.
A valley of alone-ness and solitude.
In my mountain free world I discovered
God only meant the mustard seed
to be the starting point;
not the end all, and be all of faith,
not the final parameters
but
the jumping off place.
I took on the challenge and
with the faith of a watermelon seed,
I whispered,
"Dance, mountain, dance."
The mountain lifted her skirt and began to waltz.
"Dance, mountain, dance!"
The mountain began to Cha-Cha.
It did the Meringue, and the Macarena.
"DANCE, MOUNTAIN, DANCE!!!"
It twisted and shouted, it did the Poney Maroney and the Skate and the
Monkey and the Frugue. It Pop-locked into the Robot and C-Walked.
Just imagine,
me
with the faith
of an avocado seed
shouting,
"SING, MOUNTAIN, SING!"
And me finding my slumber in a mountain lullaby.
Or even me with the faith of a mango seed,
saying,

"Make love to me mountain, make love."
Aaaaaaah, the faith of it.

http://yolantha.trubupress.com/move-that-mountain-dance-mountain-dance/

The missing element for women as the abused and as survivors is that we are often led to believe that being a "survivor" over domestic violence is as far as we need to go. That's where I find the fallacy. We as women must be VICTORIOUS over our lives. My journals full of poetry, prayers and "ghetto tales" (stories told from a Black perspective) helped me to take back my voice and led me to use my voice to discover victory over my life and to become an advocate and support system for not just the abused in America but also the less fortunate in Haiti. I have served in Haiti since the year 2000 and I've now been invited to serve in India. What makes me roar? I would say that the most empowering word I have ever heard was "NO". I never liked the saying when life gives you lemons, make lemonade. Why?...because I don't like lemonade. But I am living proof that the very thing that was my downfall I turned into my victory. And you can, too. I grew up without a voice and now am the voice through my books for abused women and for sharing Haiti in a way that no-one else has ever seen. Not Oprah Winfrey, not Sean Penn, not Kim Kardashian. And as trite as it might sound, I had to learn to crawl before I could walk, then skip then run. The crawl of my voice began as a soft purr, then a whisper, then monologues of positive self-talk, then shared dialogues of encouragement. My books are documentation of my voice. They are a celebration of "not an ABUSED me, not a SURVIVOR me, but of me recovering and celebrating my voice of VICTORY."
Just remember:
when you are down and out
as long as you have breath
you can roar
when you feel all alone and
alienated
just roar
when no one will listen
I promise they will if
you
roar

Finally, the most empowering words I have ever ROARED were THANK YOU. When all else failed an attitude of gratitude opened doors, ferreted out new pathways, healed wounds, and was an entryway to forgiveness. So when you are down and out, and feeling all alone and alienated and nobody is listening to you and you don't know WHAT to roar...ROAR...THANK YOU...come on, let's try it, hitch up your big girl panties, take a deep, deep breath and let's do it together...

THAAAAAAAAAAAAAANKKKKKKK
YOOOOOOOOOOUUUU!!!

To contact Yolantha or order her "palmettes" on domestic violence, or have her come speak or do workshops, book readings/signings she can be contacted through:

yolanthapace@gmail.com or 859-936-7313 or 859-583-9894. Her books are found through Amazon and through www.trubupress.com.

You can also read her blogs at www.yolantha.trubupress.com

Diane Latiker

Kids Off The Block, Founder

ROAR: *Youth Violence Prevention*

The mother of eight children, "Ms. Diane" as the children refer to her, is a twenty-five year resident of the Roseland community on the far south side of Chicago. She founded the award winning organization Kids Off The Block, Inc. (KOB) in her home in July of 2003. Ms. Latiker was given this vision through her mother Evangelist Ruth Jackson. Ms. Jackson, saw that the youth in the neighborhood liked and respected her daughter. Looking at the children that were always at her home, Ms. Diane saw health professionals, doctors, lawyers, professional musicians, professional sports figures, politicians, and actresses, and the list goes on. She believed that she could make a difference in the community, and in the many youth that she came in contact with daily. She became encouraged and opened up her home to get these young people off the streets and involved in programs that would benefit them for the rest of their lives. The organization celebrated ten years of service to children/youth, teens and young adults in the city of Chicago, IL. KOB started out with ten neighborhood kids, and now has impacted thousands of lives. "Some say our youth is a lost generation, I don't believe that to be true. I, Diane Latiker, Founder and President of Kids Off The Block organization think differently. I have heard the voices and they speak of hope and love. Through forms of compassion, love, and guidance, this generation can be led to discovering a spectrum of opportunities and become positive leaders in our communities".

Awards & Accolades:

ComEd Neighborhood Hero / Black History Month 2014

Received the BET "Shine Your Light Award 2013

Featured on ABC "Secret Millionaire" July 1, 2012

Red Cross "Community Impact" Award March 2012

CNN Top Ten Hero 2011

Speaker in 2011 "Festival of Thinkers" in Dubai (UAE)

CNN Hero of the Week in April 2011

NAMED TO MAYOR-ELECT RAHM EMMANUEL TRANSITION TEAM (PUBLIC SAFETY) 2011

AWARDS:

IIFWP - AMBASSADOR FOR PEACE
EBONY/PINE-SOL – WOMEN MAKING A DIFFERENCE
METHODIST YOUTH SERVICES – CERTIFICATE OF APPRECIATION
THE BLACK STAR PROJECT – STUDENT MOTIVATIONAL PROGRAM
PASTORS NETWORK OF ILLINOIS – COMMUNITY SERVICE
COOK COUNTY STATE'S ATTORNEY – VICTIM SERVICE AWARD
SUN-TIMES NEWSPAPER (AUGUST 2008) ONE OF 50 PEOPLE WHO MAKE CHICAGO A BETTER PLACE
LEWIS HINES AWARD (NATIONAL CHILD LABOR COMMITTEE)
GLOW AWARD
FOUNDER DIANE LATIKER WAS 1 OF 3 PEOPLE HONORED ON ANDERSON COOPER (CNN) FOR BLACK HISTORY MONTH.
DIANE LATIKER RECEIVED THE EPHRAIM BAHAR COMMUNITY SERVICE AWARD IN JULY 2010
DIANE LATIKER WAS FEATURED ON WCIU CHANNEL 26 (THE U) AS ONE OF CHICAGO'S POWERFUL WOMEN FOR BLACK HISTORY MONTH FEBRUARY 2011

DIANE LATIKER RECEIVED THE MARION N'ZINGA STAMPS AWARD AT THE BLACK HERITAGE AWARDS IN FEBRUARY 2011
DIANE LATIKER HONORED WITH AN "UNSUNG HERO AWARD" COOK COUNTY PRESIDENT'S OFFICE IN MARCH 2011
DIANE LATIKER WAS CNN HERO OF THE WEEK IN APRIL 2011
YOUTH ADVOCACY AWARD / FENGER HIGH SCHOOL / PRINCIPAL ELIZABETH DOZIER
DWAYNE WADE FOUNDATION "VILLAGE KEEPERS AWARD" IN AUGUST 2011
FESTIVAL OF THINKERS IN DUBAI (UAE) NOVEMBER 2011
CNN TOP 10 HERO IN SEPTEMBER 2011
LOU RAWLS COMMUNITY SPIRIT AWARD
COMMUNITY IMPACT AWARD (ALLSTARS PROJECT)
RED CROSS "COMMUNITY IMPACT" AWARD 3-15-12
ETA "RESURRECTING SPIRIT and RECLAIMING COMMUNITY" Award 9-8-12
Essence "Style and Substance Award" September 2012
Young & Powerful Group / Community Award / September 2012
Cook County Clerk Dorothy Brown "Hidden Jewel" Award / February 2013
Chicago Center "First Voice Humanitarian Award / May 2013
BET "Shine The Light" Award / July 2013

MEDIA:

N'DIGO MAGAZINE
CITIZEN NEWSPAPER (3TIMES)
CHICAGO DEFENDER
CHICAGO SUN-TIMES NEWSPAPER
CHICAGO TRIBUNE (METRO AND MAGAZINE)
THE FINAL CALL
THE CHICAGO COMMUNICATOR (2 TIMES)
CLTV NEWS (3 TIMES)
FOX NEWS (2)
WGN CHANNEL 9
ABC-7 (3 TIMES)
CBS NEW YORK
KKC RADIO
CHICAGO STATE UNIVERSITY RADIO
CNN (4 TIMES)
BET
THE GAURDIAN (LONDON)

THE VOORKANT (NETHERLANDS)
EBONY MAGAZINE
WYCC (CHANNEL 20)
BLACK ENTERPRISE MAGAZINE (TV)
WTTW CHANNEL 11 (NEED TO KNOW SERIES)
WCIU CHANNEL 26 (THE U)
GOSPEL TRIBUNE NEWSPAPER
AL-JAZEERA TV (WASHINGTON)
WASHINGTON TIMES
NEW YORK TIMES
MICHAEL BAISDEN SHOW
GARY CRUSADER NEWSPAPER
BLACK AMERICA (TOM JOYNER)
WINDY CITY LIVE
CNN TOP 10 TRIBUTE AWARDS SHOW DECEMBER 2011
BBC
TOKYO NEWS
NEWS ONE
DATELINE AUSTRALIA
USA TODAY
EBONY MAGAZINE STORY / JULY 2013
DNA.COM
ESSENCE MAGAZINE
FAME MAGAZINE

The Power of One!

After forty-six years, eight children, thirteen grandchildren and two husbands, I finally was blessed with a passion that filled my soul. My mom raised me to be independent, married or not, she always taught us to stand for something or fall for everything. I was the oldest, so I took it in the most, literally. The problem was that it was always for someone else. I was a people pleaser. You know, the one who can't be happy without others being happy. I stood for everyone's well-being, never giving thought to my dreams, hopes or goals in life. It would all be fine, I thought, if everyone around me was okay. At forty-six years old, all that changed, but in a different way.

When my mother mentioned to me that the kids in the neighborhood liked me, even respected me, and that I should do something with them, I immediately thought to myself, "no, I can't." Because I had one child left at home, she was thirteen and would be gone to college at eighteen. I would be free, or so I thought. For days after that I prayed about what my mom said, it then hit me. That's what I loved to do anyway, help people. I always wanted people to be happy. Well, here was my chance. I just never thought it would make me happy too! When I began to get involved with children from my neighborhood, something began to happen. I started to feel vibrant, useful, giving. My spirit was uplifted as the young people strolled into my apartment every day, relying on me to guide, teach, listen, love, care, nurture, and discipline them. As I began to listen to each one of their stories, I felt compelled to help, even if only to offer advice. The more they talked, the more needed I felt. Each day began to be an adventure; I would stay up nights thinking of ways to make their day better and more uplifting. I would be so excited knowing they were coming, then their friends started coming, kids I didn't know.

The other kids were telling them about this "lady," it dawned on me that "that" lady was me! Each day more and more would show up, "Hey, Ms. Diane!" they would say. The joy in my heart would fill up, just knowing they depended on me to be safe, to be cared for, it was an amazing feeling.

My family began to notice and my neighbors began to notice all the kids hanging out at my house. Even some of my children began to question my decision to allow this to happen. My husband asked with a concerned look, "Are you crazy? We can't take care of all these children." It didn't help much either that I had sold the family television, his television. Well, I couldn't explain it to any of them, how I felt, why I felt this way, but I knew I couldn't stop.

In the meantime, more kids were coming, so I moved all the furniture out of our dining room, bought used computers with the television money so the kids could study and do homework. It almost cost me another divorce. I promised my husband I wouldn't touch anything else if he just stayed. Then I noticed there were over fifty, yes fifty youth in my house and they were coming every day of the week. Some came or called in the middle of the night or early in the morning. They were even coming to sit on my porch just to wait until I came out. Those that were getting thrown out of the house and needed a place to stay for a couple of days would sleep on my floor. My husband and I would wash their clothes, feed them, take them back and forth to school. Amazingly, when my family saw how serious I was and how happy I was, they began to pitch in. We bought shoes, coats, hats, scarves and in the blink of an eye, there were seventy-five.

My husband and I moved everything out of a bedroom, solicited used music equipment and made it into a studio for them to make music.

That was when he put his foot down. "Diane, we are not going any further. I need my bedroom!" I complied as long as he stayed (smile). Neighbors were not so nice at this point, saying things like "old lady in a shoe, got so many children she didn't know what to do". They called the police on me a couple of times. Oh, but it was something in me that wouldn't let me stop and I knew what it was. The Young People! They really believed in me, and to prove it, they tried hard to show me they could do it. They got back in school, got out of gangs, stopped fighting, were so happy when their grades started improving, became empowered, all because I opened my home. I was having the time of my life! They made me laugh, cry, think, create, feel validated, it was an awesome feeling and nothing was going to stop me at this point. I took my newfound euphoria out into the community to share with others. Telling them about the kids in my home, asking for help and assistance for them. Again, I was naïve, thinking everyone wanted to help. I was running day and night in between being with the youth. Every day was an adventure. I spoke the same message everywhere I went. Soon it began to sink in, even the neighbors looked at me differently, some even offered their help. I was making progress. Each year more and more people reached out to support my vision.

After much exposure, press and 2,000 youth later, I can honestly say this is the most rewarding thing I have ever done in my life. Certainly the "Power of I" is the power of us all. Collectively, we change things, but individually we start the change. I'm glad I was one of the ones chosen to be a part of so many inspiring lives, to earn their trust and respect. I am fulfilled and leave you with this thought: "Our day begins to end the day we become silent about things that matter." Dr. Martin Luther King Jr.

Adrienne Rumph

God's Church International, Senior Pastor

ROAR: *Living Authentically*

When asked to take down a few lines to describe who I am and what I do, I was eager and ready to do so. From the outset, it seemed as though it would be easy, but in actuality it has been difficult. How do you put into words what you have been doing before you knew you were doing anything? How do you describe that what you do is what you were placed on planet earth to do? How do you capture what is so innate that it's difficult to separate from and examine to give an intelligible and intelligent answer? I'm wholeheartedly convinced that the work assigned to my hands is a ministry of elevating the human spirit and illuminating the innate, sometimes hidden potential each of us has inside through Christ Jesus. Love, understanding, wisdom, counsel, courage and knowledge from God all play in the success of an individual becoming who they are designed to be. It can be a difficult task to be realigned with whom we are called to be. Our pasts can be a collective hindrance to discovering the essence of who we really are. I believe one of the tasks God has given me is to be a lover of His people. I have always been a nurturer of people. Some of my first memories as a very young person were of me being the one who led, instructed, oversaw and corrected others. Those who seemingly had gotten off course would solicit my advice. I remember sitting in an untitled seat of counselor. Giving wisdom and instruction to those double and sometimes triple my age. It was effortless and came with ease. I was unaware that it was the divine knowledge and insight given me from God. I assumed that I was just peculiar. Family and friends often called me that and so I began to believe it. It was overwhelming at times, "this gift". I didn't see it as a gift, but as a curse. Everyone that I have met in different phases in my life, God has allowed each person that I encountered to affirm the gift and affirm my life's work. It wasn't until I was well into my thirties, that I could begin to clearly and definitively see what God had purposed and planned for my portion in ministry. Aside from realizing at an early age that I had a calling to help others, I realized later in life that I had greatly been influenced by my early experiences of faith working miracles in the lives of those who needed healing, deliverance and restoration. My first church experiences in Newark, New Jersey were at Deliverance Evange- listic Center under the leadership of the late Apostle Arturo Skinner. At the helm of this great ministry, he made suitably sure that the children were blessed, ministered to and included in every service. It was at this ministry that the love of Christ was awakened and nurtured in me. It was the foundational teachings, the pure unadulterated truth of the word of God, the charismatic and supernatural demonstrations of healing and deliverance and the impartation that helped to form and mature my spiritual self.

It is true when it is said that hindsight is 20/20. As I look back over the path my life has taken, I can comprehend with sound revelation why my path was as rocky, curvy, hindered and stagnant at times. You see, I am the product of a broken home. A home where spousal abuse from my father is what I remember most from my father. His absence in my life always caused a knot in my stomach that made me unintentionally hold my breath, hoping, wishing, wanting him to follow through this time. Yes, I have been homeless, hungry, inconvenienced, rejected, sexually abused, depressed, suffered low-self esteem, suffered panic attacks, suffered paralyzing fear and battled suicidal thoughts. I was the poster child for anyone who was scheduled to be a statistic. Even with marriage, becoming a mother and even as a minister, my change didn't fully come until I realized that no amount of therapy, no prescriptions, and no accolades from man would be able to save me and pull me out of my pit.

It took two women's conferences in 2004 and 2005 to really set me on my journey to wholeness. There I met God like never before. It took obedience, fasting, prayer and eating God's word to turn my situation around. I yielded all that I had. I felt like the rich young ruler... I knew I needed to leave my high paying position in pharmaceuticals. I knew I needed to open my heart and release the pain of the past and all the resentment toward those that I believed had wronged me. I took a two-year journey to healing and restoration and readily accepted my call to ministry in May 2006. Since then, though difficulties have presented themselves, I have not looked back. I can see clearly my role in helping others get to their authentic self and begin their authentic lives as Father God intended. I have been mentoring young women for more than thirteen years. I counsel using the word of the Lord and godly principles. I am currently certified as a "cleansing specialist". I assist in helping you uncover and become free from those things that have encumbered you in making progress in your life. I am a teacher. I love to teach, train and instruct, especially the word of God. I am a mother. I have birthed two of my own, but I am affectionately known as "Auntie A" to those who are not connected by blood. I am a wife. I am rejoicing at what the Lord has done as my husband and I will soon celebrate twenty years of marriage. (It wasn't always "wedded bliss" either) I am a singer/songwriter. I have penned more than a dozen songs that were divinely downloaded by the "Divine One", God Himself. I am an aspiring author. I hope to have my first published work out by this fall in a bookstore near you. I am a senior pastor. I pastor via the Internet along with three other dynamic women of God. At God's Church International (GCI), we offer 24-hour access to preaching, teaching and prayer. (godschurchinternational.org) I also sit at the helm of my training and equipping ministry known as Effective Weapons For The Kingdom. It was launched in February 2013 and has hosted a successful teleseminar, with many others to follow. I am oftentimes busy, but it truly is a joy to do the work I was designed to accomplish here in this earth. I find great satisfaction in watching others grow knowing that God used me in some humble way to seed, weed, water or prune in some capacity for someone else's life. I try to live each day remembering with all earnestness the motto that the Lord gave for GCI, "It's not about you. It's not about me... But It's ALL about HIM!

Angela Latoya Williams

Mothers Against Murderers Association/Founder

ROAR: *Gun Violence*

Angela Latoya Williams was born and raised in Palm Beach County, Florida. She attended school in Palm Beach and graduated from Palm Beach Gardens High School in 1978. Angela raised her three children Sonishari Bellamy, Ashley Williams and Jermaine Williams Sr. as a single mother. She is also the grandmother of four boys Jermaine Jr., Jermaris, Jermonte and Damian Jr. Her passion has always been her love for children. Angela has worked with kids in public schools, managed a successful day care, and interacted with kids as a school bus driver.

In 2003, Angela created and founded the organization known today as Mothers Against Murderers Association Inc. (MAMA) in West Palm Beach Florida 33407.

Awards/Honorable Mentions:
Recipient of the Outstanding Contributions to Crime Victims in 2009
Distinguished Victims Service Award
Service award from Attorney General Bill McCollum

The American Health Association 13th Annual American Senior Achievement Award November 11,2011 in appreciation for her community service and honoring the spirit of volunteering.

The Trailblazer of Social Justice Award 2012-2013 for leading the way in fighting crime in the community

Angela had the pleasure of meeting the First Lady Michelle Obama on February 12,2013 at the White House

Angela has served as a voice for Juvenile Life Without Parole (JLWOP) and voiced her opinion regarding the bill, which was fought through the Supreme Court of the United States in 2009.

Affiliations:
Destiny By Choice, Skyler Jett social conscious artist/vocal producer
Mayor Against Illegal Guns
Timothy E. Kitchen Funeral Home
Oscar Grant Foundation
Juvenile Life Without Parole
Preventing Crime in the Black Community
Churches
Dan Calloway
Derrick MCCray
Paul Hogan
Frank Hogan
Willie Lane
Thank You!!
Mothers Against Murderers Association

MAMA: A Place Called Hope
The week before Christmas 2002, my nephew Torrey Manuel helped me financially with obtaining video games for my son Jermaine so he could have them for Christmas. Being a single mother of three, it became very difficult financially to be able to purchase toys and gifts for my children. I have always been fearful of what could happen on New Year's Eve because of celebratory gunfire. On January 1, 2013 at 6:00 a.m. my phone rang. My sister Cora Sabrina Hays was screaming into the phone. At some point I was able to hear her say, "Torrey is dead."

My response to her was, "Repeat what you just said."

And once again, she said, "Torrey has been shot and he is dead."

I dropped the telephone went directly to the hospital, which was ten minutes away, instead of going to his apartment up the street from where I lived at the time. Either I just wasn't thinking at the time, or I was too afraid of what I might find.

When I arrived at the hospital, it was very quiet and I didn't see any familiar faces, so I figured maybe my sister was confused and maybe someone else was shot. I left the hospital and headed towards Torrey's apartment. As I got closer, I started to see flashing lights. When I arrived, I could see a crowd of people standing there with tears running down their faces. I was still in denial and disbelief. Because it was a crime scene and certain areas were not accessible, I went through the back window of Torrey's apartment trying to find out what was going on. His body was lying in the front of the apartment, which the police had sealed off. Torrey's mother, Georgie Dixon, arrived at the scene and entered through the same back window as I did earlier. She was screaming saying that's not Torrey it must be someone else.

As hours passed, we waited for the coroners to come, and they finally arrived. When they attempted to take the body away, I could see Torrey's leg come from underneath the sheet. I remember this like it was yesterday. Torrey's leg was severed in half and the only thing keeping it together was his skin. He was shot seven times with an AK47 high capacity magazine riffle execution style.

During the week of his funeral, I still found myself in disbelief as I was helping with the funeral arrangements thinking, *Is Torrey really dead?* It wasn't until Saturday, the day of the funeral, when I was standing outside of my mother's home, that it became real. When the funeral car pulled up, I realized that this funeral was really happening, Torrey was really gone. The tears began to roll down my face. I was trying to control myself, but it was extremely difficult to hold back the emotions, so I began to pace back and forth. Everyone gathered inside the house to pray, then off to the church we went.

After the funeral, things didn't get any better for my sister. I started receiving telephone calls from Johnnie, who is Torrey's brother, asking for help with my sister. The calls started coming more frequently asking for help because he would find her sitting in her car with the windows rolled up in 90 degree weather. This behavior went on for a while after Torrey's death and she had a mild stroke after losing her son. I asked God for help and he responded, telling me what I needed to do. I knew what I had to do, I just wasn't sure which steps to take. I stepped out on faith and came up with Mothers Against Murderers Association (MAMA). I asked the Lord to give me a gift to help families experiencing a crisis due to losing a loved one to murder. I had no idea it would grow so rapidly.

Now this was the next step. I started reaching out to mothers that had lost their child to gun violence and they started joining the MAMA organization – along with other family members that were gunned down in the streets of Palm Beach County Florida. I started finding myself going to more and more funerals, courthouses, homes, hospitals, juvenile facilities and graveyards ministering to families I did not know. I started having healing groups bi-weekly on the first and third Thursday of the month. The groups have been very successful in helping families heal. Mothers never get over losing a child to violence, they just learn how to live with it. There are those days such as holidays, birthdays, and death anniversaries that are the hardest. At MAMA organization, we teach forgiveness and how powerful the word is. Forgiveness may help you overcome so many things such as anger, hurt, guilt, and retaliation by taking that pain and turning it into power. Torrey D. Manuel was the second person to get murdered on New Year's Day, January 1, 2003. In addition to that, I have lost twelve other family members to gun violence in Palm Beach County over the years. I have attended two hundred and twenty eight funerals. Because of this I find myself saying that I must continue to help these families despite the things I am going through myself. I am trying to keep the doors open for these mothers and youths so they will have a place to come and share their grief, a place where they can tell their stories and be able to heal with others. We call MAMA a place of HOPE.

Our young black boys and girls are losing their lives daily. Despite whether they were involved in any misconduct or not, no one deserves to be gunned down in the streets.

Those left behind to heal:

Margaret Wilson is the grandmother of Tiara Meeks (10/15/1988-3/16/2007). Tiara was buried in Glenwood Cemetery in Riviera Beach, Florida. She was eighteen when she died. Two people were involved in the shooting. One of them was shot and killed and the other the police did not have enough evidence to arrest him. Tiara was a victim of a drive-by shooting. She was on her way to visit a friend when she was shot. The intended victim was shot five times, while Tiara was shot twice and became paralyzed from the neck down. She died a couple of years later from complications. This is a dedication to all 260 mothers that have joined Mothers Against Murderers Association Inc.

Special Thanks to Georgie Dixon, Artie Williams and Jimmie Williams.

Cheryl Fisher White

Author, Dramatist, LIMCW Inspirations, Founder

ROAR: *Holding on to hope*

Cheryl Fisher White is a saved, sanctified, Spirit-filled woman of God, gifted poet, dramatist, playwright, publisher, motivational speaker, workshop presenter and author whose anointed words have brought encouragement and hope to the single, married, separated, divorced and widowed. Since her teenage years, Cheryl has written numerous books, plays, skits, songs and poetry.

How I Got Started:

Every writer should begin as a reader. I remember at a very young age always having a love of reading. As I read each book, it was always my desire to write my very own book one day. Not really believing that was possible, I started writing love letters for my teenage friends. One day my teacher caught me in the process and took the letter. After he read it, he came to me and said that I have a talent for writing and if I signed up for the Creative Writing class he would not call my mother. Well, I signed up for the class. During the class, my love for writing was revealed even more. Not really understanding at the time that this gift was instilled in me by God, I continued to write with ease. In addition to writing, there was always a special feeling each time I participated in the drama presentations at my church. My love for drama and writing allowed me at the age of sixteen to write my first skit for the church,

"Who Will Walk With Jesus." Noticing how everyone enjoyed the skit, a desire to write more was manifested.

Vision Revealed:

A few years later, I began to pray deeply about my direction from the Lord. One night in particular, I prayed and asked the Lord what was I supposed to do with my life. That night I fell asleep praying. During the night (still not sure if it was a vision or a dream) I saw my hands in the clouds and they were very bright. I knew it was the Lord anointing my hands to write for him. After waking up, the presence of the Lord was felt all around me. I looked at my hands and they looked the same, however, they felt different. This unique experience caused me to walk around envisioning the dream/vision for the next few days. From that point, there was a strong passion leading me to pen words that revealed my inner thoughts and feelings which are words to encourage those who are experiencing frustrations in their daily walk.

My Motivation:

The motivation in my life comes from six areas. My first incentive to pursue writing came from my teacher who acknowledged it. Next, the revelation of what the Lord wanted me to do came through the dream/vision that the Lord had provided on that special night when my hands were anointed through prayer and seeking God for direction. My continued drive is my mother who supports everything I do and always encourages me to know that my work is very good. Following that, I am motivated to be a role model for my children along with reaching for the goals in my life. My friends and others that I write for encourage me to continue on this journey. All of this motivates me to write and continue performing which provides a message that will enable someone to stand up and be a blessing to others as I share my testimony of how God has delivered me in the times of trouble.

My Experiences:

For the last forty years of my life, I have had the experience of sharing my writings through books and drama presentation in churches, schools, nursing homes, banquets, workshops, seminars, conferences, bookstores, conventions and many other venues.

In the area of writing – I have had the opportunity to serve as a secretary in various capacities at church for over forty years. This area of ministry afforded me the opportunity to enhance my writing skills, note taking, correspondence, flyers, bulletins, newsletters and customer service experience. Since the 1980s, I have written eight books. The publications are as follows: "The Waiting World" (poetry), "Spreading Some Sunshine" (poetry), "Thoughts of Inspiration (poetry) and "Crown of Glory" (poetry). I have also written, "It's Okay to Go Home" a book which is a testimonial for families dealing with troubled youth. "Virtuous" is a book of encouragement for women, and "A Voice of Inspiration" shares a message of hope for those going through trials in their daily life.

In addition to my other writings, I am blessed to be able to prepare my own greeting cards for various occasions. The Lord has inspired and enabled me to be in my fourth year of publication of the magazine titled "Hope For Today." Through this publication, words of hope and encouragement are shared along with interviewing people who have a story to tell that will encourage others to continue in the service of the Lord. In 1988 I was afforded the opportunity to travel to Anaheim, California as a semi-finalist for the World of Poetry with 400 other poets from around the world. Although I didn't win first place, my self-esteem increased and I was able to go places and do great things for the Lord.

In the area of Drama – I have written over twenty plays and skits that have been shared in churches, workshops, banquets, nursing homes, veterans memorial homes, schools, seminars, wedding receptions, and family reunions.

For more than twenty years the Lord has blessed me to portray the character of Harriet Tubman. As the character of Ms. Tubman, her life accomplishments are always shared and geared towards the needs of the audience. She is also my role model. Harriet Tubman's life and mission is an extraordinary example of the road that I had to travel while working towards my dreams and goals. For the last three years, I have developed a character named "Shirley Mae" who shares a problem in someone's life and provides a solution through the Word of God. This character has portrayed a drunk, prostitute, single parent, preacher, homeless person, depressed person and much more.

In the Area of Education – The Lord blessed me in 2001 to graduate from Start Right Stay Strong Entrepreneur Class. In 2002 I graduated from the Cumberland County College and received an Associates Degree in Office Automation Management. In 2005, I graduated from Christian Research and Development receiving a certificate in Biblical Counseling and in 2008 I received a certificate in "Twelve Steps with God." Every year I attend the counseling conference to enhance my learning of how to deal with the issues people face on a daily basis.

I have also received educational certificates in Computer Information Systems and Office Systems Technology.

In the area of Ministry/Business – Writing for more than forty years, God has allowed me to utilize my gift of exhortation towards everyone I meet. Throughout the years, I have lived by Colossians 3:16-17. "Let the word of Christ dwell in you richly in all wisdom; teaching and admonishing one another in psalms and hymns and spiritual songs, singing with grace in your hearts to the Lord. And whatsoever ye do in word or deed, do all in the name of the Lord Jesus, giving thanks to God and the Father by him."

With this thought in mind, in 2001, I was inspired to establish my own ministry/business entitled: L.I.M.C.W. Inspirations. The initials are the first letters of my children's names. This ministry captures the essence of my entire life of service. Under this ministry, I visit the nursing homes to perform skits, shares poetry and cards of encouragement for the residents. I also share performances through drama which provide messages of hope whenever requested. Under this ministry a magazine is published titled "Hope for Today" periodically sharing messages of hope and testimonials. I also assist others in the area of publication through support and providing workshops where they can gather information to move forward in their endeavors. My gift is also shared by writing poetry for others in any occasion. The poems are always uplifting and a source of inspiration and encouragement which is my purpose in life.

Future Plans:

My future endeavors are to continue writing poetry, books of encouragement, drama to encourage the hopeless, providing hope and to launch my own line of greeting cards.

In closing, Cheryl serves as a Church/Clerk, Deaconess, Missionary and Women's Fellowship Convener at Union Baptist Temple, Member of the Church Secretaries Alliance and Poets Vineyard Organization. She is the proud mother of five children: LeAnne, Isaiah, Willie, Matthew and Christopher, and the proud grandmother of seventeen. My testimony of living more than two and a half decades as a single parent has been to "hold on, because help is on the way."

Desiree Lee

Ex-convict, Author, Speaker, Activist

ROAR: *Prison Prevention*
A Phenomenal Inspirational Story

Desiree Lee is a renowned keynote speaker, author, and philanthropist. Using herself as a visual aid, Desiree has committed her life to providing a prison prevention workshop, with resourceful tools others can apply to their lives, in an effort to overcome life's most difficult lessons. It is designed to derail young people from making decisions leading to crime and transforming our youth into rewarding citizens of society.

"I wouldn't want any teen to go through what I've experienced in prison! I wouldn't want any parent to experience what my parents went through seeing their child in prison!" – Desiree Lee

She delivers a high energy message which helps the audience retain the image of heading down a criminal path, with a message of inspiration wrapped in a package unlike any we've seen before. Not the typical "Scared Straight" approach, she shows people how to eliminate fear, seize opportunity, and live up to their greatness. Desiree is one of the nation's leading authorities in connecting and stimulating human potential, utilizing a powerful delivery and newly emerging insights to awaken, inspire and channel people to new heights of achievement. Desiree's personal mission in life is to provide inspiration to individuals who feel that their current situation is hindering them from accomplishing greater. Desiree continues to travel nationwide presenting her presentations, "Imagine, Create, Become," "Eliminate Fear and Become Fearless," "Season of Preparation: Seize Opportunity & Step into Your Greatness." Ms. Lee is also committed to hosting an Annual Prison Prevention Tour nationwide and welcomes the opportunity to offer her presentations worldwide.

Invite Desiree Lee to share her story with your audience today! www.IamDesireeLee.com | Office: (404) 919-0396 | Email: hilary.cole72@gmail.com

It is our faith that moves mountains, not our hands.
Written by Desiree Lee
In Short…

My story began in Riverside, California where I was born. I was raised in Atlanta, Georgia. I am a convicted felon who has managed to turn my criminal background into inspiration for many to find inspiration to overcome life's most difficult barriers. This life-altering decision happened in May 2002. A high school student, 3.8 GPA, two basketball scholarships, on my way to college in pursuit of THE AMERICAN DREAM. About two weeks after graduation, I've found myself on the other side of the law. Soon I was charged with eleven counts of armed robbery and five counts of aggravated assault, with the possibility of spending 135 years in prison. A ten minute decision that severely affected my parents, brother, others and ultimately my future. There were many times that I had thoughts of committing suicide. Faced with many limitations with a criminal record on my background, I felt like giving up during the crucial time of my transition into my breakthrough. During the six years since my release from prison, I've tried to secure employment, an apartment, transportation, and to pursue a college education. I even attempted to obtain a license in cosmetology, and to my surprise, I was denied all of these opportunities due to my criminal background. Many know that if you commit a crime, the result is doing time in prison. I wasn't aware of the aftermath of disappointments that I would encounter following my release from prison. If I knew of this at the age of seventeen years old, I am certain that I would have made an alternative decision. These trials could have been avoided if I had taken the time to think. While in high school, I wasn't classified as an 'at-risk' teen. I guess it was because I wasn't showing any of the familiar signs of not-so-good behavior and somehow I still ended up going to prison. I wasn't exposed to criminal behavior and somehow I still ended up in prison. I didn't get an opportunity to hear the mistakes of a convicted felon, nor knew of the negative connotations of a criminal background. It is my belief that there shouldn't be a category of at-risk teens, a segregated line of the good teens over here and the bad teens over there. The truth is EVERY child is at-risk!

After failing countless times in search of rebounding from my past mistakes, I quickly found myself in a really dark place. In this dark place is where I found the brightest light. I realized, all of this time I've been trying to move the overbearing mountains out of my path with my bare hands, instead of using my faith to overcome life's most difficult barriers. It was in this moment that I began to embrace what I went through, in an effort to prevent others from experiencing the same pain, the same regret, the same fear. I believe that every child, teenager, young adult and parent has an equal chance to go beyond their limitations or the circumstances that surround them. It's then that we will begin to see the resources that were available to us all along. With my story I intend to inspire those who may feel as if their situation is hopeless, to imagine so intensely that their imagination creates a new reality. I'm not saying that I will change the world, but I guarantee you this, I aim to spark the mind of those who will. By faith, I can!

"Never doubt the POWER OF FAITH" –Desiree Lee

Elayssandria Kasongo

Minister, Author, Activist

ROAR: *The "throwaway youth."*

Better Than Tomorrow

"We urgently need much more action and much less talk in the practice of living for the sake of others!" That has been the slogan and belief that I and my husband have lived by for almost the last thirty-nine years. We have not been able to take a vacation in the past two decades, not because we did not want to or could not afford it, but primarily because we could not stop the roll. Sometimes it has been incredibly challenging to do this type of outreach, because you rarely hear the words "thank you," but to see even one person reverse destructive behavior and habits for the sake of good, is worth every bit of suffering that I have ever experienced.

I was born in the early '50s in Southern California to Captain Richard Alex Zander, and my mother who was an extraordinary Home Economics teacher for The Camarillo School for Girls. Her name was Ida Odessa Williams. She was a completely selfless mother, who loved us unconditionally. She had a heart of gold and was always busy in her life tending to all of her eight children, but also having enough kindness to assist others in the community whenever anyone needed help. I don't know how she was able to do that. Most parents I knew had only enough love for their immediate families, but I remember my mother's heart being big enough to love the whole world. When I would wake up in the morning as a child, I would see my mother on her knees in deep tearful prayer. I was awestruck by her example and it humbled me beyond words. Consequently, I believe it was my mother's unselfish, loving example in how she served and loved us that was the primary reason I decided to pursue a spiritual path to love and to serve others.

My father died when I was two, which left our entire household devastated. Mainly by him being a high ranking officer in the Army, this allowed our family to live a wonderful, comfortable lifestyle, but now all that would end within days after his death. Everything would now depend upon my mother, with eight children to keep alive. Caring for all eight of her children at one time, would prove to be too challenging for my mother, so she eventually had to send four of us younger children to live with my Aunt "Too Sweet" in Northern California. To this day, I do not know why they called my Aunt "Too Sweet" because she was tough as nails and didn't take any mess from anyone. Her character could be so frightening that it was enough to make a grown man quiver in his boots, but I bless God for her because it was in her home that I learned to grow up about several years faster and tougher than a normal child should have, thus my real journey begins.

Everyone in my life played such an important role in what I have become today. I have not mentioned all my struggles and challenges because time will not permit me to do so at this moment, but because of the incredible people in my life, I decided to become a mentor and advocate for "At Risk Youth." I ran an after-school program in Harlem at a facility called "Rosie and Harry's Place, would teach the fundamentals of education to children from ages 6-12, and in the evening I taught at risk teenagers, ages 13-19, Character Education.

I was astounded how the public would come in great numbers to donate toys, new clothes and money for the little children in my care, but when it came to the teenagers, most people were weary of helping them, or seemed to be drastically uninterested in helping youth over the age of 9. This hurt me tremendously, because from my own perspective, I felt it was the teenagers that needed the most help, since young adults can be very fragile, and vulnerable to the wrong influences and bad choices. They cannot be classified as adults, but yet, they are not children either. I believe that it was during this period that I decided to create a ministry that centered around helping to address the needs of youth in the inner cities.

While I mentored in Harlem, our program consisted of one on one give and take with at risk teens that were having serious learning issues at school, or they were kicked out of classes and could not attend school because of behavioral issues. I had two women volunteers that would come and help me with these kids every day. I love these women with all of my heart because together we created such a powerful trinity of love, we were able to help influence these kids to make better decisions for their lives and most of the kids went back to high school and many went on to college.

My volunteers were both white, their names were Linda and Mary Ann, and the kids that attended the program were predominately African American or Puerto Rican, but our love for each young person was so sincere and powerful that eventually attendance in my program doubled, and sometimes we didn't even have enough room to house everyone. We had incredible success with this program and it became my model that I continued to follow in years to come.

Mary Ann, Linda and myself decided early that we did not want to run our youth program like most programs. We realized to help anyone change their lives would require our complete investment of true love and not words, but our actions. Rather than lecture the teens about how important it was to stay in school, Linda would go with the teens to school and support them one hundred percent in their activities. This worked miraculously! This showed our young people that we sincerely cared about them, and that we would not throw them away because they had problems. Their grades began to improve, and classroom attendance became consistent. The confidence of each of the young people began to soar as they began to discover the power of their own potential within themselves. Mary Ann taught them how to make gorgeous jewelry, and other art pieces that they sold daily within the program (by the way, their jewelry pieces were beautiful!) so they could learn the power of entrepreneurship and not end up on the streets selling drugs. My husband and I took charge of teaching Character Education and held interactive Life Skills Workshops that were fun and interactive for young people. We also had people come from the community and speak about their professional occupations. They shared about their professions, and how they were able to become successful without turning to crime in order to achieve their success. This made great impressions on the young people because it demonstrated how they, too, could "achieve and succeed" without turning to a life of violence and crime. The speakers came from diverse backgrounds such as construction, banking, small business owners, cosmetologists, dentistry, nursing, painting, stock brokers, chefs, bank tellers, and they shared their incredible testimonies with the kids, sometimes the challenges of these professionals was so compelling, it brought the young people to tears.

This has been the core of my entire life. My husband and I would sometimes open our entire life to help a young person that was down and out. At one point we had twenty-two young people living in our home at one time, and this included our own three children! It is the dream of my husband and I to open several group homes and centers for "throw away" youth. When young adults have caring parents, or parent figures in the home to create a safe environment, then they, too, can begin to discover their own value. We have seen with our own eyes how quickly young adults can turn their lives around if they are given a chance. I cannot say that every youth that we tried to help are success stories. Some young people have walked away still as angry as when they first arrived, but the few that we were able to inspire by our example went on to achieve their dreams, and they went on to live respectable lives.

At the present time, my husband and I run a ministry in New Orleans. It empowers young men and women to discover their true identity and live by positive principles of giving back to their own communities. Young African American youth are constantly exposed to negative images by the media, which creates tremendous levels of "self-hatred" and insecurity within themselves. The Black family is also in crisis by the very fact that our own government promotes the destruction family by not allowing the male to be a part of the healing process of the family. Our organization promotes Traditional Family Values, African and African American Reconciliation, Identity Advancement Mentoring, Positive Imaging and Reclaiming Our Original Heritage Seminars with no apologies. I am honored to work with such beautiful young people and seeing their zeal, passion and determination for a brighter future lets me know without a doubt that we will truly build a future that will be "better than tomorrow."

Geraldine Alshamy

Activist, Community Organizer

ROAR: *Youth Advocacy*

I am a grassroots organizer, and great grandmother from the rural South in Wilson, North Carolina. The city's history is that it once held the title of Tobacco King. It was the tobacco capital of the world. It was a place greatly divided by bias, socio-economic class and race discrimination. Wilson is a community deeply entrenched in internalized oppression, better known as the "crab in the bucket syndrome; or the Willie Lynch Syndrome." This culture of oppression and discrimination is still very prevalent today in every aspect of the city and the larger society. This is why I do the work.

I am what is called a Gadfly Organizer. A Gadfly Organizer is a person who upsets the status quo by raising their level of consciousness, as well as, sometimes their blood pressures. These organizers are fire starters in the social justice realm, they are usually a part of community affected or have been directly affected. There are many of us, but outside of our communities, few of our names are known. We are seldom recognized or honored for the work we do; it is for this reason, I am highly honored to be featured in Ariel Rising. I see this book as a way to reveal the phenomenal work done by so many women and the divine power in which we stand. I have organized and advocated around issues of environmental injustices, welfare reform, education equality for Black children and children of color, and youth incarceration. These organizers are fire starters in the social justice realm, they are usually a part of community affected or have been directly affected.

I fight against oppression in any form. More than thirty years of active research and social justice work has taught me that though people can move out of poverty, they have not found the answer to freedom from oppression and the bondage of mental slavery. Our children have been caught in a vicious cycle of what I term as the Home/School/Prison cycle. It first started with testing and holding children back two and three years for failing standardized tests without remediation and due process. Then next abuse of position and power by arbitrarily using policy to rid schools of unwanted students and building alliances with the probation officers in an effort to further destroy their lives through arrests for frivolous infractions. This book is very timely, in that President Barack Obama, has recently acknowledged the School to Prison Pipeline and has made recommendations for districts throughout the nation. Arne Duncan said the School to Prison Pipeline must stop, or face severe consequences. I do this work because it is a spiritual call on my life. I am destined by ancestral duty to assure that poor children and children of color receive a quality education. I do it because poor children and children of color need those who will stand in the educational gap for them as our ancestors stood in the gap for us. It is an obligation and show of appreciation for the gifts and sacrifices so that Black children could be educated. We can't afford to stop now, we have not arrived. My great grandfather built a little church where Black children were educated during the week and services were held on Sundays. My grandmother continued providing education for children in Johnson County by making sure the school had teachers. In fact, the teachers for the school lived in her home. My great uncle sat on the board of education. I do it because of my mother, who even in the late 1800 and 1900s, fell through the educational cracks. Educators did not understand hyperactivity; they had low expectations and it was believed that she could not learn, so she was pushed out of school to work the farm. She lived in the shadow of a mulatto sister, and became rebellious. She only went to school through the third grade, but her education level was equivalent to a student today in the first two years of high school. I do it for myself who was born the year that Brown versus Board of Education decision was handed down. I was promoted to the ninth grade when the federal government sent in troops to end desegregation in southern states that had held out in massive resistance. There was much violence and rioting to prevent integration. Because I was not prepared for integration in 1969 and experienced so much discrimination I quit school with no objection from my mother. I do it for all children because too many are still falling through the educational cracks.

As I struggled to educate my own children, I learned that there were many parents like myself, who didn't how to navigate the educational process. I vowed to learn everything I could and pass it on to my peers. I grew tired of my sisters lamenting over their children and fighting a fight they could not win. They all knew that something was very wrong, but felt helpless to do anything. I will keep buzzing, bothering and speaking truth to power until someone does that which I don't have the ability to do. Hundreds and thousands of young Black, Latino and poor children have fallen through the home/school/ prison cycle. I do this work because students like these don't have a voice unless we as parents and a community give them voice. As long as I can, I must continue to educate communities around the issues that keep our children caught up in a vicious cycle of rebelliousness, violence and incarceration. I must continue to call out the injustices done to our children. I must continue to work towards freedom from oppression, justice and a quality education for all children.

'If you want something said, ask a man; if you want something done, ask a woman.'

-Margaret Thatcher

Roar

4

Business | Literary | Motivational

I've always believed that one woman's success can only help another woman's success.

-Gloria Vanderbilt

Mildred Muhammad

Domestic Abuse Survivor, Author, Consultant

ROAR: *Domestic Violence*

Mildred D. Muhammad –

Domestic Abuse Survivor, Advocate, Consultant, Life Coach, International/National Speaker & Author of "Scared Silent...When the one you love, becomes the one you fear" & "A Survivors' Journal"

Today is a blessing to behold, as every day has become for the past thirteen years. As I reflect on my life, I am blessed to be alive to witness the goodness of Almighty God, Allah. My life has been filled with blessings, favors, anointings, trials and tribulations... everything needed to put me in the right place to be used by God to assist others.

I am Mildred Denice Muhammad...Child of a true and living God, mother of three adorable children, Executive Director of After The Trauma, (a nonprofit organization that assist survivors of domestic violence) and the other attributes listed above. I am also the former wife of John Allen Muhammad...the convicted and now executed D.C. Sniper. My life took a different path once this situation occurred. You see, I believed I was headed towards a 'simple' life of being a wife, mother, grandmother, friend, etc., like most of my friends. Instead, my life has become everything but simple.

My memoir, "Scared Silent, when the one you love, becomes the one you fear" documents my emotionally abusive relationship with John Allen Muhammad. The unfortunately killing of innocent people, in October 2002, as determined by law enforcement, was a cover to hide my murder. I was John's target. The theory was he was killing innocent people to cover up my murder so that he could come in as the grieving father to gain custody of our children. It was a domestic violence/child custody case. He had been honorably discharged from the US Army; he was well trained as a combat engineer. He was capable of tracking, making a weapon out of anything and killing whomever stood in the way of making sure I was no longer alive to be a part of my children's lives.

Prior to the killings, in 2000, we were separated moving towards getting a divorce and visitation with our children. I was a victim of domestic abuse, which society doesn't look at as being as serious as a physical altercation. Domestic abuse includes verbal, mental, stalking, economic, psychological, spiritual…all of the abuses that lead up to the physical altercation. 80% of women, who are in an abusive relationship, do not have physical scars to prove they are being victimized. 75% of women who try to leave an abusive relationship are killed. Although it is very dangerous within the relationship, it has been reported that the most dangerous time, for a victim, in an abusive relationship is when she leaves. The reason is because while a victim is in the relationship, control is still in effect by the abuser. Once the victim leaves, he has lost control and will do anything to regain that control. The most dangerous person in the world is one who does not have anything to lose.

Often children are used as pawns in divorce proceedings. Our children were used, by their father, to gain information about me as well as my activities. He would use them to give information to me as well. Once visitation was established, he had them for a weekend visitation and did not bring them back. It would be eighteen months before I heard their voices as well as held them in my arms again. He took them out of the country to Antigua. He needed help to get them out of the country and so those, who claimed to be my friends, knew where my children were and did not tell me. They assisted him in his efforts to isolate me from our children because he told them I was not a good mother to our children, and it would be wise to take them from me. They believed him and assisted.

Since August 2001, by the grace and mercy of Allah (God), I legally retained custody of my children. In October 2002, the shootings began in the DMV area, where several people were killed. Once law enforcement told me I was the target, they put me and my children in protective custody until he was caught. He was tried and found guilty. He was executed November 2009.

I began speaking about the abuse I suffered in October 2006. It is important for me to convey my message because society does not understand that you don't have to have physical scars to be a victim or a survivor of domestic abuse/violence. The psychological effect of abuse can be so severe that you can become mentally impaired. It has a devastating effect on your well-being and how you move about in life. It has become my passion and my purpose to bring more awareness to the 80% of us who are walking around traumatized and in pain.

There are those who say you can never recover from being a victim of domestic abuse/violence. I would say to those individuals...you are wrong!!! I recovered and I'm thriving. In Ephesians 2, it says God created you to be a Masterpiece. Masterpiece means a person's greatest piece of work. You are God's GREATEST PIECE OF WORK! Understand your value and you won't allow anyone to treat you other than what God has created you to be. I have moved from victim to survivor to warrior on the issues of domestic abuse/violence and child abuse/custody. It is not an easy work, but it is a work that Allah placed upon my heart to do.

I've joined the fight with many, worldwide; as we strive to bring a resolution to an epidemic that continues to grow because so many don't understand how much this affects all of us. Domestic abuse/violence doesn't have an educational/financial status, race, creed, color, gender or sexual orientation. This social disease can happen at anytime, anywhere. As you are reading this, the statistics are that every 9-15 seconds a woman is abused. Someone is being abused right now. Help us to help those in need of help. This makes me roar!

Visit my website, www.MildredMuhammad.com to find out more about my work and my speaking engagements. You can also order an autographed copy of my memoir, Scared Silent. My organizations' website, www.AfterTheTrauma.org will give you resources to assist you, should you decide to leave. Click on resources and the first line item is a safety plan. It is a comprehensive plan...fill in the blank. Don't take it home...leave it at work or give it to one trusted friend. Should you decide to leave, you will need a plan. Modify it as you need to and execute your plan when you are ready. I will never tell a victim to leave, but I will tell you to plan, because in your planning, you will know when it is time to leave. Above all, be safe and strategic telling only one person what you are planning to do. Because you don't know whom your abuser knows, your plan may get back to him. You may not get another chance. You have the element of surprise, use it wisely.

Thank you for taking the time to read my story. Should you need to contact me directly, use this email address, afterthetrauma@yahoo.com. I will respond within 24 hours after receiving your email. You can also call the National Domestic Violence hotline. That number is 800-799-SAFE...800-799-7233. You are not alone and the abuse is NOT YOUR FAULT!

Susan Elizabeth Brown

Documentary Filmmaker/Founder, Beyond The Fog

ROAR: *Education and children with learning differences*

Born in 1958 in San Francisco, California I had an electric upbringing. San Francisco had been the national focus of the United States at several points in history. However, in 1968, when I was ten years old, San Francisco was exploding off the map! The country was coming into its own with the ending of the Vietnam War, the beginning of Black Pride, the emergence of Female Empowerment and alternative education, Rock and Roll and the freedom of expression, the beginning of gay and lesbian acceptance and a deeper sense of guardianship for the earth with the introduction of recycling. It was the end of innocence and the beginning of a sexual revolution. And it all started in San Francisco - in the Haight Ashbury!

We lived on Masonic Avenue four blocks from Haight and Ashbury and I was soaking it all up at age ten!! So my childhood was rooted in a dynamic melting pot of innovative ideas. It was an amazing time. My father, Former Mayor of San Francisco and Former Speaker Willie L. Brown Jr., was an up and coming politician and although we had a normal upper middle class life, my father was in the middle of this cultural explosion, defending peoples civil rights, marching against the war and creating laws that to this day change the lives of so many people. My mother, Blanche Brown, is a choreographer and instructor in Haitian dance. All of this rich history coupled with my parents' response to what was happening at the time and their parenting choices remains at the core of who I am today.

As children, we were encouraged to be a part of everything, to be in the middle of everything and to express freely not only who we are as people, but to stand up for ourselves as well as stand up for those who were unable to stand up for themselves. This is how we were raised it was as natural as breathing. I now work for my father in his nonprofit, The Willie L. Brown Jr. Institute On Politics and Public Service, where I founded and now run a scholarship program that gives under-served boys the opportunity to sing with the Pacific Boys Choir in Oakland California. I am also a documentary filmmaker and my focus is giving a voice and a platform to people, particularly children. I create a platform, an opportunity for them to tell their story. I am also developing a program at a local arts high school that will help identify and support kids with learning differences.

I have a company called Beyond The Fog where I create interesting behind-the-scenes experiences of San Francisco and the Bay Area for visitors and locals. Unique experiences that offer an exclusive perspective of the area and very often, an experience that is way off the beaten path. I have always had a number of interests: I initially wanted to be an actress which led me to my bachelor's degree in Theater. In turn, my love of film led me on to my master's degree in film as a documentary director. However, in more recent years I discovered a deep passion for education, particularly focusing on under-served children and children with learning differences. I truly believe that given a chance—and the right supportive environment—all children can thrive and exceed their potential. I know that our future is in the hands of our children, and if I can help in any way create an environment where all children are supported and encouraged to create to their heart's content, then I will stop at nothing to make this a reality. My parents provided this for my siblings and I, and I want to do what I can to provide this for other children in my community.

Patricia Duncan

Author, Professional Photographer

ROAR: *Perseverance*

I am a professional photographer and over the years I have photographed President Obama and the First Lady Michelle Obama numerous times. I had been thinking for a while about doing a coffee table book about the journey of junior Senator Barack Obama becoming the first African American president.

My project began in early 2008. I had assembled a wonderful team of photographers, writers, and an art director. Prior to getting a team together, I started a publishing company. The name of the company is IJABA (meaning A Wish Fulfilled) Publishing Company. It is a full service company.

Stories started rolling in. I met with the photographers asking them to contribute some of their pictures. Even though I photographed 97% of the pictures, I needed their pictures to fill the voids. My art director worked for our local newspaper laying the pages which made her a perfect art director for the book. We were on track to have the book finished and published right after President Obama's inauguration. That didn't happen. Matter of fact, the book went to print two years later.

During those two years, my project was nicknamed "A Labor of Love". I put my heart and soul into it, hoping it would show it in the end. I wanted the book to be about his journey through Colorado, because many major events evolving around the presidential race happened in

CO. We had made progress with the layout when I realized I didn't have money to get the book printed. So I called a family friend and asked him would he meet with me. I was dreaming big (large number of books) and that meant big dollars. He loved the layout and asked me the title of the book. I said, "Colorado's Defining Moments".

He said, "No, that's not the right title for your book. From what I can see here, you are giving your book a national appeal."

I said, "Okay, give me a title."

To which he said, "A Defining Moment". Now we began to discuss the finances for the book. He said, "We are headed towards a recession and our economy is very sluggish. Unfortunately, at this time I can't help you and I don't know who can." Needless to say, I felt crushed and decided this project wasn't meant to be. Now I had told people I was doing a book coming out around that December. My team members were pumped up because they had finished their parts and were waiting anxiously to see the finished product. I didn't have the courage to tell them that it was on hold indefinitely. There were times I would work for hours and then stop.

This went on for months. By this time, President Obama was now the 44th President of the United States. Coffee table books were coming in droves! I purchased ten books and starting comparing them to each other and my book. I realized I had to revamp my book making different than any other book published because my book was coming out so late. So I started making changes. Once again, I spent hours working on the book and then stopped. Now the economy was better. Should I try one more time to find investors? I was talking to a friend of mine about the book. I was telling him it was on hold because I didn't have any money. I asked him if he knew anyone that would invest in the printing of my book. He said he did and gave me their names. I called and set up my first meeting. I said a prayer prior to going in. After seven successful meetings, I convinced seven wonderful people to invest in my dream and goal. Final results were I had enough money to get "A Defining Moment" printed! God does answer prayers. I worked diligently on the book making the necessary changes in order to make it one of a kind. I would work on the book during my visits with my mother while she was in hospice.

On August 15, 2010, while visiting my mom, I told her I had finished my part of the book. She had a huge smile on her face and said, "Oh, Pat, I am so proud of you! You have worked very hard on this book." Eight days later, my mom went home to be with the Lord.

On February 27, 2011 (my deceased mom's birthday) I received four review copies of my book "A Defining Moment". All I can remember is I sat on the couch; I opened the package and pulled out one book. Before I knew it, I was jumping up and down, hollering, "I Did It" with tears rolling down my face. Then I went into the bathroom, held the book in the mirror up and said, "You have finally accomplished your goal! You started it, got to the middle and finished it. Pat yourself on the back and know that the only person who can validate you is YOU!" My book arrived on March 30, 2011. It was that moment I had achieved my own defining moment.

I would like to conclude with this dedication to my daughters, Shania and Shyra, I am living proof you will achieve your life's desires, if you keep God first in your life, work hard and ALWAYS HAVE SELF BELIEF!

Shawna Stepp-Jones

Divaneering, Founder/President

Miss Maryland Plus America 2013

ROAR: *Youth Entrepreneurship*

STEM's Not Just for Them

It is with much excitement and enthusiasm that I utter these words "STEM is Not Just for Them." I say this profoundly, I say this with great conviction, and I want the world to know. As a result, I have made a commitment to community service and contributing to the advancement of our nation in the global competitiveness in innovation and technology. I have dedicated myself and platform to educating, nurturing, and mentoring some of our nation's future leaders in the fields of science, technology, engineering, and mathematics. By marrying two of my very own beloved passions, engineering and fashion, I founded "Divaneering: Where Girls are Engineered into Divas," an avant-garde, K-12 STEM initiative to get more girls interested in STEM through fashion, health, and beauty design challenges. Divaneering was ambitiously established with the vision to triumphantly break through the barriers of male dominated technical professions, by providing young females with the mental, emotional, and intellectual artillery for success.

Divaneering is my way of giving back to the world and inspiring girls who came from backgrounds such as myself to think big; to innovate; and, to stop being just a consumer. Oftentimes, I'm asked how did a young lady from Baltimore, raised by a single mother, a heroine addicted father, who was sexually abused, and homeless become an engineer (well a Divaneer rather). What comes to mind is the fact, that in life you are either going to sink or swim, and I have been swimming my whole life. It is now time that I give out some swimming lessons. When I think of Science, Technology, Engineering, and Math (STEM) it's all around us. Whether we are learning about it, using devices that are extensions of it, or hearing about it from our President, we are surrounded by it twenty four hours a day, seven days a week. Just take a moment to think about how paralyzing your day would be if you didn't have access to your personal electronic devices for just one day (I'll wait because I know it's going to take longer than a moment to fathom the thought). So it's important for us as parents, as people, as minorities, to get engaged in these initiatives so that we are not further left behind. As a double minority in a STEM profession, I know that it is very important for both African Americans and women to get involved in STEM because science is the language of the universe and innovation is what drives the global economies. How can we make a difference and be a part of the great things that STEM is doing for our lives as humans if we don't know how to speak the language and aren't represented in the rooms that the language is spoken in? The statistics are alarming. According to a 2013 report from the national science foundation, in 2010 women only accounted for 28% of the scientist and engineers working in science and engineering occupations, while Black and Hispanic women only make up a mere 4% of the population. So, I echo the words of First Lady Michelle Obama, "If we're going to out-innovate and out-educate the rest of the world, we've got to open doors for everyone. We need all hands on deck, and that means clearing hurdles for women and girls as they navigate careers in science, technology, engineering, and math."

Through Divaneering I want to get more girls interested in STEM through things that girls like to do. Most girls think of STEM as boring or masculine, but in fact they just aren't aware of the beauty of STEM and the STEM behind beauty. So I figured I would capture their attention by showing them how STEM is used and how they can use STEM in fashion, beauty, and health Divaneering demos. Once I engage them, I believe I can increase their interest and at least getting them to start looking at STEM from a different perspective and ultimately pursuing education and career paths in STEM fields. Additionally, I adopted Divaneering as my platform for "Miss Maryland Plus America 2013" as I wanted girls to understand that beauty is not just external, but internal as well, through cultivating a beautiful mind, a beautiful heart, and a beautiful soul such as me and the rest of these phenomenal women in this book.

Divaneering was launched in 2013 at the Black Engineer of the Year Awards conference in Washington, DC. Over the year I have conducted Divaneering Design workshops including: the Divaneering Design: Lip Balm workshop where elementary school aged girls were challenged to make lip balm out of crayons to expose them to chemistry as they explored various properties of the mixture including melting points, texture, and color. The Divaneering Design: Hair Dye challenge exposed middle school aged girls to biochemistry as they make hair dye out of Kool-Aid. Participants were educated on the biological structure of hair and the natural chemicals that determine a person's hair color that is chemically processed and coated with Kool-Aid in this workshop. Finally, the Divaneering Design: LED earrings challenge in which girls were exposed to the fundamentals of electric circuits in the creation of their very own bright LED earrings. In 2014, I will be hosting my very first Divaneering STEM Summit with the theme of "Redefining the STEM-age" with the addition of four new workshops for the participants to participate in. In addition, I am launching a series of children's eBooks centered around the Divaneers, a group of girls who solve fashion, health, and beauty problems for students at their school.

Professionally, as a patent examiner at the US Patent Office I use my technical expertise to examine patent applications pertaining to display systems. From applications for bright plasma and LCD flat screens, to applications for the small and portable e-book readers, to applications for Apple's cool touch input user interfaces, and similar patent applications, I spend much of my time researching these inventions and determine the patentability of the invention. Ultimately, I work diligently to provide the innovative inventors with protections for their intellectual property. The coolest thing about my job is seeing all of the latest and greatest ground breaking technology before it actually hits the market.

In closing, after reading my story I hope you too are convinced that STEM is Not Just for Them, in fact it is for everyone!

LANIYAH BAILEY
Award Winning Author

LaNiyah Bailey

Author, Activist, Speaker
ROAR: *Anti-Bullying*

Nine-year-old, author/youth advocate LaNiyah Bailey was ONLY six years old, when she was introduced to the world by way of NPR Radio. Shortly thereafter, her phone began ringing off the hook from major media outlets such as CNN, FOX, NBC, BET, WGN, AOL, ABC, Huffington's Post and many others throughout the world including London and Korea. They wanted to know more about this young girl's "inspiring courage" after she penned the highly-acclaimed children's book "Not Fat Because I Wanna Be" along with her mother LaToya "Toyiah Marquis" White and illustrator Laura Pérez Ricaud.

The book detailed the story of fictional character Jessica, who was bullied because of her weight due to an underlying medical condition. The condition caused her to gain weight even though she was healthy and active. At such a young age, Jessica had to endure some painful and unhappy times. Finally, she decided to stand up for herself.

The story was based on LaNiyah's personal experience with being bullied and teased because of her weight. Since the books release in March 2011, LaNiyah has been featured in magazines, interviewed on hundreds of radio shows, blogs and TV shows. The book has garnered "5-star reviews" across the board and is currently in lesson plans at schools throughout the United States and Korea.

At the precious age of nine, most children are in that fairy tale stage and enjoying playtime with their friends. Well, nine-year-old, LaNiyah Bailey has a different song to sing. She's an award-winning author at nine. It all started when she was four years old. That's when her parents noticed her weight spiraling out of control, gaining more than twenty-five pounds in one year. Sounds crazy? Well, it's true! Instead of enjoying life, LaNiyah was becoming introverted, shy and very self-conscious about her protruding belly and bow legs. Adults and children alike began teasing her, calling her names like "fatso," "elephant-girl"; telling her she walked funny and looked like she was pregnant. These acts tormented her so badly that LaNiyah would come home crying almost every night. She hated the sight of any doctor's office, because the doctors said mean things such as "she's just fat because you feed her the wrong things," "Stop feeding her," and many other assumptions were being made on LaNiyah and her parents' lifestyle choices.

Being stigmatized led LaNiyah to believe that she was everything doctors, bullies and teasers said about her. One day she came home crying and mom vowed "this has to stop; we have to find a solution." She suggested LaNiyah use art as a form of expressing her feelings and thoughts, maybe on canvas or even in a book. LaNiyah liked the idea of a book. She then came up with a title that really fit her perfectly, "Not Fat Because I Wanna Be". Jokingly, her mom said, "Well, that works, and it is your story." Over the next week LaNiyah and her mom would sit down every night after dinner and homework writing LaNiyah's story with pad and pen. Her mom says, "It was never a thought to distribute the book beyond family and friends; my thought was to use it as a form of therapy for LaNiyah." Advice from LaNiyah's dad and other family members encouraged LaNiyah's mom to find a way to get her story heard. An editor found the story exceptional but the plot boring and suggested making it more "kid-friendly." LaToya ran it past LaNiyah who said, "No, it's not supposed to be funny." They came to a compromise. Going back to the drawing board, LaNiyah created the fictional character Jessica and created a few fictional events to help bring it to life. After three re-writes and suggestions from the editor, the story came to life.

Currently, LaNiyah has two anti-bullying books ("Not Fat Because I Wanna Be" and "Stand Up! Bully Buster's Coming to Town") in the market. Both are being sold on sites like Amazon, Barnes & Noble, Author's Den, and via her very own website:

www.NotFatBecauseIwannaBe.com.

Things are going well for LaNiyah. Her books are international, her self-esteem and confidence is soaring, and she's feeling much better about herself. "All we wanted was a happy, healthy and normal kid," said Songo Bailey, LaNiyah's dad. LaNiyah says that she never imagined she would be "famous" for telling her story. Currently, the nine-year-old is developing the world's first ever educational anti-bullying app. Eventually, she wants to write more books, start a clothing line for girls and get into acting, all while she's become an advocate for other kids that may be teased or bullied. She also hopes to visit more schools and children's hospitals around the world, giving her book away for free and talking to kids.

Dreams are often built when adversity strikes and LaNiyah has proven to be a true hero who is now living out her dream. Tweet #NoBulliesAllowed to @LaNiyahBailey to receive an autographed copy of LaNiyah's book!

Maddie Pelgrim

Maddie's Blankets, Founder
ROAR: *Needy children and pets*

Maddie Pelgrim is the founder of the non-profit organization Maddie's Blankets. She started this organization at the age of ten, after finding herself unable to find volunteer opportunities for those her age. In the seven years she's been running Maddie's Blankets, Maddie has worked with nearly 6,000 kids making nearly 12,000 fleece blankets, all of which have been donated to animals in shelters and kids in need. When she's not making blankets, she's an average seventeen year old high school junior, varsity cheerleader, and volunteer EMT at the Vienna Volunteer Fire Department. When she grows up she hopes to be a pediatric oncologist, and ultimately make her mark on the world, but until then, she hopes to continue helping her community as much as she possibly can.

"Looking back to my ten year old self, I just wanted to do something. It didn't have to be big, and I wasn't seeking any awards; I just wanted to find some way I could help people. In the seven years since, I've received many awards, been given the opportunity to speak on many occasions, and have even inspired other young girls to start their own organizations. I could never have predicted the implications of my actions, the day I decided to make a blanket.

"I began my non-profit whenever I was ten years old. Looking for somewhere I could help out, I found no opportunities available for me. Fundraising was all that anyone wanted me to do. I was ten. I had no allowance, no job, and hadn't won the lottery, so clearly fundraising was not my thing. However, I was a very persistent ten year old, and wouldn't take no for an answer. I finally found a job cleaning out cages at the Reston PetSmart with the help of my mom. I was allowed to do this once a week on Friday nights. Spending my Friday nights scooping cat poop for Lost Dog and Cat Rescue Foundation, however, was not my ideal way to give back.

"I kept my eyes peeled for some way I could get involved, and my inspiration came while doing the very activity I was trying to get out of. I noticed the cats had only a thin towel or pillowcase to sleep on. Curious as to how this could possibly be comfortable, I climbed into the biggest cage and curled up. About five seconds later I knew exactly what I was going to do. Blankets. Twenty prototypes later, I had my two layer, double knotted fleece design.

"My organization, creatively named Maddie's Blankets, gives kids like me the opportunity to volunteer in a hands on way. Since our creation, we have worked with nearly 6,000 kids, teaching them the importance and simplicity of community service. We have middle and high school students fringe our blankets for us to help them earn community service hours. We then take the fringed blankets to Girl Scout, Brownie, Daisy, and Church Youth Group events to be tied. We will work with anyone who is interested, and although it's not the best way to grow a business, I think it's the right thing to do. Maddie's Blankets has also expanded from just donating to animals and we donate blankets to kids in transitional housing, child protective services, police departments and government subsidized day care. We have donated nearly 12,000 blankets to other organizations from Oklahoma to New Hampshire.

"In the future, I hope to expand my organization fully nationwide, and even globally. Partnering with the Red Cross would be one of my ultimate goals. Getting my blankets to orphanages in China and earthquakes in Japan would be absolutely incredible. I also want to make Maddie's Blankets a national staple in all the schools in the U.S.

"These may seem like lofty goals, but I've had such an exponential learning curve since creating Maddie's Blankets, that I believe I can learn how to do anything else I set my mind to. I've learned all about making an organization an official 501(c)3. I've learned how to deal with other business owners and write grants, because I'm in charge of writing all the grants that fund my organization. We want to enable any kid who can tie their shoes to make a blanket, so we don't charge anyone any money. This enables everyone, no matter what their financial situation, to give back.

"I've also had the unfortunate experience of learning the negative image held about teenagers by so many adults. When I started my organization, I had to make all the phone calls trying to donate blankets. Nearly every person I called hung up on me, or didn't have the courtesy to call me back. They all thought I was a prank caller and no one took me seriously. I was disheartened by this and appalled by the fact that no one even took the time to listen to me, yet alone take the blankets I was donating for free. Rather than giving up, or yelling at the people ignoring me, I thanked them for their time and got my mom to help me. With her help, she made the introduction, and I followed through. Luckily, now, most of our communication with people we are donating blankets to is through email, allowing me to interact with them much more.

"I have made such an impact at only seventeen and it goes to show how community service is truly for anyone. If you don't have time, donate money, if you don't have money give time. Everyone has some way they can give back, it's all about finding your niche. Scooping cat poop wasn't my thing, but helping kids make blankets is perfect for me. Whether or not you've discovered your passion for community service, we all have it within us to change the world, we just have to find out how. It took me seven years to build up my organization and I faced opposition every step of the way. The inspiring part of this journey came just recently. I have just now begun to be recognized by other non-profits and other organizations receiving awards and grant funding. Now, rather than calling everyone in the phone book, people call me.

"The best part of this is the kids I get to interact with. Working with a group of passionate girl scouts who truly love what they are doing makes everything worthwhile. I believe that a quote by Walt Disney perfectly sums up my entire journey and creation of Maddie's Blankets – 'If you can dream it, you can do it. Always remember that this whole thing was started with a dream and a mouse.' Well, for me, a blanket."

Jasmine A. Jennings

Author/Advocate For Education

ROAR: *Reading and writing for fun and learning.*

Jasmine Jennings is a trailblazing Kindergartner from Southern New Jersey. While in preschool, she wrote her very own ABC book because "it helped her learn them better." She loves spaghetti, the color pink, and washing dishes! Academically advanced for her age, Jasmine says that reading and writing will help her get from Kindergarten through twelfth grade and on to college. She enjoys her teachers and considers school her favorite place in the world. Although she loves baby dolls and video games like any other little girl, Jasmine would rather read than do anything else! She loves going to Sunday school and desires to be an Olympic gymnast when she grows up. Inspired by gold medalist Gabby Douglas, she is making mental preparations to compete in an Olympics games. She plans to write several books like her favorite author Dr. Theodore Seuss Geisel, better known as Dr. Seuss.

Tsheli Lujabe

Medical Professional, Consultant, Athlete
ROAR: *Transformation*

Tsheli Lujabe BA, ADE, BA (Hons), MA

Tsheli Lujabe is an Organisation Development and Change consultant at Ashridge. An experienced practitioner with more than thirteen years experience in Leadership and Organisational Development and Change Management, she believes in the importance of building deep relationships with clients. Tsheli adopts a practical approach to working with teams and one-on-one to assist people in managing the tensions, dilemmas and complexity that exist between their individual identity, their role and the organisational dynamics. Using interventions that leverage individual strengths and a Gestalt-based style, she brings about results for the individual, the team and the organisation.

Before joining Ashridge, Tsheli worked across industries, such as Financial Services, Utilities, Mining and a number of NGOs. She worked extensively with MAC Consulting, YSA, and Gemini Consulting in South Africa to implement large scale organisational and business change with various clients, spanning safety, building the brand and leadership development. Her work included:

- ➤ Enabling strategic / difficult conversations with senior management teams in various organisations
- ➤ Transformation, culture change and building the brand through people in a tourism organisation in South Africa
- ➤ Using Action Learning methodology for leadership development in a large South African bank
- ➤ Organisational Development, HR Business partnering and Leadership Development in an electrical utility in South Africa and Uganda
- ➤ Talent management and Leadership development in an Aluminium asset in Mozambique
- ➤ Leadership development and Coaching with a department of a German funding agency
- ➤ Balanced scorecard implementation with an emphasis on collaboration of teams and individuals to ensure effective individual and business performance management

Tsheli's varied career started as a Clinical Psychologist in Cape Town, South Africa, where she worked as a therapist with survivors of violence and torture as well as refugees in the NGO sector. She has worked with human rights organisations in the NGO sector. In addition, she has worked as a Management consultant in the private sector and with State Owned Organisations (SOE's).

Tsheli has a BA in Psychology from Richmond College, The American University in London; an Advanced Diploma in Education (Child development) from the University of London; a BA (Hons) in Applied Psychology from the University of the Witwatersrand (Wits University, Johannesburg); and an MA in Clinical Psychology cum laude from the University of Cape Town. She is a registered Clinical Psychologist with the Health and Professions Council of South Africa.

"I am going to use the metaphor of a triathlon to tell my story. In 2010, I decided that I wanted to do a triathlon, in fact, I wanted to do Ironman. That is a 3.8km swim, 180km cycle and 42.2km run. In September 2010 I did my first sprint triathlon, November 2010 an Olympic distance triathlon, January 2011 Half Ironman and in April 2011 I completed Ironman South Africa. Triathlon taught me about honouring the relationships with others and the relationship with myself. It taught me how to Push Past Possible.

"I believe that my identity is formed by multiple realities. My multiple realities show up as daughter, mother, friend, cousin, niece, Godmother, Clinical Psychologist, Consultant, executive coach, social athlete, wanna-be-entrepreneur and former refugee. I am sure there are others."

Swim:

"Before I was born, I had a brother that passed away. His name was Vuyani, which means be joyful. He brought joy to my mother in particular, and when he passed away that brought sadness to the family and my mother in particular.

"When I was born, I was named Matsheliso, Xoliswa, Nontutuzelo. Matsheliso / Matshidiso is the Sesotho / Setswana word meaning to comfort. Xoliswa and Nontutuzelo are Xhosa words meaning to comfort. I was given the names by my parents and grandparents.

"I was born in Nigeria in 1972, to South African parents that were in exile. From a young age, I learnt to identify myself as South African despite the fact that I was not going to see this country till 1990. When I was seven years old, I remember drawing a picture of Solomon Mahlangu, a South African freedom fighter that was hanged.

"My early memories were of travel, my mother made sure that I got to know that I was part of a bigger world. Education was important and went beyond the confines of the classroom; ballet lessons, music lessons, political education lessons (African National Congress (ANC) Pioneers), travel and conversation. We had to be 'vigilant'; we were at risk of being attacked by the South African Defence Force (SADF). My mother always emphasized that I had to be awake when they came to kill us. I never knew who to trust, so I became good at keeping secrets. I learnt quite early on that life is dynamic, you form relationships, you maintain relationships and you lose relationships for a whole variety of reasons.

"We moved from Nigeria, to Botswana (deported in 1985 after SADF raid), to Zimbabwe, to Norway (my mother was appointed the ANC Chief Representative to Norway), to England (to study), to South Africa in 1994."

Cycle:

"I chose to study Psychology. Could this have something to do with the fact that my name means to comfort (multiplied by three, I might add)?

"My curiosity about the mind and why people do the things they do started in my early years when I had to go to school and live the reality of enjoying dancing ballet, playing the piano, learning and being with my friends; but where I was unable to share my reality of my family being part of the ANC etc. I remember my mum dropping off one of my friend's at her home and she walked through her gates, I wondered what happened once she got behind those gates.

"I did a Masters in Clinical Psychology and worked for the Trauma Centre for Survivors of Violence and Torture in Cape Town, South Africa. Although I worked with survivors of violent crime in Cape Town, I focused on refugees. The people I worked with had fled from the conflict in Rwanda, Burundi and the Congo in the mid to late 90's. I enjoyed this work. The most significant thing I learnt from doing this work was that I could not sit in an office and wait for people to come to see me to talk about their trauma. I had to understand their context and work in a creative way that would allow me to connect with them individually. I often had to go to where they lived and work with them individually or in groups. I had to develop relationships with the broader networks of organisations and institutions that were a part of their lives.

"The next part of my journey sees me joining the South African Human Rights Commission (SAHRC), where I worked with Child and Disability rights. There are two significant moments for me. One where we did some research into how children affected by sexual violence are treated in the justice system; we still have a long way to go in dealing with this issue so that children (male and female) are empowered in a situation where they are already vulnerable. The power dynamics at a formal and informal level that are at play in this situation are incredible. The second was participating in the Conference against Racism, Xenophobia and other forms of intolerance in 2001 in Durban, South Africa. I learnt about modern day slavery from a young West African woman; about unity in diversity from a couple from Rwanda (husband – Hutu and wife – Tutsi); about how pharmaceutical companies treat indigenous medicine from a South American man; and how to keep going even when you are 'sick and tired of being sick and tired' from an African American woman.

"I became a mother in January 2000. I have a fourteen year old son, whose name is Jemelle Vuyani. Yes, he is named after my late brother. My son carries the burden of being named after my late brother, his father's late brother and his late paternal grandfather. His first name was given to him by me, and it is his own name. I also chose to spell it differently. It is the same name as the Arabic Jamal. He had to have something that was uniquely his. He brings a lot of joy to me.

"I also chose to change my surname from Rankoe (the paternal surname) to Lujabe, my mother's maiden surname. I identified more with this name and my mother's family. I decided to change direction in my career. I wanted to use my skills in a business context. Why? I don't know the answer to this question.

"My consulting life started at Gemini Consulting, where I was in the Human Capital discipline. I learnt how to be a consultant at Gemini, where I worked for five years on various projects in various organisations. I moved to a consulting organisation called Yudelowitz, Shannon and Associates (YSA). At YSA, I did Leadership development, organisational development, change management and Executive coaching. I currently work for Ashridge in Berkhamsted, Hertfordshire, United Kingdom. Ashridge is a Business school and Consulting organisation.

"I really enjoy working with a variety people on a one-on-one level as well as in groups / teams. I enjoy the complexity of organisations and the variety that comes with the work that I do. Things are changing all the time and it becomes about making 'change feel like progress'. Leadership is at the heart of all that we do. I have a great leader in my mother. How I lead my son is important to me. I have learned from other great leaders that have been present in my life, and I have learned from people who have not shown great leadership, from my lens. Understanding leadership is also about learning how to be a follower. The first follower has a role to play, as do the other followers. Understanding what roles we play in relationship to each other is also of interest to me.

"A lot of the work that I do happens through conversation. It is also about managing the dynamics between, individuals, their roles, the collective and what happens in between. People's values and self-esteem lie at the heart of work. I believe that over the years I have transformed. I am still on my journey of transformation.

"During the time that I worked in South Africa, I became curious about the word transformation. Due to the changes that took place from 1990 and especially post 1994, transformation has become a truly fashionable word. You get transformation managers in organisations. In most cases they are there to ensure that organisations comply with the National affirmative action policy. I found myself being impacted by this.

"Whenever the compliance agents came to do their work, I was classified as not being South African according to the definition. "The definition of Black according to the B-BBEE Act is African, Coloured, Indian and Chinese South African citizens by birth, descent or naturalisation only if the naturalisation was before 27 April 1994. Black according to the B-BBEE Act no 53 of 2003 excludes all foreign citizens. Ms Matsheliso Xoliswa Lujabe was born in Nigeria and is classified as a Foreign Citizen." Every year, despite my upbringing, I have to prove my South Africaness by producing all my documents and mother's documents etc.

"While this infuriates me, part of my role is to understand this and the colourful South African context in which it has arisen. We are transforming as a nation, I am transforming as an individual and all the experiences I have told you about here, the people that have touched my life, have all had an impact on my journey and in creating who I am now.

"I enjoy being with family and friends, reading, travelling, being a social athlete and constantly challenging myself in various ways. I recently moved to the UK to start the job at Ashridge and I went sky diving last year."

Run:

"I completed the Comrades marathon (87km from Durban to Pieter-maritzburg, Kwa Zulu Natal, South Africa) in June 2014. Running outdoors is a lot of fun, the environment has a lot to offer, you never know what to expect, and you have to use your body, mind and heart.

"My greatest challenge is being a mother. I love it. It is the easiest and most difficult thing that I do on a daily basis. So what does the future hold in store for me? Continue being a mum; I look forward to my evolving consulting practice journey; Travel and climb a few mountains (Kilimanjaro, Machu Pichu…); Write a blog on transformation; Get a PhD in Organisational Change; Start my own company (wanna-be-entrepreneur); Be happy; Love; Value the time I have with the people that touch my life and whose lives I touch; and Push Past Possible."

One of the poems I like is Ithaka by Constatine P. Cavafy. The last part of the poem states:

Have Ithaka always in your mind.
Your arrival there is what you are destined for.
But don't in the least hurry the journey.
Better it last for years,
so that when you reach the island you are old,
rich with all you have gained on the way,
not expecting Ithaka to give you wealth.
Ithaka gave you a splendid journey.
Without her you would not have set out.

Arkay Evans

Author, Spoken Word Poet, Photographer, Blogger
ROAR: *Spiritual Solutions For Women Of Faith*

BULLYING: Blessed Are the Peacemakers.
By Arkay Evans

As a kid who had to fight bullies both in and outside of my family, I'm thrilled to see a sweeping, worldwide effort to stop bullying at home, in the schools and in the workplace. It's tough when the first people you're taught to be able to trust prove themselves to be the last ones worthy of it. This is the case in many families. People lacking compassion are running amok with influential ignorance. When the bully is a parent or sibling, the victims are often trapped in silent horror until someone intervenes, or learns to fight back. Then all bets are off.

As the new kid in school, it can be a little tough to learn the ropes. But when a new kid is targeted, parent/teacher apathy can result in terrible consequences. In recent times, we've seen extreme examples of what can happen when a kid feels isolated and defined by the clutches of a bully. But God can work through any storm and make all the difference. With swift parental and school intervention, I believe from my own experience that any weeds feeding on the dignity of flowers in the academic garden can be plucked and re-trained to be compassionate for the people around them. It is the job of an elder or authority figure to promote unity in families and groups. A woman of purpose knows that unity and peace gets a lot more good done than war and division. It is my nature to be a peacemaker. It's unapologetically who I am. And so are many of you – by default or desire.

Growing up in a hostile environment exposes kids to the intimate evils of familiar warfare, and this plague is damaging to the perception of all it touches. It takes faith in God to identify some of the many meanings and methods in this madness, as well as how to overcome. As a child, there were times when fighting back was my first and only line of defense, and I was willing to do whatever I had to do to be left alone. This was my first lesson in passive aggression. Then there were a few school bullies who thought I'd make the perfect target. They were wrong. By the grace of God, I was caught with the weapon I'd taken to school in response to their threats. Bring it, I thought. I'd been fighting that ignorance my whole life. They had no idea, and did not know me. I just 'looked' like a good target. Proof that it's true – You never know what a woman has had to withstand to stand before you. I was one who wasn't afraid of confrontation after dealing with people just like them in my own family. The potentially explosive event was intercepted right on time by the school's vice-principal, who caught me waiting in the halls and questioned me until I broke. The school year had just started, so I didn't know their names – and I didn't care. But the vice principal talked to me. She had me describe them, and knew right away who they were – disturbers from way back. She called them in immediately and got in their faces with full intent to expel them. With stern authority, Rev. MacDonald shut all our garbage completely down. She shared her wisdom with us along with a few words of encouragement. She also followed up to keep the mess straight.

When I think of what my intentions were that day and what could have happened, I know that we all were saved from what could have absolutely been a life altering incident. One day, after years of physical abuse at home, I'd finally had enough. A fight was started, and I cracked the bully in the head, breaking my mother's yet to be installed ceramic bathroom sink on the yellow streak that raced down her back. I was absolutely mortified. I was sickened to have been cornered and forced to fight back so viciously against someone who was supposed to love me. I left that house and ran home as fast as I could through a flood of tears. I burst through the door to talk to my grandmother, hoping that she could help me make sense of it all; or maybe just show me how to bring peace to this awful situation - but she just looked at me intently and shook her head. "You," she said, "are the only person I know silly enough to cry after giving somebody a beating they deserve."

This is the mentality that threatens to destroy us from the inside out. We no longer just have to endure the ignorance of bullying; we can make decisions today about our identity that changes things instantly. Those who are bullies were likely bullied by some other coward. Those of us who choose apathy only serve to encourage cowardly, bullying behavior. To those who are enduring, I say this: Child of God, know and enforce your boundaries. Put your confidence in Christ. Get help when you need it – from colleagues, instructors, bosses, supervisors; even the police if necessary. Educate yourself. Fight back with prayerful intention and follow-up action. Trust your instincts, and that you or the situation will be changed or removed by faith. It is my way to refuse the inclusion of foolishness and drama as a part of my life, because what is not of God is not for me. From Vice Principal Rev. Mrs. Ann MacDonald, I learned who truly fights my battles. Sometimes the woman of purpose has multiple scars just like these that cannot be seen. Over time, she has learned many lessons, and she believes by faith to be whole and healed of a hurtful past; she shares the lessons she's learned to empower herself and others. She is beautifully human. She doesn't blindly follow – she is watchful and aware of games and power plays displayed by bullies. She resists greed, manipulation and selfishness, and not only believes to see God among us in word and deed, but that she too can be a blessing. She questions fear and loathing, so that negative emotion cannot imprison her honor, her ambition, her integrity, her authority, or the joy of her spirit. She is not defined by the misogynistic darkness, or political and religious legalisms that threaten to and do oppress women in every faction around the world. She does not let another make her feel smaller. A woman of purpose is aware of the power of her prayer. She waits and listens for the time to take action. She honors the change in her spirit by pressing through pain, chaos, confusion and oppression to arrive at this amazing place: A direct relationship with God. She knows it is of the utmost importance to uphold and defend her universal religious freedoms without imposing on others, so a woman of purpose defends her honor, and focuses on what works for her life. This is not good news to everyone. In every aspect of life, there has always been and there will always be darkness thriving in the void of hopelessness, greed and ambition. Political types, industry leaders and authority figures have a lot invested in controlling the things and people around them, and often confuse confidence with arrogance; and fear with respect. This confusion reflects in their actions. Many leaders in church, community and state fall prey to the twisted, idle perspective demanding unearned rights, and to abuse their power and position for sex, money, etc. while dismissing responsibility, accountability and consequence. Oppression experienced in the home, and greedy power games in business, politics and the church has left many of us damaged, cynical and angry at these particularly distasteful betrayals. Over and again we hear about bullying and sexually inappropriate behavior in institutions that promise to motivate for good and inspire unity among us. True leaders do not undermine the gifts and talents of others, or manipulate for gain, or fostering fear and hatred among friends. Bullies do. And when we run across them, sometimes faith is the only way a woman makes it through the day with a smile. Your faith is nothing to be trifled with, for herein lies your familiar peace. This is available to us all – even those who have been coerced and hurt by the leaders and loved ones they expected to be able to trust. It is a terrible thing to see people who want a closer relationship with God give up and turn away in anguish from their spirituality because of chaos, baiting, bullying or seduction by popcorn players who see the world as one big safari and those closest to them as their prey. No matter where the bully lies, you are not a victim. You are a person. One who does not confuse the rancid actions of man with the promises of God.

BULLY

Beware the 'leader' dancing to the beat of war. A woman of purpose knows that genuine leadership motivates and inspires the best in others, and comes from within.

From twisted, feckless, vile intent
Emerged the bully's fecal scent,
Contemptible, despicable, completely predictable,
Clammy and stinking and miserable,
Comes to brutally castrate
The joyful dreams they asphyxiate,
And of their tainted foul, infested cognition,
Great things die; dead
Blocked from fruition,
Then out of the cowardly muck they slither
Seeking talents and gifts to wither,

Beware, the self-appointed rebel,
Hiding and plotting for the devil,
And the foul motive queen bee
Here to rape you of your dignity
For they fail their putrid crown
Finally destined to go down
To the skink mire from whence they came
Discarded, forgotten, and
Insane.

Arkay Evans' inspiring novel, 'A Woman of Purpose: Secure In Faith Through Difficult Times' is a global movement keeping the peace within of heart, mind, body and spirit through the power of poetry and music. Arkay shares an intimate poetic journey of love and life through the eyes of faith that leaves readers wanting to hear more from this truly unique perspective. You can check out some of the author's spoken word recordings on Soundcloud or Reverbnation, and connect with her on Facebook, Twitter. Stop by for her 'Thought for the Week' at arkayevans.com

Brenda Jones
Hug Wraps, Founder
ROAR: *Comfort for Cancer Patients*

Every single one of us, is born with inner strength. God supplies us with enough to last us our lifetime, however long or short that may be. Many can't possible fathom exactly how strong we are, until faced with adversity and life's challenges. Some may give up too soon, instead of having the patience to wait and dig deeper to find that hidden source that is tucked, waiting to be unlocked. True believers know, the well never runs dry. God replenishes it, as needed. He always has, he always will. Never give up, the answer may be just around the next bend. The most important thing that all women should also remember, is that our gender is unstoppable.

Of all the challenges in my life, I was most brought to my knees in October 2008, when I first heard the ugly words, "you have breast cancer." Sitting in the doctor's office, I remember the sound of a nurse yelling somewhere in the background "Brenda, breathe!" This is where my story starts, yet it's also not where my story ends.

A cancer diagnosis is different for every person. Each handles it differently, in our own way. It doesn't define you, but it definitely tests strength, patience, endurance, love, compassion, resilience and about a million other things. There is no particular order, no promise of outcome. You also come to realize that doctors don't always have all the answers.

On 10/09/08, I found my lump in my left breast, on a self exam in the shower. Deep down inside, I instantly knew it was cancer. I called my primary doctor for an appointment that morning. What happened next was a rapid succession. I was sent to a breast surgeon, who just so happened to have an immediate opening. An exam and biopsy in her office confirmed cancer.

Within the next three weeks, I had undergone so many tests and procedures that I thought my breast had been seen and examined by every doctor and nurse in NJ. I had a lumpectomy surgery first, then later an auxiliary node dissection. There was a surgical complication after the second surgery that went undiagnosed for some time. I was unable to lift my left arm and the pain was intense. I was scheduled to start radiation treatments and this caused a delay because I was unable to raise my left arm over my head. A position that was needed for radiation of my left breast. The radiation doctor actually thought I was faking not being able to lift my arm, because she thought I was trying to delay and stall treatment. When I complained about the constant pain and limited movement, she actually looked me in the eye and said, "Suck it up, Princess." It was that day that my anger hit full force and I let her have it.

After finally being diagnosed with false winging, a complication due to surgery, I was sent to physical therapy for treatment. By the time I was able to start daily radiation treatments in 1/09, I was the angriest cancer patient you never want to meet. I was scheduled for seven weeks of daily radiation. On my first day of treatment, I walked into the radiation department and was greeted by a nurse who looked at me and pointed to the dressing room while uttering the words "Go on in there and change. You will be wearing a hospital gown for the next seven weeks," there was no "Welcome" "Hello" or anyone who introduced themselves...just someone pointing me to the changing room. I felt like a patient on a conveyer belt being pushed along. As I numbly walked into the changing room, I opened the door and saw three stacks of those hideous, nasty, itchy, wrinkled blue hospital gowns...and I lost it. Putting on a hospital gown was telling the world and me, I'm a patient and I'm sick.

Looking at those gowns, and with tears streaming down my face, I said out loud, "Oh, no! I'm not wearing those!" My next thought was something of a miracle. I instantly had a vision in my head of my perfect hospital gown alternative. I saw a kimono style wrap that opens in the front and ties with a belt. It would be bright, colorful, comfortable and warm. Something that would give me back dignity during my treatments. I could not control cancer, but I could control what I wore! I laughingly called this my Vera Wang moment. As I put on two hospital gowns to cover myself, I also put on my coat because it was so cold in the treatment area. By the time I sat down in the waiting room, I continued to think on what I was going to make in this new gown. I was now on a mission to change something, for myself.

When I left the treatment center, I drove home. Still angry, still talking to myself, still frustrated. As I turned the key in my back door, I heard the phone ringing. I grabbed it and yelled, "What!" It happened to be a good friend of mine, Judy, wanting to know how my first treatment went. She patiently listened as I yelled, ranted, screamed and cried. Next I told her of my image for a gown alternative that I wanted to make for myself. I told her that I had one problem, I didn't know how to sew. She then said, "You're in luck, I'm a seamstress and I'll teach you how to sew." Judy told me to get a sewing machine and then directed me to the fabric store to buy fabric. She suggested flannel material because I told her how cold it was in the hospital. I put my coat back on and went out and bought a used sewing machine from a sewing center and some cheerful flannel fabric. I was set! I spent the next three days at Judy's house learning to sew. Together we spent some time designing a pattern for my perfect wrap. We made so many changes before I had what would work best. I designed it to open in the front, tie with a belt, had 3/4 length sleeves and came to my thigh in length. Breast cancer patients can wear their pants to treatments so I did not need a long length. I did not add any snaps, hooks or metal so it could be worn inside to radiation. It was also designed larger so I was able to get it on and off with my limited arm movements. The flannel material was ideal for the softness, comfort and warmth.

The first time I put on my finished wrap, I smiled to Judy and said, "This feels like a nice warm hug." For that reason, I lovingly called it my "Hug Wrap".

With a finished product, I put my Hug Wrap on at home, put on my coat and drove to treatment. I walked in and went to sit down in the treatment waiting room. The technician said, "Aren't you going to change?"

I stood up, took off my coat and said, "I did." My colorful wrap started to cause heads to turn and jaws hit the floor. I was actually surprised at the response. There was another patient there named Millie. Millie and I had become friends as we both had treatments at the same time.

When Millie saw what I was wearing, she asked, "Where did you buy that? I love the colors!" When I told her I made it, she smiled and said, "I bet it's warm, too!" When she made such as fuss, I asked her if she would like me to make her one to which she replied an enthusiastic "Yes!" I asked Millie what pattern she would like and she said butterflies. So I picked out a pretty butterfly design and started on a Hug Wrap for her. As I began sewing, I realized that making this for her somehow took my mind off my own cancer. I was now making something for a friend to comfort her through her battle. When I handed her the new Hug Wrap, she immediately went into the changing room to put it on. She came out, wearing a smile. Together, we became fashion statements as other patients looked on. I then started making them for others. One patient, then another, then another, and I have not stopped. I never dreamed that something I made for myself, to get me through a difficult time, would also be a comfort to another, and I'm glad they are. Sewing also had become the perfect therapy, to help me get rid of my anger. Each time I sat down to sew, every stitch started to chip away at the rock of anger. I was now working to help another patient. To somehow ease their burden. It was not about me, but about how I can put more smiles on the faces of some very frightened patients. To be able to give them back their dignity. To make them feel like a person, not a file or a chart, or just another cancer patient. Wearing a Hug Wrap says "I matter". They are made with love from one patient for another. With understanding of their plight. I've been in their shoes. When someone contacts me for a Hug Wrap, I ask for favorite colors and patterns they would like. Then I try to find the perfect material to make their Hug Wrap. I also will make them in a longer length for patients with ovarian or colon cancer or men with prostate cancer. Hug Wraps are most known for the bright, fun colors that I choose. My favorite motto is "you need to wear something LOUDER than cancer!" I began contacting local newspapers asking them to do a story on Hug Wraps. The response was heartwarming. I then began work on turning Hug Wraps into a 501c(3) nonprofit. Word of Hug Wraps has spread through social media as well. I have made Hug Wraps for patients of all ages with all types of cancer. They have been mailed to patients all over the US and in Canada, England, Poland and Australia. I began making personal visits to cancer centers and hospitals to hand out Hug Wraps to the patients I meet.

In May 2012, I was surprised by the NBC TV show *George To The Rescue*. They had heard about what my nonprofit does for cancer patients and that it was started by a cancer survivor. The show's host, George

Oliphant, came knocking on my door, to surprise me with a room makeover for Hug Wraps. The show was here to answer a wish and turn a spare bedroom into a full sewing room. They heard that I sew at my kitchen table and had fabric and supplies splattered all over my house. I needed organization and they wanted to help. Along with their team, they brought in Interior Designer Susan Hopkins, from Philadelphia and Amiano & Sons construction company from Tabernacle, NJ. They put me up in a hotel for two weeks and these wonderful people transformed my home. I was unable to watch their transformation, until the reveal. They built custom shelves, sewing table, chairs, hardwood floors and painted a beautiful design on the ceiling. They brought in Olde City Quilts from Burlington, NJ, who supplied me with two Bernina sewing machines, a sewing chair, fabric and all sewing supplies. When they brought me home for the reveal, I cried when I opened up the bedroom door. But wait, it wasn't over. They had another surprise for me. They took me to another spare bedroom, opened the door, and revealed a full and complete office. More tears, more hugs. They had a custom built desk, full office supplies, new laptop computer, fax, hardwood floors and even a TV in both rooms. You could feel all the love and work from every pair of hands that went into this makeover. I am so blessed and grateful to all. So many people write me to tell me what a good thing I do. But, I always tell them I don't do this alone. I have been so blessed with help along the way. I never ask for a hand out, but simply a hand up. For every person who had reached out and joined my journey, I call them my "Angels In The Wings". We all need Angels, they are what keeps us going. God puts the right people in front of us, at the right time. So, keep doing the good things you do, you never know who is listening or needing your help. My ultimate goal is that for every patient that is handed a diagnosis of cancer, I would like for them to be handed a Hug Wrap. There is nothing better than being wrapped, in a nice warm HUG. Taped to my computer and refrigerator are the words I live by "Be the answer to someone else's prayers". So many people have answered mine, and the circle continues.

Brenda Jones
www.hugwraps.org

Dr. Dorie McKnight

Cover Girls In The Church, Founder/Executive Director
ROAR: *Transformational Change*

"What makes me roar, is when I find others void of purpose. I roar as an example to help the silenced find their voice. I roar to fight causes and injustices. I am like Harriet Tubman and Sojourner Truth combined, seeking out the bound in need of deliverance. I am God's Cover Girl hear me roar!"

Dr. Dorie McKnight is positioned as a well-respected thought leader in the empowerment of women around the world. On a daily basis, Dr. Dorie provides transformational change, leadership knowledge and experiences to an ever-growing core of women leaders from diverse communities, instilling them with best practices and practical techniques they can implement in their own communities to inspire and support women to become more confident, conscious, empowered and purposeful in all aspects of their lives. Dr. Dorie Mcknight is inspiring women and men around the globe to pursue their passion for living. Dr. McKnight is helping women and men alike to positively change their lives. She does so with a unique blend of ministry, personal enrichment seminars and life skill workshops. Simply put, her gift is in helping others to transform their lives from the broken places to a place of fulfillment and purpose. Dr. Dorie is also an author, playwright, a national motivational speaker, counselor, community activist, a women's and leadership conference workshop presenter, does corporate speaking, a defender of faith and a life balance coach. Through her work as founder and executive director of Cover Girls in the Church, International/Help A Sistah Out, thousands of women have embraced life long transformations. She conducts a mentoring program to help women in leadership as well as the incarcerated to develop and seek out their purpose, potential and skills.

Introduction:

Cover Girls In The Church is dedicated to those who have been cover girls, but have never received recognition for their sacrifice. To those who have covered in love and refused to cover lies. Thank you for your courage. Cover Girls, yes, that's who we are. Yes, I said we. Everybody knows one or is one. Cover Girls have been around since the beginning of time. Did you know that even Eve, the mother of creation, was a cover girl? Oh yeah! You know the story about the forbidden fruit thing. When God told Adam not to eat, and Adam told God the reason he disobeyed was, "That woman you gave me told me to eat!" Eve had to cover for her man Adam. She was just the beginning of a long list of cover girls in the Bible, which includes Esther, Deborah, Rizpah, and Mary, the mother of Jesus. Some of these women not only covered, but were covered. But the greatest cover girl of them all is the Church. God called the Church a woman. The Church is the ultimate covering for all mankind. So you see, covering can be the right thing to do when it is done in a positive way that displays strength, loyalty, confidentiality, or unconditional love. Therefore, ladies, don't feel bad if you're a cover girl, because it speaks of your strength. Women are a special breed, because they don't sell-out very easily. They are loyal. Women know how to keep secrets, and many times are the secret (secret lover that is)! Isaiah 4:1 says, "In that day seven women will take hold of one man." I believe we are in that day now, because some cover girls will tolerate their man having women on the side as long as he's home on Friday. They call these brothers players, but they cover for them anyway. This is an example of covering being displayed the wrong way. As you read the reasons why people cover, you will have a better understanding of her reaction. It means to cover from attack, to hide from sight or knowledge, to spread over, to appear one way on the surface, to invest a large amount of something, to have sufficient stock of something, to deal with or treat something, to handle or care for one's territory, to pass over, to defray a cost, to pay a debt or place yourself as the ransom, to conceal something illicit, blameworthy, or embarrassing, or to be a substitute or replacement. Brothers, I'm sure you, too, can identify with the meaning of cover. This teaching will provide you with some cover-up lessons that King David learned as you read his story. Plus, it will help you understand the cover mentality. So get ready, because this book would level the playing fields so we all can come out of hiding. I pray that it will unlock your prison doors and free you from captivity. I pray it will open up some graves that contain promises and dreams that have been assassinated by the spirit of abuse. I pray it will speak to the dead and dry bones. I declare you shall live and not die. There is hope. You can get out from under your past or your present situation. The anointing of God will destroy all yokes of bondage. Be free in Jesus' Name! Isaiah 61:1 –The Spirit of the Lord GOD is upon me; because the LORD hath anointed me to preach good tidings unto the meek; he hath sent me to bind up the brokenhearted, to proclaim liberty to the captives, and the opening of the prison to them that are bound. – God's Cover Girls have nothing to do with make-up, but what you are made of. ~ Dr. Dorie McKnight

drmcknight@rocketmail.com www.godscovergirl.wordpress.com

Margarita Lopez

Cancer Survivor, Hero of Hope, Spokesperson

ROAR: *Living Beyond Cancer*

My name is Margarita Lopez, forty-eight years old, living with stage IV metastatic breast cancer. I am a woman, a survivor, a spirit filled with gratitude. My life changed drastically in October 2008. This is when I heard those three words that no one should hear "You have cancer." I decided, almost immediately, that cancer is simply a 'word' not a 'sentence' and although I'd be in for the fight of my life, literally, I knew, in my heart, I would be just fine. This belief and unwavering faith resonated with my entire being and my soul. This is what has made my journey easier and has given me the strength to advocate for greater awareness.

Had I known in March 2008 what I know today, regarding breast cancer, perhaps my life would be very different. Had I known about dense breast tissue and how dense tissue appears white on the results, as do tumors and the best way to detect an abnormality would be with an ultrasound and not an MRI. Maybe with this one little piece of knowledge, I could have taken that one little extra step and possibly caught this cancer early on. Instead, I realized I had cancer when I stumbled upon a lump on my breast in August 2008. After an ultrasound, biopsy and numerous tests, they found two tumors, one was 5.2cm and still not detected with an MRI. I had tests done in March due to hormonal changes and just not feeling well, the doctors, even after an MRI and blood tests, discounted it as perimenopause. I was on top of the world, living my dream, married, three wonderful children, successful entrepreneur, traveled, lived in an amazing custom house we built, driving the car of my dreams, you get the idea. I did not know that those three little words were the beginning of a LIFE journey. It changed everything. Recently, I realized that those three words and the journey that followed, filtered much unneeded negativity and unrealistic ideals about life, what I thought I wanted and the people I held closely. When I was faced with my own mortality, I had a choice . . . BE with the reality of it and choose to create something beautiful with my life . . . or live the rest of my life in fear. Having and living with a life-threatening or terminal illness will either wake you up to the beauty that life is or freeze you into constant worry or depression. Happiness IS A CHOICE. Choose to stand in your essence. Choose to see and hear all of life's gifts we are surrounded by daily. Let go of what you do not have control over and simply look at it and persevere on!

Chemotherapy is no fun! My first rounds of adriamycin / cytoxan (they have the word toxin for a reason!), were painful and nearly life-draining. It is an indescribably feeling to have these 'toxins' administered by a nurse dressed in protective clothing, mask and gloves as they very carefully, slowly and patiently manually 'pushed' this drug into my veins. I could feel it going into my bloodstream like a cold, unwelcome, haunting guest. One nurse would be moved to tears as she watched me meditate during this process. I would visualize the cancer cells being eliminated as quickly as the AC entered my bloodstream and new, healthy, vibrant cells reproducing in their place. So many changes occur to one's body, mind and spirit... it is very very difficult to stay optimistic and faithful. There is no feeling quite like the vulnerability that cancer treatment leaves you with...there I stood...hair-less, pale, food was flavorless, touch was at times painful, cold, thin and my spirit was completely challenged.

During my most difficult months, I found myself more alone than I had ever been in my entire life. I had heard it would not be an easy road and that was the honest truth. My husband, whom I loved with all my heart, could not be my emotional rock I needed him to be and I became even more alone and devastated. There is an unspoken fact that over 24% of women diagnosed with cancer go through separation or divorce once they are diagnosed. I never imagined that I would fall into that statistic. I never thought I would live through cancer treatment and a heartbreak simultaneously. Strength, determination, gratitude and FAITH pulled me through. Every moment of despair, as I sat on my balcony through countless sleepless, painful nights, I would thank God and the universe for the beauty surrounding me. Tears of heartache would turn into tears of gratitude. I chose to avoid mirrors often, hug myself daily, more importantly, I chose to see my children's eyes and smiles as signs of hope. I mourned many things, including the life I once had and the life I thought I wanted. I did not realize or expect the transformation I was embarking on. It wasn't the cancer . . . it was what the cancer and the journey opened. In other words "Whatever opens us is never as important as what it opens" {Mark Nepo}. What it opened made me realize that there are no experiences wasted in this journey of life. "To be broken is no reason to see all things as broken." {Mark Nepo}

My Story:
    I am LIVING with stage IV metastatic breast cancer. Newly diagnosed in August 2012. Since my original diagnosis in October 2008, I've received many rounds of several types of chemotherapy, radiation, several surgeries to remove a tumor, my breasts, skin and lymph nodes. My last surgery (a mastectomy of my left breast due to new IBC) was one month ago today as I write this (Feb 2014). Although I am now diagnosed in 'temporary visible remission' from the cancer INSIDE my body, it is now in my skin's lymphatic system. I continue to beat the odds, statistically speaking. I must add that I was in remission from May 2010 through July 2012. I go into the infusion center every twenty-one days, for the rest of my life, for treatment. Countless MRI's, PET scans, X-rays, blood tests, Echo-Cardiograms, tests, tests, and more medical tests. Something 'new' shows up, a biopsy is done. And with each one, there is a waiting period . . . waiting for the results. Is it true what they say that waiting is the worst part? Is it simply fear of the unknown? The stories and worst case scenarios can steal my joy during this waiting period. I choose not to worry and simply 'be'. Worry gives me no power, its a robber of power and joy. I tell my body to reproduce only good, healthy cells as part of my daily meditation. I ask my spirit to help my body heal. We have choices every day, and our choices create our experience in our journeys of life. Be mindful of your choices and the words you speak to yourself. I am so blessed and grateful for everything! Not allowing the negativity of the pain, the stigma, the social image of a cancer patient to become my identity is critical. The scars across my breast-less chest, the protruding portacath (the catheter implanted under my skin to connect

needles for IV or blood tests) near my shoulder, the numbness in my toes and other parts of my body, they are all reminders of the battles I have fought, reminders of how grateful I am daily for the gift of life. Cancer is already all-consuming, the thing to remember is to not let it consume your spirit. Continue doing what you enjoy in LIFE. Soon you will nearly forget you have cancer. This is a great thing to allow. I say to simply stand and live in your essence. Our spirit is much more powerful than we allow it to be. Allow others to help you, it takes courage to ask for help! I would not have made it to today without the love and support of my children, family and friends. What does this all mean? More importantly, why do I continue to beat the odds?! Bringing awareness to women of all ages regarding where to go, what to do, what to ask... being your own advocate, letting them know they do not have to embark on this journey alone or helpless... we all have the power within to overcome our fears... this is my mission, what makes me 'roar'. You'll find me speaking at Legislative campaigns supporting a healthier environment, American Cancer Society events, Spanish TV and radio, cancer awareness campaigns or organizing breast cancer awareness campaigns and fundraisers. Being featured in numerous print material from magazines to newspapers and having received several awards for my determination is not what drives me... I simply desire to bring a message of HOPE or a flicker of inspiration and knowledge to you and maybe it will bring you encouragement or maybe even save a life.

Here is what I've learned:

1. Get your mammograms! Ask the technician if you have dense breast tissue, and if the answer is yes, get an ultrasound, do not rely on a mammogram.
2. You have the right to a 2nd and 3rd opinion after diagnosis. If you're not comfortable with one team, seek another.
3. Be your own advocate. Get educated and stay aware of your specific condition and become an active part of your medical team.
4. Declare, with unwavering faith and clarity, what it is you want your body to do. Enroll your mind, spirit and heart.
5. Speak it, meditate, pray, and visualize your desired outcome daily. There is power in doing this!
6. Find people around you that will lift you up, make you smile and keep you optimistic.

7. Discover what brings you joy and do more of that!
8. Above all… love yourself, forgive yourself… see the beauty that you are… and smile.

www.MargaritaLopez.me
Hero of Hope, American Cancer Society
CA Legislative Ambassador, ACS CAN
Spanish media event spokesperson, cancer awareness
Speaker & Advocate for breast cancer awareness
Stage IV cancer survivor
Mother of three, I would not be here today if not for my three children, family and friends ~ I love each of you dearly.
Lover of LIFE

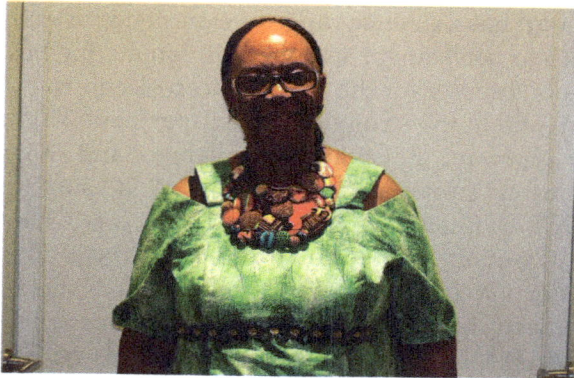

Thandi Lujabe-Rankoe,

South African Ambassador and Diplomat

ROAR: *Diplomacy and Human Rights*

Her Excellency, Thandi Lujabe-Rankoe the former South African High Commissioner to Mozambique is one of the first Black women Ambassadors and Career Diplomats in South Africa. She has led and represented the foreign and diplomatic strategy and relations of South Africa in Tanzania, Botswana and Mozambique. She is a pioneer in many respects, having started the first South African High Commission in Tanzania and being one of the first women to document her experience of being exiled from South Africa. Thandi has strong negotiating, lobbying, administrative and coordination skills. She is excellent at forming relations with leaders within governmental, business, and non-governmental sectors to ensure that she effects transformation and has the necessary impact and influence required in her position of leadership. In her capacity as an Ambassador, she has worked with a number of key African institutions, namely SADC and the AU, amongst others. She has also worked with other key International organizations such as the EU and some UN organizations. She has used her diplomatic, foreign relations and foreign policy skills to lead transformation in South Africa.

She has facilitated Trade and Industry relations at governmental level. She has facilitated South African businesses such as Murray & Roberts, Sasol, and Standard Bank, operating in Tanzania, Mozambique and Botswana. Thandi has spearheaded the coordination of various reconciliatory actitivities, women's initiatives and social investment initiatives. Thandi has a diverse range of experience over the last 20 years that contributes to her being a seasoned diplomat. She has experience as an Independent Observer for the Mozambican elections.

She was pivotal in the struggle against apartheid, having represented the ANC in Norway, Botswana, Zimbabwe and Nigeria. She has coordinated various projects within various ANC structures, especially within the ANC Women's League, where she was Chairperson of the ANC women's section in Botswana and Zimbabwe. Her International organisational experience began with the United Nations Development Programme, where she was programme coordinator for scholarships for ANC and SWAPO students. She then coordinated various projects working for NORAD in Botswana and the Norwegian People's AID in Zimbabwe. Thandi has recently published her second book – "Two Nations One Vision" which documents the close relations between South Africa and Mozambique through the Apartheid era to present day. Her first publication and autobiography "A Dream Fulfilled – memoirs of an African Diplomat", was launched in South Africa, Mozambique, Tanzania and Botswana. She has published two other works, namely, "ANC History Booklet 1912 – 1991" published in Oslo, Norway in December 1991; and an article on Child Labour in Africa, published by UNESCO in 1987.

Marcelette Anderson-Pearson

Business Professional/Military Veteran

ROAR: *Unconditional love for family, life, and the joy of living.*

I am passionate about my family, my career, and my life in general. I thank GOD when I wake up each morning for allowing me to see another day! I have been on a wonderful journey that I call LIFE! I have been blessed to wake up each morning and begin a new day that starts with a "SMILE" and ends with "PRAYER".

My family began with a loving set of parents (John and Bessie Anderson) growing up in Brooklyn, New York. I was blessed to have parents that were disciplinarians and ruled the household with a stern hand. Although we (my sister, brother, and me) did not have everything that we wanted they supplied us with everything that we needed. Oftentimes, the wants outweigh the needs and they had to determine which was more beneficial for us. I have found that as long as I am giving people what they need and not necessarily what they want, I am providing them with what is beneficial for them. I use my childhood experiences as tools for me to grow each day. I am blessed to have a wonderful husband and together we have five beautiful children and five precious grandchildren ages six, three, two, and twenty months. Our oldest daughter lost her baby during the fifth month of her pregnancy and although it has been two years, we are still adjusting to this change and loss in our lives. I have learned to use her loss as a strengthening tool to help others deal with their losses. My family (biological, immediate, long-term friendships and in-laws) is very important to me and I treasure each of them and value our relationship. Family makes me "ROAR" because there is unconditional love and never-ending stories, learning tools, and friendships.

I began my career at the tender age of fifteen working in Woolworth in Roosevelt Field, New York as a waitress. This was the first responsible job that I had besides babysitting. I treasured this job because it taught me that working hard pays off and gives you a sense of honor and self-respect. I had a feeling of power because I was able to go to the store and buy my own school clothes and shoes; I was able to buy my own lunch and help my parents out with smaller bills in the house. Although, my parents never asked me for money, I felt the need to contribute to the household because I was working and my father always brought his check home and gave it to my mother (who was a housewife until we entered high school) to pay the bills and buy food. He instilled in me a great work ethic and that has stuck with me my entire life and helped me maintain a sense of responsibility that extended into adulthood. After graduating high school, I joined the military (U.S. Army) when I was only sixteen years old (my parents had to sign me in). This was one of the best career decisions that I made and one of the best experiences of my life.

While in the military I learned what true friendship is, how to depend on ME, and that I controlled my destiny. I had the most wonderful experiences while in the military and was trained in the Communications field where we climbed telephone poles and laid cable to establish telephonic communication for the entire battalion while in the field. Although this would not have been my first choice for a military job experience, but doing this job taught me to be disciplined, to always finish what I start, and I can be anything that I want to be. I always put my best foot forward while in the military and earned many medals, honors, and accolades while assigned to various military bases. I learned to believe that quitting was never an option!

My career continues now that I am working for an insurance company in South Carolina for sixteen years. I am a manager in a call center where I am responsible for sixty-two employees. I began with an entry level position and worked my way into the management field. Throughout my career, I have learned that there comes a time when you have to be a servant, soldier, mentor, coach, trainer, counselor, friend, confidant, disciplinarian, and most importantly, a listener. My career makes me

"ROAR" because of all the beautiful friendships, discipline, loyalty, work ethic, and learning tools that have made me the worker bee that I am today. I value my experiences and am proud to be able to share them with others that may be able to use them to enhance and grow in their career. My future holds great things for me and my family and I hope and pray that GOD continues to allow me to mentor and share my experiences with others.

One other thing that makes me "ROAR" is LIFE and the JOY of living. I thank GOD each day that he wakes me up and allows me to see another day. The one thing that I do not do is take life for granted. I know that I am not promised tomorrow; therefore, I live each day to the fullest. I live, love, and laugh daily. I tell those that I love daily, not when it is a special occasion or because I feel obligated to do so, I do it because when I love, I love hard and for real. So many times, I find that people say things that they do not mean and I have learned to say what I mean and mean what I say. I do not think that people should "sugarcoat" or "tell people what they want to hear" to save face. I think that honesty is the best policy, even if it may not be what they want to hear. There is a way to say everything as well and we should think about what we want to say before we say it, so that it does not come out as unsympathetic or hurtful. Respect other's feelings because respect is earned and not given and over the years, I have learned that respect goes a long way in life. I am also a firm believer that you should treat people like you want to be treated and we should lead by example at all times.

Oftentimes, people emulate what they see from those that are considered to be leaders and we are all leaders in one way or another. Life is a journey, and the journey is what you make of it. If you want your life to be pleasant and joyful, you have to make it pleasant and joyful. Life is not always about what or how much you have, but what you do with what you have. My life has been wonderful, I have no regrets, and I would not change anything that I have experienced. I learned from my mistakes, experienced the joy of life growing inside of me, taught my children right from wrong, let go and allowed them to grow, I continue to pray for them each day, and I actually live and love my life! At the end of the day, I say a prayer for my family, my friends, everyone else, and me because I truly believe we are all blessed and highly favored! Ultimately, you have the POWER to be all that you can be and do what inspires you to strive to be the best YOU possible.

If there is one thing that I would be allowed to say in hopes to inspire one person, it would be to LIVE your life to the fullest every single day.

LOVE hard and strong with all your heart, and LAUGH as much as you can because laughter is good for the soul! You should make it a point to find what makes you "ROAR" and live life to the fullest!

Sherryl A. Carey

Entrepreneur/U.S. Army Veteran
ROAR: *Stepping Out On Faith*

I've come this far by Faith…

What makes me roar is stepping out on faith. There was a point in time where I knew what faith was, but wasn't sure about stepping out on it. As I grew in size, age and in knowing God, I learned how to step out on faith, but at times wasn't sure that faith could hold me and all of my baggage. But God filled my path with an everlasting light, and brought me out of darkness.

I became saved at the age of eleven years old. I would always question God about why he had me here, I felt unloved and different from other children my age. I would seek out God's face by walking over ten city blocks alone to the tent service with no fear. I believed that Jesus Christ was my Lord and Savior and He had the answer. So now I am a believer and I knew that God could change things, but He couldn't possibly stop the things that were going on in my life. Well, I made it through my teen years oftentimes forgetting about God, although He had not forgotten about me. Looking back, I can now see that I was reckless with the gift of life that He had given me. Sometimes I was mad at the world and wanted to be called home, "Why am I still here, haven't I learned my lesson?" His answer was 'Not yet.' I was married and had my first child at the end of my teen years, second child at twenty-two.

My husband was not the man that God had planned for me. So, after unbelievably difficult times, I slowly tipped out on faith and did what I had to do to raise my children. I took the Army entrance exam knowing in myself that I did not pass because I only took it because I was angry. When the recruiter called and said, "You passed," I almost passed out. I actually went to talking to God about this one, "Lord, what should I do?" I slowly stepped out on faith and He guided my footsteps right down to the MEPS station to be sworn in. I was fully stepping out on faith and counting on God to get me through Basic Training and the training for my job, Wire Systems Installer. Although I was doing this to provide for my children, I had a few choice words for my recruiter, God is good and never allowed me to see him again to be my blessing blocker. I met some amazing women in AIT who are my sister friends, that's a whole other story.

At my first duty station I got a divorce, went home and got my children from my mom and remarried. On the latter, what was I thinking? I picked him, my family liked him, so he was number two. When you don't have God in it, all I can say for right now is wow, and not a good wow. Things in my life had really spun out of control, my health took a dramatic turn for the worse. I went from being on the cross country team and the basketball team to not being able to run a block. I was diagnosed with Pulmonary Sarcoidosis. I had so many questions. How did I get this and what caused it? The doctor's response was, "No known cause and no cure." It was not what I wanted to hear, but I knew I had to return to my first love, and that was the love of God. In all things seek him first and he will direct your path. So, yes, I had this disease, but I did not allow it to have me. I have had many health issues where the doctors didn't know what to do, so I learned to pray and to step out and stand firm on faith. So now the family is sent to Germany because of my wonderful Army life. By this time the second husband is causing me to pray even more. I don't like fighting, but if you start it, I will surely be the one to finish it.

My growing up with four brothers and a dad who boxed really taught me to defend myself. I remember one of our crazy days. I saw the Mr. Hyde character building up, I started praying and singing spirituals. I was hit, I then blacked out. When I came to, there was a knock on the door. I opened it and it was Mr. Hyde standing there bleeding and scratched up. I was looking at him, wondering, *what in the world happened to him?* I finally realized what must have happened, till this day I do not remember touching him. I told him this is it, because he could end up dead and I would end up in jail, not knowing why. I still say God saved him that night. I hate to think what would have happened had I not been praying that night before. From Germany to Texas maybe life will get better. I started school and going to church on a regular basis. That brought on the 'you think you are better than me' attitude. Lord, give me strength. I am tired of begging, pleading, cussing, fussing, fighting and crying for something God had not planned for me. For the last time I prayed to God to tell me what to do. I listened hard and I actually heard a voice say, "I did not put you here to be abused." God said it, I believed it. I packed a bag and left everything. I can get more stuff, but I may not be able to get my sanity back if I lose it. Good bye to heartache and heart breaks, "I'm done".

I prayed and found number three, although it took a while to trust. I didn't want to take care of another mother's son. At the same time I had become so independent, not being able to trust anyone to be responsible for me or my belongings. We dated for four years and have been married for fourteen years, and are very happy. He is my friend and makes me laugh every day and we love and take care of each other. Trusting and stepping out on faith is why my marriage is filled with joy. I can tell you so much about prayer, miracles and God's love. Praying and stepping out on faith is what keeps me living. Stepping out on faith makes me roar when I see how God brings me through whatever storm I am going through, I am truly blessed.

Laura Ahlstrand-Gwin

Voice Training/Vocal Rehabilitation

ROAR: *The Voice*

Laura Ahlstrand Gwin has been training singers internationally since 1996, and has had a successful professional singing career even longer. She has studied the art of teaching vocal development extensively with the masters. Her clients include: Artists signed with Epic and Universal Records, and finalists in the "top five" of *American Idol* and *America's Got Talent*. "The voice. My deepest passion is this most special and wondrous instrument. And so I study it. I use it. I help others to discover the beauty and mystery that is within their own voice, and teach them to develop it to its fullest freedom of expression. There is no other instrument like it - that can so uniquely pass the forces of Creativity and Truth, and move us to the core of our being."

Charley Gabrielle Thompson

Sassy Me Bowtique, Founder/Owner

ROAR: *Conquering Challenges In The Pursuit Of Dreams*

I used to think that dreams were only wishes that could never come true, but I now know otherwise. I remember being in preschool and loving to draw and color. Creating things was something that I enjoyed and knew early on that it made me happy. I dreamed of making clothes and owning my own company. I dreamed of traveling to faraway places and seeing and creating designs that people would love.

Playing dress up and sketching visions of fashionable clothing was something I enjoyed as a very young child. I've always been very girly and loved to wear the big hair bows to match my outfits. In fourth grade, I finally decided that I didn't want to shop for hair bows, I wanted to make my own. I used my computer skills and went on YouTube to see if I could find a video to show me how. After hours of video watching and wasting rolls of ribbon, I finally got the hang of making a hair bow! My materials consisted of ribbon, hair clips, scissors, hot glue gun, needle, and thread. I went to work making these bows and I wore them to school. I loved matching my bows with my clothes and was very proud to wear a bow that I knew I had made myself. My friends started asking me where I got my bows and I was so proud to say that I made them. Soon, they started asking me to make bows for them and this is how it all began! My mom and I figured out what it cost me in materials and time to make a bow. Orders started coming in and I decided my business would be called, "Sassy Me Bowtique."

What some would consider work was fun to me because I enjoyed what I was doing. I soon outgrew my small container of materials and my grandmother bought me my first sewing box. My mom turned an extra room at home into my own bow room to make sure I had plenty of workspace.

Over time, my interests in accessories and fashion led me to jewelry. I truly believe that my confidence with the bow making gave me the drive to expand my business and do even more. I did more research and began making bracelets, necklaces, and earrings. Of course with a business, I knew I needed some way to advertise. I created and ordered business cards and made my own website. I wanted a way that people could see my products and order even though I don't have a shop.

Word spread about me being such a young entrepreneur and I was asked to speak to a business class at a local college. The professor wanted me to share with the class how I got started and talk about my motivation. It was such an honor to be looked at as a designer and business owner.

After my visit, the professor challenged his students with a special assignment. They would partner with me and come up with a way to create a video to advertise my business. It was so fun and it also allowed me to encourage others to go after their dreams! Part of my dream has been to add monogramming to my business. For Christmas, my grandparents surprised me with a monogramming machine. This has allowed me to offer monogrammed clothing, hair bows, towels, etc. I have never taken a sewing class, but together, my grandmother and I learned how to use my machine and my dreams continue to come true!

For every dream, there's a challenge. I've realized that as I conquer each challenge, a new dream comes out of it. I dream to continue my business and hope to expand until one day I have a private shop of my own by the time I am in high school. I dream of going to college and majoring in design. I dream of traveling to other countries and designing all over the world. Because of my self-motivation and the support of my family, I know my dreams can be achieved. I have been successful and I will continue to be successful as long as I believe that I can achieve my dreams! I know that to achieve my biggest dream, I will have to continue to be self-motivated and disciplined. I am an "A" student and am fully aware of the balance that it takes to run my business, stay on top of my academics, and participate in extracurricular activities. I consider it a blessing to have realized at such a young age that dreams DO lead to success and I hope to share this with others!

Glenda A. Wallace

Pink Kiss Publishing Company, Founder/Owner

ROAR: *Uplifting, inspiring, and empowering young girls and women to discover their true potential, so they may achieve the highest level of success!*

Because I descended from a family of business owners, I knew from an early age that I didn't want to work for anyone else. I wanted to "own" the business. My grandparents were farmers. They raised everything from cattle, chickens, and hogs to every vegetable imaginable. They also grew sugar cane and made and sold homemade sugar cane syrup. They were self-sufficient and lived off their land.

My dad, has been an entrepreneur all his life. While growing up on their farm in Butler County, Alabama, he owned livestock, and before he was even twelve years old, he had established credit from a local bank and was able to obtain loans. When he was only fourteen, my father got his calling into the ministry. In addition to the many churches he has pastored over the years, he also still owns several successful businesses.

My mom, who also grew up in rural Alabama, was raised to be a housewife. She and my dad married young and started our family. I am the oldest of four children. My passion for reading and writing began at a very young age. As a child, I was fascinated with words. I was told by my mom that I could write before I even knew how to speak. Reading and writing, for me, were an escape, allowing me to tune out the rest of the world. Through words, I could write my own happy endings. Those written words had the ability to transport me into another world. And, as I grew older, they provided me with an escape from the madness I encountered in my everyday life.

When I was fifteen, I witnessed the breakdown of my parents' marriage. Then, a messy custody battle ensued—not because my dad wanted his children, but because he didn't want to pay any child support to my mother. It was difficult to watch my mom being penalized by the judicial system for being what she was raised to be—a housewife and a mother. Because my dad was deemed the sole breadwinner, custody was, ultimately, awarded to him.

My brothers, sister, and I were basically forced to live with our father and his new wife after the courts decided that our mother could not provide for us financially. This was a valuable lesson for me because it inspired me to use my writing to educate women on the importance of being financially self-sufficient. And, as a result, I found myself writing about issues that affected and pertained to women and relationships.

Life with my father wasn't easy. He was very strict, and he ruled with an iron fist. We didn't have a normal childhood when we lived with my dad and his wife. While our peers enjoyed their summer vacation, my siblings and I had a strict daily routine. We got up at five o'clock in the morning, made our beds, and cleaned our rooms – all before having breakfast, which was served at five-thirty sharp! After breakfast, we washed the dishes. By six o'clock, we were in the field—picking peas, beans, corn, tomatoes, collards...whatever came out of the ground, my father grew it, and we picked it. We worked until noon, then broke for a half-hour lunch. Afterward, we were back in the field until dinner time at six in the evening. After dinner, we washed and put away the dishes, then we had one hour to do whatever we wanted before getting ready for bed. This went on for an entire year. In the meantime, my mom found employment and remarried. And, at some point, my dad decided that he and his wife didn't want us anymore, so he agreed to allow us to return to our mom.

My first paying job was in a trendy clothing store in the mall when I was sixteen. Since I was no stranger to hard work, I excelled at my job. I was an overachiever. I was the type of employee that would always do anything that needed to be done without being told. My district manager was extremely impressed with my initiative and drive. He said, "One day, you're going to make an excellent manager."

To which, I replied, "No offense, sir, but I'm not trying to *manage* anything. I'm going to *own* the company!"

As I grew older, so did my ambitions. I joined the US Army when I was twenty. This was one of the best decisions I ever made. I took to the military quite well because I was already self-disciplined. Thanks to my father and my strict upbringing, I was no stranger to hard work; therefore, I excelled. After several years in the military, I still felt there was something else greater in store for me. I just had to strike out and learn what that was. After leaving the military, I worked in several fields. I worked in retail sales management, obtained my real estate license, worked in healthcare, and, finally, settled into a position as a casino table games dealer. As a table games dealer, the money was awesome, but I hated the job! Nothing, up until that point, had given me the personal fulfillment that I was yearning for.

So, in June 2008, I decided to incorporate my publishing company (Pink Kiss Publishing Company, Inc.) and publish my second book. I had previously published my first book through another company, but I was extremely disappointed with the results, so I wanted to publish my second book through my own company. While working on my second book, I still kept that job that I loathed. Every day, I would stand in line at the time clock, and, while waiting to clock in, I would say, "Lord, one of these days, I'm going to step out on faith and run my business full-time."

I said this for many years, but even though I knew what I was capable of, I still had that *fear* inside that prevented me from leaving a job that I hated. But because I was earning an annual salary of $65,000 and only working part-time, I held on. I soon learned that what they say is true—"What the Lord has for you, is for YOU!"

In October 2008, after fifteen years of being stuck in this dead-end job, I guess the Lord decided that I wasn't moving fast enough. So He pushed me out there in the form of a layoff. *Thank you, Jesus!* But I was scared. What was I going to do? I had a $1,400 a month mortgage. I had just purchased a luxury vehicle. How was I going to survive and pay all of my living expenses out of $180 a week in unemployment benefits?

I got my Bible, went into my closet, dropped down on my knees, and prayed like never before. I prayed for strength, direction, and clarity in my life. I prayed and asked God to show me *His* will for my life. When I walked out of that closet, I took my hands off the situation and gave it over to Him. I knew, without a doubt, that I hadn't orchestrated this chain of events. He had orchestrated it, and He'd done it for a reason. I went to work full-time on my second book, and, nine months later, it was done!

When I laid eyes on my second book, I realized that it exceeded my every expectation. It was more than I ever imagined it would be. It was perfect and so professionally designed! I fell on my knees and thanked God for blessing me with the ability to do something of this magnitude! I was filled with so much pride that *I* had done this. People who saw the quality of my work began asking me to publish their books, but I still didn't know everything about the publishing business. At that time, I still wasn't knowledgeable enough to take on any authors, so, for two years, I went underground and learned the publishing business. I took classes, read books, watched video tutorials, and consulted with attorneys about contracts. I also learned about business structure, investment strategies, and book design. Then, I assembled my team.

In February 2010, I officially opened the doors of Pink Kiss Publishing Company, Inc. to the public, to provide a platform to assist aspiring authors in achieving their dreams of becoming published authors. For me, this was a huge accomplishment! I had taken something that I loved and had a passion for and turned it into a successful business.

In 2012, our gross earnings doubled what I earned punching someone else's time clock. But the biggest reward of all is when I hear from all of the new authors who have just received the first copies of their books. While crying tears of joy, they thank me because they never imagined they could achieve such an accomplishment. That is confirmation that I have found my true calling. Everything that I've gone through in my life—failed marriages, surviving breast cancer, unfulfilling job choices—were just stepping stones to get to where I am today—where the Lord intended me to be. And, every day, I thank Him!

To date, we have signed over sixty authors, and we currently have over one hundred titles in print. In addition to the authors signed with my company, I also work with other self-published authors and aspiring publishers, and have assisted in launching several successful publishing businesses.

In short: Most people don't reach their full potential because of fear. But, fear of what? Fear of the unknown, or the fear of failure? In order to succeed, it is important to conquer that fear. Fear has the ability to paralyze us. It can keep us trapped in bad relationships or marriages. It can keep us trapped in a job that we absolutely hate. I've heard people say that it took almost drowning for them to learn how to swim. I have found this to be true. In my previous situation, it was either sink or swim. I chose to swim because failure was not an option.

I have a passion for working with women and young girls, because as females, we are unique and fabulous. We are strong and resilient. We have no limits, no boundaries, and we are a powerful contribution to the world!

BIO:

Glenda A. Wallace is the Founder and CEO of several businesses under Pink Kiss, Inc. She founded Pink Kiss Publishing Company in 2008. In addition to being a publisher, she is an author, entrepreneur, educator, and business consultant.

Ms. Wallace is dedicated to uplifting, inspiring, and empowering young girls and women to discover their true potential, so that they may achieve the highest level of success. She lives, works, and plays on the beautiful Mississippi Gulf Coast.

Where words leave off, music begins.

-Heinrich Heine

The Dream Team

Talent behind the production of the Ari'el Rising Theme Song, *"We Have The Power To Change The World."* From Left, Skyler Jett, Shana Morrison, and Sylvester Burks.

Skyler Jett

Songwriter-Lyrics-Vocal Producer

As a singer/songwriter and social conscious music producer I'm proud and honored to be a part of such an epic contribution to women's empowerment. Denice and I were co-hosts of an Internet radio show dedicated to finding solutions for three years called the SNR network (Solutions Now Radio). Once Denice explained to me about her idea of writing a concept book about the accomplishments of women who disconnected themselves from the norm, I was blown away. This was serendipitous because nine years ago I collaborated on a songwriting project about this very subject entitled WE GOT THE POWER TO CHANGE THE WORLD, written by myself, Shanna Morrison (Yes, Van Morrison's daughter), and my dearest friend and songwriting colleague, producer Sylvester Burks. Thank you, Denice, for inviting me and my songwriting colleagues to be a part of such a historical book, bless you for that.

Bio & Discography:

Skyler Jett is an award-winning, Grammy Recognized vocalist and one of the most sought after Singer/Songwriter and Background Vocal Producers in the Music Industry. Skyler's impressive resume includes some of the biggest recording artists of our times. His accolades include receiving a Grammy Award-embossed plaque from NARAS for singing with Celine Dion on the Grammy-winning hit song "My Heart Will Go On" from the blockbuster hit film "Titanic." This was also Record Of The

Year (1998) and is still the highest grossing movie theme song of all time. Skyler's other movie credits include Background Vocal arrangement on "I'm Every Woman" from the blockbuster hit film "The Body Guard", also Movie Of The Year (1992), featuring Whitney Houston; "Tap" with Gregory Hines and Sammy Davis Jr.; "A Smile Like Yours" with Greg Kinnear; Disney's "Hercules"; James Bond 007 "License To Kill"; "Big Bully" with Rick Moranis and Tom Arnold; and "Ghostdad" with Bill Cosby. From 2003-2007 Skyler also played a pivotal role in reintroducing Sly Stone back to the World Stage for a European tour. Skyler performed with Sly in such venues as: The Montreux Jazz Festival; North Sea Jazz Festival; Cannes; Olympia, Paris; The Love Box Festival in London and the George Wallace Show, Las Vegas. Skyler has recorded and performed with the following Legendary Stars:
- Stevie Wonder, Celine Dion, Patti Austin
- Quincy Jones, Ricky Minor, Lionel Richie
- Sting, Ray Charles, Al Jarreau
- James Brown, Al Green, Paul Anka
- Lou Rawls, Chaka Khan, Oleta Adams
- Barbara Streisand, Christina Aguillera, Tina Arena
- Diana Ross, Whitney Houston, Taylor Dane
- Aretha Franklin, Jennifer Lopez, Pia Zadora
- Mariah Carey, Patti LaBelle, Tom Jones
- The O'Jays, Todd Rundgren, Marc Anthony
- The Commodores, Kenny Loggins, Rick Martin
- The Temptations, Steve Winwood, Walter Afanasieff
- Curtis Mayfield, Eddie Murphy, Boyz To Men
- Peabo Bryson, Kenny G, Tevin Campbell
- Michael Bolton,
- New Kids On The Block … and many more…

His beautiful lyrics and vocal production can also be found on recordings by the following artists:
- Al Jarreau, The Commodores
- Patti Austin, Tevin Campbell
- Eddie Murphy, Cori Lerios
- Shana Morrison, Lenny Wiliams … to name a few

In 1982 Skyler replaced Lionel Richie in The Commodores, touring 31 countries.

He performed live at The Kodak Theater, Hollywood, for The Lou Rawls 25th Anniversary of The United Negro College Fund with the following Gospel Artists:

- Donnie McClurkin, Smokey Norful
- Fred Hammond, Yolanda Adams
- Shirley Caesar

Skyler Jett is Founder and CEO MUSIC FOR GLOBAL CHANGE. Skyler is also the co-host of SolutionsNowRadio with S. Denise Newton — a high ranking Blog Talk radio show offering dynamic solutions for some of today's most pressing issues.

"About my social conscious mission. Below are the building blocks to my vision for 'MUSIC FOR GLOBAL CHANGE'. I'd like to incorporate these points into my mission statement.

"First on my list would be to put music school teachers back into our schools and fund music programs all over the world with this model. We can't let the lack of money kill a child's dream simply because it costs too much to educate them. As a child growing up on welfare I understand the terrain well, raised with three other siblings by my mother who was a single parent. I feel blessed to have been actively involved in the music industry for forty-two years now and I understand how change can come about. My incentive to Songwriters and Artists in this mission statement is to outline various ways to provide for your family and effect social change, while at the same time promoting music for the cause of your choice.

"In my opinion, music is the number one language of the world. Music is not only an educational tool, but a healing tool as well. My idea is to take some of the funds and profits from our music industry and bring awareness to social causes all over our planet. My ultimate goal is to start a 'good news' channel, if you will, called "Music 4 Causes" a radio Internet network. It is a place to showcase songwriters' music and their messages for the purpose of changing our world for the better, giving musicians a platform where their music can affect social change. In addition, I see monthly interviews to promote products that better our lives, inventions that save the consumer energy and money from some of our worlds best and upcoming innovators. Knowledge is power and sharing it empowers all of us. Are you ready for the next positive news channel? It's time to give the bad news some healthy competition – may the best news win! My goal is to travel the globe teaching ways to improve our music industry and provide cause-based institutions more visibility via our conscious music services. I also want to improve the state of our music industry and bring awareness to some of the outdated, discriminative practices that we no longer need, since the old way of doing things have all but vanished due to the Internet revolution … give thanks! Here are some examples of internal changes that need to be made expeditiously to our music business. 1) Image – since our industry injected image onto the scene, it has become discriminative to artists that don't fit the commercial 'look'. For example, there may be a child dreaming of becoming a star, but they don't believe they're attractive enough due to some music executive dictating the marketing brand of the industry. Music isn't something you look at, it's something you listen to. Think about it – if you're in your car listening to the radio and you surf the channels and find a song that SOUNDS GOOD TO YOU, you don't care about how that artist looks… do you? If we keep supporting this brand imaging, we are going to miss the next Mozart's music because we judged them on how they looked before they could blossom. We need to stop this practice immediately. 2) Racism – Why is it more difficult for African Americans songwriters and artists to pursue their dream of being a Country music or Rock artist? The expectance is closer to nil, but you can find Caucasian artists thriving in the music industry in Jazz, R&B, Hip-hop and even Rap music, check out the equilibrium for yourself. Music is a language for all of us, not just some of us. It's time to break down the barriers and open the doors to all who seek to pursue any genre their heart desires. 3) Age discrimination in music. Remember music is something to listen to, it has nothing whatsoever to do with your age. I have demonstrations for all three of these points that will change these very important issues that have plagued our industry for years. 4) Bring the human sound back to the forefront… because "YOU CAN'T BEAT THE SOUND OF A HUMAN BEING." Last, but not least, this demonstration will prove this poignant point. Technology has destroyed the human element – the emotion – from music. I invite you to test the difference for yourself. Computers have no emotion – emotion can be only be provided by humans. "Frequently imitated but never duplicated" fits the bill perfectly in this instance. 5) Where is the respect for musicians nowadays? I'm dismayed by dancers getting more respect than musicians these days. Take a look at any one of the awards shows for our industry like the Grammys or American Music Awards shows, they stick the musicians behind a curtain somewhere while the artist and dancers get the glory. News flash!!! Again, without the music what are you going to dance or perform to? And the disrespect is getting worse by the minute. With these points above now in writing, I've learned it's not about the problem it's about the solution. Funds are one of the most important components to such an undertaking, however, it's people who make the world go round and with the help of people all things are possible. There's much more refining to do, but hopefully, I've made it hard to argue that the future is all ready here ... but only for those that are ready for it."

Peace Always,

http://skylerjett.com/

musicforglobalchange.com

Sylvester Burks
Songwriter & Co-Music Producer

I've had the honor of working and touring with twelve Grammy artists, mostly in the Gospel genre. Edwin Hawkins (Oh Happy Day – 7 million copies sold), Patti Labelle, Platinum artist Donnie McClurkin, BeBe Winans, Shirley Ceasar, Yolanda Adams, Rafael Saadiq, Dwayne Wiggins, etc. I've played the Apollo Theatre and Lincoln Center with Tramaine Hawkins in New York, did a special for BET there and proceeded to the island of Bermuda. After a seven city tour, we went to L.A. to shoot a music video with Tramaine for A&M Records, which was presented at the Grammy awards telecast by the late Luther Vandross. I was the music director for the wedding of "Friends" sitcom star, Courteney Cox.

Concerning your book, I must say that this is indeed an honor and privilege to make a musical contribution as co-writer with Skyler Jett for such a worthy cause and endeavor. It has long been my opinion that not enough has been done towards the parity and brilliant contributions of women on the front of multiple issues and I think that this book will serve as a beacon platform to enlighten and jolt the "world".

Bio:

Sylvester Burks is a Keyboardist/Producer in the San Francisco/Oakland Bay area that has worked and toured with over ten Grammy artists and many Stellar award winners. He began his musical interest at the tender age of nine years old and was inspired at his church, the

Ephesian Church of God in Christ by the organist and pianist brother tandem of Edwin and Walter Hawkins (Oh Happy Day – 7 million copies sold) who would go on to be legendary Grammy artists.

He began to progress at a rapid rate and by the time he was twenty years old, the legendary late Rev. James Cleveland heard him as he played for him at a music workshop and he was offered to tour with him. Shortly after this, he was called into the office of his early musical idol, the late Bishop Walter Hawkins, asking him to be the organist of the world famous Love Center church. Although he graciously declined the offer he was able to work with this musical association later by touring with the former wife of Walter Hawkins, Grammy artist Tramaine Hawkins. This tour included performances in New York at the famed Apollo Theatre and Lincoln Center and doing an interview with BET television. This East Coast tour continued to Philadelphia, Atlanta, Cleveland and on to the island of Bermuda. It ended with doing a music video for A&M Records in Los Angeles for the single "Wake Up Singing" which was introduced at the Grammy telecast by the late great Luther Vandross. After this tour, he was privileged to work with some of the greatest artists in gospel music such as Yolanda Adams, Donnie McClurkin, Donald Lawrence, Shirley Caesar, Kim Burrell,Vanessa Bell Armstrong, Tamela Mann, Norman Hutchins and was also hired by Edwin Hawkins to be the MD (musical director) of a concert working with Patti Labelle and BeBe Winans. His dream came true when he was able to record with Edwin on the project "Have Mercy" which produced the worldwide praise anthem "I Love You Lord Today" and later was a co-writer on the project "Church Time". He has also been blessed to work with many renowned ministers such as Bishop Noel Jones, the late Bishop G.E. Patterson, Pastor Jamal Bryant, Apostle Richard D. Henton, Rev. Jeremiah Wright and many more. He has been blessed to also work with many in the idiom of the popular entertainment industry such as Saxophonists Kenny G, Gerald Albright, Raphael Saadiq and offers to do session work with Frankie Beverly. He was also hired to be the M.D. (musical director) for the wedding of "Friends" sitcom star Courteney Cox which was attended by such stars as Brad Pitt, Nicholas Cage and also meeting Jennifer Aniston and many more.

Sylvester currently owns and operates his own recording studio, Slykeys Recording. He enjoys serving as an engineer and being a multi-talented musician being a session bassist and drum programming. He is also excited about the career of his step-son Jonn Hart, who was discovered and signed to Epic Records by L.A. Reid. Sylvester currently enjoys working and writing with his music group "Kingdom Business" and teaching young musicians through instructional videos which have been viewed and downloaded by over 200,000 viewers. He takes pride in being humble and loving everyone.

Shana Morrison

Songwriter- Lead Vocals- Lyrics

My passion grew from being raised in a family that loved music. All of my relatives were collectors, players, singers, dancers, and my stepfather worked on the technical side of the music biz. My parents were rehearsing and recording demos in the house, and at my grandparents' record store. I could play promotional copies of records of every artist imaginable, and I have been attending live concerts since before I can remember. So, music came naturally to me, probably just by osmosis. By the time I was a teenager, I had learned so much about the creative process, the different relationships between industry professionals and artists, and all of the instability in that life, yet, against all sense of reason, I began my career as a singer/songwriter in 1994 after I graduated from Pepperdine University with a business degree. I had a song in my heart, and I decided that I was going to sing it. So many blessings have come into my life since I chose this path. The musicians, writers, engineers, producers, and audience members are all collaborators in this project, and I consider myself very fortunate to have their support and encouragement over the past twenty years.

Bio:

Shana Morrison's musical style has been called pop with a side of blues and a side of rock. She has also been known to include other ingredients, like country, R&B, and jazz into the mix. Her material seems to be ever-changing and hard to pin down categorically. What always remains the same is Shana's unique and wide-ranging voice. Shana's international exposure includes a live broadcast for the BBC's Kelly Show and an appearance at the BRIT Awards in 1996, when her father was presented with a lifetime-achievement award. This has been broadcasted on A&E in America several times since. She also participated in a VH1 Father's Day special and was featured in *People* in 1997, *Rolling Stone* in 1999, and in *Interview*, as well as on the Oxygen channel's *Pure Oxygen*, and on *The Howard Stern Show* in 2002. Since 2002, the band has been busy with tours across the United States, Germany, Italy, Ireland, and the U.K., playing radio shows, clubs, theaters, and festivals, most notably playing the Warfield in San Francisco, the Viper Room in Los Angeles, the House of Blues in Cambridge, the Bottom Line in New York, Meinisfree Open Air in Germany, the Arezzo Wave Pop festival in Italy, the Borderline in London, the Cork Jazz Festival, the Galway Arts Festival, and The Late Late Show in Ireland. 2006 through 2008 saw Shana singing beside Van Morrison again during his U.S. and U.K. tour dates.

Twelve years have passed since her beginnings singing duets with Mr. Morrison his infamous Rhythm and Soul Review, which featured artists such as Jimmy Withersoon, Junior Wells, and John Lee Hooker. Since her first foray into recording on the Van Morrison releases A Night in San Francisco (1994) and Days Like This (1995), Shana Morrison has grown as a singer, a songwriter, and an artist. Her self-produced 2007 release, the R&B-flavored CD That's Who I Am, is on Belfast Violet Records. Joyride, produced by Kim McLean, was released in April 2010, also on Belfast Violet Records. Both albums are available online at iTunes, Amazon, and CDBaby.

Joey Blake

Background Arranger

Raised in a family of musicians and gospel singers, Joey's multiple skills include singer, producer, recording engineer, instrumentalist (piano, guitar, bass, percussion), composer, dancer and choir director. He studied classical voice and vocal jazz arranging at Phil Mattson's School for Vocalists in Spokane, Washington, developing his deeply resonant and expressive bass vocals. Joey is one of the founding and current members of Voicestra, the a cappella ensemble created by Bobby McFerrin in 1989. He is a founding member of the ensemble SoVoSo, a six member a cappella ensemble that spun from Voicestra. Joey has recorded & produced five albums for this group, (Precious - a European release, Bridges and Seasonings for the US, as well as Crack the Nut and Then and Now). He also holds numerous arranging credits to his name, including his work with SoVoSo. His discography includes recordings with Bobby McFerrin (Medicine Music, CircleSongs, Vocabularies & Spirit You All), Kenny Loggins (Conviction of The Heart), Mickey Hart (Supralingua, Mondo Head), to name a few. Joey also has four self produced solo recordings, Through My Eyes, Come Inside The Circle, Songs From The Singing Soul and Reaching Back. Joey is also a renowned teacher in the San Francisco Bay area. His desire to teach is motivated by his need to give back to the music that fills his life with so much joy.

Joey has taught at the Oakland College Prep School as The contemporary Vocal Instructor, and has served as Director of music at

The Golden Gate Academy in Oakland, California. He was commissioned by the Oakland Youth Chorus to write and arrange for its professional touring ensemble, Vocal Motion. Joey was on the faculty of The Berkeley Jazz School for four years, as the Conductor of the Berkeley Jazz School A cappella Ensemble, a course which he designed himself. He taught and held a Board position for Young Performers International, a San Francisco based non-profit organization for youth music & education and is currently working with Musicians Without Borders Based in the Netherlands. Joey teaches alongside Bobby McFerrin during his summer residencies at the Omega Institute in Rhinebeck, NY, called "Spontaneous Inventions". Joey currently holds a position as an Associate Professor in the Voice Department at Berklee College of Music in Boston, where he continues to develop his teaching methods. Joey is a vocalist with an unmistakable style, fluid as it is unique, full of surprises and delivered with masterful grace. His instrument-like approach to the voice gives him a musical vocabulary heard only in the rarest of singers. Joey's current projects are We Be 3, an improvisational vocal Trio comprised of himself and two other members of Voicestra, Rhiannon and Dave Worm. Back to the Band a five piece band consisting of all Berklee Graduates focusing on Improvisation within the live band experience. "Sung Deep" an eight piece A cappella ensemble is Joey's latest recording project, an International Group of singers, with an emerging self titled CD coming this summer 2014! Joey also has begun an A cappella choir he calls the "Singing Tribe" the focus of all these ensembles is to model what we believe is possible in the world by functioning as an international community of people working together for one purpose, global unity!

www.joeyblake.com
www.fizzkicks.com/joey
www.reverbnation.com/joeyblake
www.webe-3.com
www.reverbnation.com/sungdeep

Kim Fleming

Lead Vocals

A native of Nashville, Kim Fleming got her education in music through the Nashville educational system. She attended Fisk University, Belmont College, and Tennessee State University, receiving a Bachelor of Science degree in Music. During her years of study, Kim was also touring and performing. One of her first monumental stage performances was at Carnegie Hall in New York City. There, she appeared with world renowned Fisk Jubilee Singers, under the direction of Dr. Matthew Kennedy. Then, Kim began her professional career in music, touring with Amy Grant. The experience with Grant launched a very impressive and extensive career in music.

Fleming has been the number one call for contracting and arranging background vocals for master recordings in film, television & radio, to date. Kim has had the opportunity to work with some of the industry's greatest artists: Patti Austin, Patti Labelle, Bette Midler, Jon Bon Jovi, Michael Jackson, B. B. King, George Harrison (The Beatles), Keith Richards (The Rolling Stones), Billy Joel, Garth Brooks, Vince Gill, Reba McEntire, Shirley Caesar, Andre Crouch, Stevie Wonder, Arif Martin, Desmond Childs, Michael Narada Walden, Ray Charles, Isaac Hayes, Motley Crue, Will Downing, Alex Benoit, Jean Carne, Michael Bolton, Paul Simon, Brian McKnight & Kelli Price. Kim's vocal ability is not limited to just one genre of music. She has appeared on hundreds of recordings, jingles, and film scores, and variety shows such as: *Johnny*

Carson, Arsenio Hall, Jay Leno, David Letterman, Ellen Degeneres, The Today Show at NBC, Good Morning America, Regis & Kelly and *The View.*

She has sung on the television series, *Touched By An Angel, ER,* as well as the television special *Music In High Places.* Kim Fleming sang in the remake of the movie, *Footloose.*

Ms. Fleming has performed on the Grammy Awards with Amy Grant, The Dove Awards, the Stellar Awards, the Billboard Awards, the CMA Awards and the ACM Awards. Ms. Fleming has performed at the opening ceremonies of the Paralympics with Stevie Wonder, Donnie Osmond and Wynonna Judd.

Kimberly Fleming has performed for four Presidents. She has also done very well in the world of theater, as an actress, a casting director and songwriter. One of her most memorable roles was that of "Armelia" in the Broadway Musical "Ain't Misbehavin." In recent years, Fleming was asked to be the casting director for the musical "Marrying Up" based on the novel written by Nina Fox. Kim cast "American Idol's" Melinda Doolittle in the leading role as "Paris". And as a songwriter, Kim wrote the melodies and lyrics to all of the songs performed in the play. Kim was assisted by the great composer John Forbes (Tyler Perry film *Diary of a Mad Black Woman*). Together they wrote a wonderful score for the play, which was revived in 2009.

If you are a country fan, you will know Kim from her fifteen years of touring with Wynonna Judd. Kim has also toured with Trisha Yearwood and Randy Owens, who is the lead singer for the famed country group "Alabama". Ms. Fleming sang at two of Wynonna Judd's weddings. She sang at Ashley Judd's wedding at Edinburgh Castle in Scotland, singing "Ave Maria" Kim sang at Will Downing's wedding in New Jersey. Kim sang at Tammy Wynette's funeral and Carl Perkins' funeral (with George Harrison of the Beatles.) Kim Fleming sang at Bob Hope's "Bag Full Of Christmas Memories" last special. This is what Kim does to make a living. But, Kim grew up singing jazz and gospel. She has been in the studio working on her own record, which is a mixture of Smooth jazz, smooth R&B, with a Neo-soul edge. Her record is being produced and co-written by Aaron Mason & Chris (Big Dog) Davis and the Hamilton Brothers; Tim, Tyronn, and Walter Jr. The lyrics and tracks of this project are all state of the art performances. Kim's mentor & inspiration on this project has been the great jazz saxophonist Joe Johnson & jazz trumpeter Rod McGaha. Kim has also been touring with Joe Johnson, Phil Perry, Maysa Leak, Chrisette Michelle, Glenn Jones, Howard Hewitt, and Angela Winbush. Kim is the vocal contractor for the Stellar Awards

Orchestra, for the past ten years. You can see Kim on BET's *Bobby Jones Gospel*, which is celebrating its 33rd year in existence. Be on the look out for Kim Fleming's new CD, which is soon to be released.

Kudisan Kai
Lead Vocals

Kudisan Kai, the artist formerly known as Natalie Jackson, has made an incredible journey from opera to alternative metal. Kudisan graduated from Howard University in Washington, D.C. with a degree in Voice. She received additional training at the Tanglewood Summer Music Program then entered graduate school at The Eastman School of Music in Rochester, New York and New York University in New York City. This classically trained singer got her commercial music start in jazz on recordings with the Howard University Jazz Ensemble. As a result of this exposure, she received Downbeat Magazine's "Best Jazz Vocalist" Award. She later toured with Anita Baker and Natalie Cole. Then, she did an about-face and toured for six years with Elton John. Kudisan also worked extensively with Chaka Khan.

Kudisan has also appeared with Beck at the Cochella Festival and on MTV's *Total Request Live*, as well as with Sting on *The Tonight Show* with Jay Leno. The range of artists with whom Kudisan has recorded reflects the depth of her experience, and includes Bette Midler, Diana Ross, Joe Cocker, Saliva, Mary J. Blige, and Salif Keita. The list of producers include, George Duke, Arif Mardin, Narada Michael Walden, Don Was, Patrick Leonard, and Glen Ballard.

This versatile artist can be heard in a host of television and radio commercials, as well as movies. She performed on the soundtrack of Dreamworks El Dorado, Disney's Dinosaurs, Ali, Eddie Murphy's film

Pluto Nash, and John Singleton's *Dark Blue*. Her recent film work was for the Sergio Mendez/John Powell collaboration, *Rio II*, which was released this spring 2014. Kudisan was featured with her own alternative-metal band in CBGB's, Cat Club and the Bitter End, three of the hottest New York Clubs.

On the west coast, she graced the stage of L.A's Viper Room, where she showcased her songwriting talent as well. Recently, Kudisan produced and performed in a 3-day Artist-In-Residency at Berklee College of Music where she was an associate professor in the voice department for ten years. It was entitled, "Women In Rock", and included recording artists Nona Hendryx, Joyce Kennedy, Me'shell Ndegeocello, Siedah Garrett, Cindy Blackman, and Felicia Collins.

"Singing with these women proved to be one of the most magical experiences of my life," says Kudisan.

"WHAT IS MY PASSION? WHAT MAKES ME ROAR? Through my voice/music, I encourage people to embrace every personal experience as a gift and an opportunity to self-heal and emotionally connect."

Currently, Kudisan is promoting her new EP Transcend and is touring with Chaka Khan.

Taylor Burrise

Drums

Taylor D. Burrise has accomplished quite a bit in his young eighteen years of life. Being a drummer, producer, songwriter, fashion designer, businessman, and entrepreneur, he has really pushed himself and proven that a young man can do anything in his life, and be a positive influence on anybody young and/or old. In his music career, Taylor has had the honor of sharing the stage and performing/recording with artist such as Analysis, A.D. Burrise (his father), Marion Meadows, Wayman Tisdale (RIP), Paul Taylor, Jessy J, Lil Twist, Diggy Simmons, Dean James, The DrumAddictz, Michael Lington, Gerald Albright, Chaka Khan, Chico DeBarge, El DeBarge, Norman Brown, Black The Beast, Darnell Robinson, LeA Robinson, and more. Taylor is now into the behind the scenes part of the music business, which is producing/songwriting.

Taylor has been into fashion his whole life as well. With his older brother Anthony Burrise being a fashion designer, Taylor learned how to appreciate fashion even more while growing up. At age thirteen, Taylor started a clothing line with a childhood friend called "Get Active". Of course, it didn't really work out, but that was just a start, it was a door that was slightly open for Taylor in the fashion game. However, once that was finished, Taylor ventured off to do another line with another friend of his called "UnKnown". That line was very nice and competed with any company out there. But, again, it did not go through. He cut ties, and decided to go on his own and start his very own clothing line called TML

(Taylor Made Line). TML will be in fashion shows, and will be sold online, and in stores. You can say Taylor has come a long way from being a twelve year old kid who started performing with his father on a big stage, to a young adult who is playing with a variety of artists in the music industry and a young man who has and runs his own company. Music, business, and fashion is what Taylor is all about. Taylor D. Burrise is a young businessman if you ever want to see one.

Leslie Ellis

Lead Vocals

Leslie Ellis, Singer/Songwriter, Working Jane Music

My Roar:

Using my Music to inspire people to find their place in the world. Believing in what you know you know. Finding your place in the world is one of life's most difficult journeys. Not just figuring out what profession you will pursue, but genuinely discovering who you are and how you fit into society and the world around you.

Most people discover many ways of defining themselves over their lifetimes: mother, wife, sister, daughter, lawyer, painter, tennis player – you see what I mean? Who you are is rarely defined by just one thing. The same is true for me. I have many levels of my character and abilities that make me who I am. However, my first foothold on this cumulative journey, was the most important definition of all. I am a singer. I am often asked, "How long have you been singing?" I say that I've been singing since before I could talk. That may not be exactly true, but I don't remember a time when I didn't sing – children's songs with my mama, chiming in with the radio in the car, enacting the songs from records in my parents' living room. It was just something I did. But, I wasn't a happy child. I was very timid and insecure. I was bullied and teased throughout my school years. Much of the time I felt terrified of the world outside my home; afraid I was inadequate in every way. I felt I wasn't pretty enough, smart enough, really likable – much less, extraordinary in any way. I didn't recognize any significant ability in myself at all.

Music was an escape for me. I knew, I knew how to sing, and that I could do it well, but I didn't understand that it made me special. Apparently my parents did understand. They heard something in my voice, before I was aware of it. They heard identity and confidence and did everything they could to support and nurture my natural abilities. After school activities gradually changed from failed sports tryouts and Girl Scouts to singing lessons and auditioning for and being accepted into State Choir!

That summer was spent not swimming and playing competitive sports with the same children who looked right through me – as if I were a ghost – during the school year, but rather singing and learning about music and eventually, integrating into a different community of kids. A quirky, creative bunch who believed in ghosts... in a good way. I had always assumed everyone could sing. But, as I grew up—and thanks to the unwavering support and belief of my parents—I realized that what I could do so easily; what I could "hear" was very special and unique. It did, however, take several terrifying leaps of faith and years of hard work before I knew what I knew, but gradually, I began to "own" my gift as a singer.

Not long after that, I had a very special summer. I went to an arts/music/acting camp my mama had discovered. I knew it was going to be fun, but socially I was so insecure. Who knew what kind of kids would be there? Bullies? Confident kids with posses and enough friends already? For the first week I kept to myself, only carefully opening up to the other campers. Then one afternoon, a very gregarious girl named Karen Fern, started singing in a group of kids who were all hanging out by one of the cabins. Without thinking about it, and without any fear, I started singing with her, full voice, trading harmonies and leads on "Let Me Be There In Your Morning" and "Breaking Up Is Hard To Do". Within six minutes we were best friends and the most popular kids in the whole camp, and I stepped into myself – who I really am – for the first time. I had found my place and I was finally in my element. That was how it started; my lifetime journey, constantly experiencing new strengths and abilities. Learning each day about another piece of me. It began with my voice and everything I am is anchored by what I believe I know I know. I am a singer. I graduated from one of the most competitive Acting/Music schools in the country. I landed lead roles in Broadway musicals (La Cage Aux Folles, CATS, City of Angels). I've acted in films, sung for 28,000 people with Michael Crawford, worked with legendary "Hit Producer" Walter Afanasieff at SONY Music and have sung with many artists. I even had the distinct honor of singing with Celine Dion on "My Heart Will Go On" for which I received a Grammy® Award. I've been an award winning songwriter and all of these wonderful accomplishments were achieved by believing in what I know and persevering – no matter what obstacles presented themselves. I've been given great advice and mentored by amazing, inspiring people. But, I've also been devastatingly discouraged. I've been told I was too young, too old, that my voice was too much of this and not enough of that and on and on. I had to perform very difficult songs like "Memory" from CATS, under less than ideal conditions; whether I was in "good voice" or not, eight shows a week. I've mysteriously lost my voice, been turned down for jobs, and sometimes suffered horribly from second-guessing myself and stage fright.

What I learned from those obstacles was that I needed to shift my thinking from relying on others to validate me, to looking inward for support. I've learned to give myself the right to cry, take a break or even quit when absolutely necessary. I finally figured out that I need lots of sleep to be mentally, physically and emotionally prepared to handle this life I've chosen. Rest is vitally important. And, I continue to learn, every day, to be my own best friend. To speak kindly to myself when the world doesn't. To reward myself when the business doesn't. To laugh at my own mistakes, and above all, to stand solid in my resolve that I know I know what I'm doing, that I really am good at it and that it's OK if not everyone thinks so.

My voice taught me this about me and yet it radiates through every other aspect of my life. What I know I know is how to measure tones, words, notes and melody to build a rich palette from which I pull colors and paint for the audience a sonic picture of who I am and what I'm singing. It's my safe place and my most vulnerable. It's pure and very genuine and when I experience these moments of musical connection, it's the best kind of happiness – I am in a completely blissful place – that's my place in the world. These days, one of the things I do is work with young singers, helping them learn to write and grow as artists. It is my vision to continue writing music with these young ladies that touches people – women – with a strong female message or a positive, hopeful lyrical content. When I hear one of my "girls" singing a song we wrote with content like this, delivered with complete connection, confidence and passion, I am so happy to hear the roar of another lioness who has found her place in the world. The triumphs and defeats in my life of being an artist are balanced by the joy and peace I find when I'm there, in my zone, singing. I may be working, but I'm fully in the moment and beautifully alive. NO ONE can take that away from me... because I know I know what I know.

Ashley T. Lewis

Background Vocals

Ashley T. Lewis is a singer, songwriter, and actress, born on the Island of Jamaica, raised in the State of Connecticut, USA. She is currently a student at Berklee College of Music in Boston, MA.

Shania Wilcox

Background Vocals

Shania Wilcox was born and raised in Glen Cove, NY. As a Music Business/Songwriting Major at Berklee College of Music, the nineteen year old singer enjoys performing, recording, dancing, and playing piano. Her soulful sound has blessed a plethora of events such as homecomings, church events, nursing homes, opening school convocations, Carnegie Hall, The Cotton Club, and the Berklee Performance Center. Ms. Wilcox is a God-fearing woman who is grateful for every blessing, yet, excited to see what her future holds.

Noel Braganza
Background Vocals

Music and design have always been the main driving force behind Noel's creativity. Having grown up in India, he was fortunate enough to be a part of a fairly musical family, the kinds that sees relatives and friends bang around on an untuned guitar or a clunky old piano. Fortunately enough, this initiation to music wasn't where all the fun would end, it grew through school and college and eventually he joined various music groups and bands. This is where his love for A cappella jazz grew. Unfortunately, growing up in India and being a practical person, he decided it was important to have a back up plan, i.e. a full time job. He began working as a copywriter in the day and continued being a musician by night. But as all real stories go, his life's plans slowly began drifting away from music and nudged their way towards his back up plan. Soon his job as a copywriter pushed him into the field of Interaction Design. From Mumbai, he moved first to Milan and then finally to Boston to work at a design lab at MIT. He has, however, kept indulging himself in singing no matter where he went by joining bands and other music groups to keep his true love always in tune. So when he was asked to lend his voice to this wonderful theme song, he most willingly agreed. Why should music ever take a back seat?

Genevieve Goings

Lead Vocals

Born to musician parents, Genevieve has been creating music since childhood. Her recording career began in Hip-Hop & R&B in the San Francisco Bay Area, and she can currently be heard on over sixty-five albums. Recording voice-over work for video game and toy companies such as DreamWorks, The George Lucas Company, Hello Kitty, X-Box and Leapfrog expanded the artists' realm of performance, and ultimately led her into the world of Children's Television. Through a partnership built from doing voiceover work, "Choo Choo Soul" was born; a high-energy, soulful music album that expanded into a live-action & animation music video segment that airs daily on Disney Channel's "Disney Junior." Since Disney Channel's pre-school programming block was expanded into its own network, Genevieve has become the voice of the network, singing the Disney Junior Theme song, as well as various songs paired with original Disney animation. To date, Disney has produced twenty-three Choo Choo Soul videos, eight of which are re-makes of Disney Classics, which premiered in November of 2012. "Choo Choo Soul –with Genevieve" tours regularly across America and Canada. Genevieve is also the narrator of the Disney Princess stories on princess.disney.com.

Genevieve is currently living in the Los Angeles area, writing musical curriculum for one of Disney's newest ventures; schools in China that teach English to children. She began her partnership in 2008 and has written over 100 songs for the initiative, as well as developing and producing an entire Phonics program for the curriculum.

In the summer of 2012, Genevieve began working with Fisher-Price on a complete brand refresh of the "Little People" toy line. Originally approached to write a new theme song for the brand, her work with the Little People expanded as she wrote six original songs introducing each new character, voiced the Teacher, "Miss Hugg" in the new "Litte People Place" animated webseries, and scored/composed all of the music for the webisodes. Her partnership with Fisher-Price continues to grow with the release of an interactive iPad app featuring Genevieve's music and voice as the narrator, which was the top selling paid app of the day of its release. She is currently working on new music for the brand for 2014 & 2015, and is also scoring an additional webseries for the Fisher-Price brand "Imaginext."

From her many shows around the country, Genevieve noticed the true power that music has in motivating children. In April of 2010, she and her skilled team created "The Happy Hearts Club" a fitness/exercise show for kids. Originally pitched as a television show, Genevieve has since expanded the brand into a community outreach organization, mentoring tweens to perform the HHC exercise moves for crowds of children ages 4-8. Rehearsing with selected performers weekly, Genevieve helps to coach the Happy Hearts Club members to perform, and encourages the crowd to "Join The Club!" The Happy Hearts Club grows as children are exposed to the upbeat, fun, and futuristic dance moves, and the concept keeps them engaged in physical movement and fun!

While focusing primarily on Children's Entertainment and education, Genevieve also continues to write R&B & Pop music for artists in LA as well as working with artists and children on vocal production and voice coaching. She is working on her first independent Children's Album, which will release in early 2014.

Bryan Matheson

Guitarist

Bryan Matheson is the owner/operator of Skyline Studios, now in its 22nd year of operation. Bryan has had extensive experience on both sides of the glass, as a recording engineer and as a session singer, and has won numerous awards for his film TV, and radio work.

As a vocalist, Bryan has a long list of radio and TV and CD credits, as well as a 2006 Grammy nomination for his work with The Pacific Mozart Ensemble on the Leonard Bernstein Mass, performed and recorded with Kent Nagano at The Berlin Philharmonic. In November 2005, The Pacific Mozart Ensemble performed at Carnegie Hall with renowned New York composer Meredith Monk. He's sung with Bobby McFerrin, Bob Weir and The Marin Symphony.

Bryan is also the founder and CEO of iMusicast, which from 1999 to 2005 produced live webcasts from its concert venue in Oakland. By creating a unique hybrid of a webcast studio, recording studio, video sound stage and concert venue, iMusicast was able to bring DVD and streaming media production services within reach of independent record labels and artists. Through six years of concerts, iMusicast became the epicenter of a vital East Bay music scene, enjoying enormous support and goodwill from fans, local bands and national touring acts.

Bryan is a faculty member at San Francisco State University, and Chabot College, teaching recording technology, music business and live concert sound technology.

Lauren Jennings

Lauren Jennings, a graduate of Cornell University, is a young entrepreneur on the rise. She is the Co-Founder of Lauren Michelle Events, an event management, production and media relations firm located in San Francisco, California. Aside from producing memorable events, she is also a worship leader at Kingdom Builders Christian Fellowship in Oakland. Her passion lies in hospitality and using her God-given talents to give back to those in need.

www.laurenmichelleevents.com and
www.kingdombuilderscf.org.

Ari'el Rising Theme Song

We Got The Power To Change The World

Skyler Jett: co-writer, lyrics, vocal producer

Sylvester Burks: co-writer/co-producer

Shana Morrison: co-writer/lead vocals

Joey Blake: Background Arrangements

Leslie Ellis: Lead Vocals

Kim Fleming: Lead Vocals

Kudisan Kai: Lead Vocals

Ashley Lewis Background Vocals

Shania Wilcox: Background Vocals

Noel Braganza: Background Vocals

Lauren Jennings: Vocals

Taylor Burisse: Drums

Genevieve Goings

Lauren Jennings

Bryan Matheson: Guitar

conscious music ENTERTAINMENT

Ari'el Rising Empowerment Song

Ari'els Rising

Produced by Conscious Music Entertainment

Writer: Milliea Taylor McKinney

Vocalist: Candice Joy

Musicians: Patrick Stevens
Ray Monyana

"Good habits formed at youth make all the difference."

-Aristotle

Cubs Rising

Keep true to the dreams of your youth...

-Friedrich Schiller

The Reasons I Am Not Joining A Gang

There are no positives to being in a gang. According to the North Carolina Gang Investigators Association, gangs issue unique forms of writing, colors, symbols, and hand signs to identify themselves and create a sense of unity within their groups. Is that really worth risking going to prison, losing the trust of your family, going through initiations, or even losing your life?

To become a part of a gang, you have to go through an initiation process. Street gangs use a variety of acts of initiation such as being "beat in," "sexed in," or even committing murder. To be "beat in," the initiate or inductee has to endure a severe beating by a number of members for a certain amount of minutes. To be "sexed in," usually a female inductee has to have intercourse with someone they don't even have deep feelings for or even risking contracting a sexually transmitted disease. I especially wouldn't be able to kill someone innocent for no reason!

When you join a gang, you are pretty much starting yourself a record and putting yourself at risk of going to jail or prison. I have goals that I would like to accomplish such as going to college, pursuing a career, and one day starting a family. Being in a gang does not help me, in any way, accomplish my goals. If I had a criminal record, I especially wouldn't be able to pursue a career, or even get a decent job, all because I wanted to be a part of a group that has absolutely no benefits.

Lastly, if you join a gang, you could possibly lose the trust of your family. I would feel as if I let my family down. They have raised me to be a very successful young lady. The last thing I would want is to hurt them. I don't know how I or anyone else would be able to visit or even see their family in a jumpsuit and handcuffs. I wouldn't be able to live with myself. I would feel like I betrayed my family. They raised me right, so to them it would be a disappointment or like a slap in the face. I have no clue what I would do if I lost their trust. From writing this essay, my feelings are simply confirmed that I would not ever want to join a gang. Gangs are not beneficial for anyone. They are bad for society and promote violence. Being in a gang is not worth any of the consequences.

Charley Thompson
Grade 8

I Love Reading

I love reading. I read every day. I love reading the Bible. My favorite character is Mary. She loves Jesus, that's her son. She is always brave. Some books make me sad. Some books make me happy. I read to my sister and brother, but they don't listen. I am a good reader and go to the public library every day.

Na'Tya Elliot
Grade 1

I Love Writing

I love writing because that is what you have to do in school. You have to write when you do homework. Homework is the best thing that you should do in school. I am almost in second grade. Writing has helped me in school. I wouldn't come to school if I didn't like writing. I would learn by myself at home. But I do like writing, so I will go to school every day.

Raquil Rouzard
Grade 1

A Girl Police

I am four and going to Kindergarten. I can write the words. I can add the numbers. I like my iPad too. I will be a girl police and make the bad people behave and be nice. I will tell them no hitting and no shooting guns to make people die. Then they can have some friends.

Madison Greene
Grade Pre-K

The Roar of Thunder

Five years ago, my family adopted a family friend's dog named Thunder. Yeah, I know it's a funny name. Thunder was a Pit Bull Terrier that was already six years old. Even though he had such a tough name, he had the heart of a kitten. We were told he got his name from being so afraid of thunderstorms as a puppy. I was only three years old when we got Thunder. We became quick friends immediately. I think one of the reasons I loved him so much was because he would let me do just about anything to him, including riding him like a horse.

As I got older, we spent many nights together cuddled up as I read. He was just the sweetest dog I have ever been around. This past summer we noticed our eleven year old Thunder was not feeling well. When we took him to get checked, we found out he had cancer and needed to be put down. It was one of the saddest days of my life. I knew Thunder was hurting and I didn't want to see him suffer, so I gave him lots of hugs and told him I loved him. We had made lots of fun memories together!

Today, I still think about our long walks, cuddling up, and going for rides. And each time it storms and I hear the roar of thunder, I think of my Thunder and how much I will always remember him. He taught me how important it is to make good memories with people I care about. In memory of Thunder, we got a new puppy named Thor. My mom says that in mythology, Thor is the god of storms and lightning. This helps me never forget my sweet Thunder!

Camryn Thompson
Grade 4

Chick

I am as smart as a duck
I am as tall as a flower
I am as funny as a fish
I am as fast as a bunny
I am as bright as the sun

Ann Thorne Webb
Grade 2

Ms. Newton

Ms. Newton is great
Ms. Newton is loving
Ms. Newton is awesome
Ms. Newton is kind
Ms. Newton is nice
Ms. Newton is like my FRIEND!

Madalyn Walls
Grade 2
Her Loving Butterfly

You Can Do Anything

You can do anything
You can change the world
You can be a superstar
And be a first place girl
It does not matter what they say
It matters what you think of you
So keep on going do what you want to do

Caroline Whitley
Grade 2

Don't Give Up!

My name is Jada and I play softball. I also pitch. I got hit in the shin with the ball when somebody hit it and I didn't want to pitch anymore. We had more tournaments, but I just tried not to do good because I was scared. I've been practicing and I am pitching well now. So, what I am trying to say is...
    NEVER GIVE UP ON YOUR DREAMS!

Jada Lamm
Grade 4

Singing

I love singing. I started singing when I was two years old! A lot of my friends also liked singing. So we would just sing along with each other. Singing is like my superpower that I am really good at using. I was once in the school talent show. I was singing " Let it Go". When I was singing it, people said that I sang beautifully. It was very exciting to find out that I was really good at singing. I got the idea of singing from my mom. She liked singing when she was about my age.

I am so glad that my mom liked singing and not something weird. Something weird is that I sing almost everyday! But singing is my passion that I just can't stop. Singing is the number one thing that makes me happy. People say that they don't want to challenge me because I am so good. That really cheers me up! So that's basically why I love singing.

Emerson Fitch
Grade 3

Hard work, focus, and discipline is the way to have academic success. Sometimes you have to turn off the phone, computer, games, and Internet to make it happen. In the end it will work in your favor. My dream is to become a lawyer. I'll have my own law practice and prose-cute people that love breaking the law. I have a lot of years to go to school, but it will be worth it. Stay focused.

Emilee Yeager
Grade 7

Sometimes I wonder what the world will be like when I become a grown up. All I ever see is fighting, fussing, and mean people. There are too many wars in the military and on the street. I don't like gangs. They hurt and kill. I don't like white hate black and black hate white craziness. I try to study hard so I can become a counselor. I want to teach kids how to say no to the stuff that is not good for them. I know I can help. That's what I will do one day if I live to be a grown up.

Simone Lister
Grade 5

I hope somebody finds a cure for cancer and AIDS. People need a cure. I hope they make medicine one day that will make it all stop. They can test new ideas about cures on some animals to see if it works. If it works there won't have to be so many funerals. I went to a funeral last year. It was my Aunt. She had cancer and AIDS. Maybe I will be the one to find the medicine. I don't care. I will do it if I can.

Destiny Rush
Grade 4

True Friends

If today was my last day
I would like to thank you, my best friend
For being there from beginning to end
For always staying a true friend
We have gone through our ups and downs
And at the end of the day, you were still around
Now that our time together is coming to an end
Just know that you are my best friend
And I will love you even if this is the end

Masiah Amari Boyce-Hinnant
Grade 9

The Smart Leader

Lanie Jinks is a great student. She is very helpful to teachers and her classmates. Lanie is smart, athletic, and a natural leader. Good things are headed her way!

Submitted by Ms. S. Denice Newton
for Lanie Jinks
Grade 4

"Open the doors of opportunity to talent and virtue and they will do themselves justice."

-Ralph Waldo Emerson

Roaring Supporters & Testimonials

We would like to thank the following people for giving love and support to the Ari'el Rising book project and grassroots movement:

"I have had the opportunity to read several of S. Denice Newton's books and I must say, I couldn't turn the pages fast enough! Her writing is truly a "blow your hair back" reading experience that can be instrumental in the lives of every reader. She has a style that will make you forget your surroundings and become one with the characters in her books. I love her writing and I am a life-long fan of hers!"

~Kimmberly A. Carter-Nichols

I've had the privilege of reading Sandra's books and I have never read such books that drew me in as if I was there. I felt as if I took the journey with her. Her books captivated me to the point that I could not stop reading them. Sandra has a very special anointing from God that enables her to bring words to life. I can't wait to read her next publication. Much success Sandra, continue to let God use you in your writing!

~Patrena Pettaway

"S. Denice Newton is by far the greatest author I've ever known. Her writings have inspired even my own children to use the talent God gave them to write their own books. God has truly blessed her with a special gift and I am truly proud of all her accomplishments. May God continue to bless S. Denice and please, get every last copy of her books. You will be so glad you did! "

~Tierra Jennings

.

About S. Denice Newton

S. Denice Newton is an inspirational speaker, author, radio host, activist, and founder of Ari'el Rising Ministries, a grassroots movement designed to empower women and girls around the globe to pursue their purpose and aspirations.

Denice was born and educated in eastern North Carolina and enlisted in the U.S. Army as a communications specialist. Her military tours of duty include Germany, South Korea, Louisiana, Georgia, New Jersey, and other interesting locations. Denice studied communications at Regent University and UMUC. She later earned a certificate in radio broadcast from the American Broadcast School. As a radio host, she has interviewed such phenomenal individuals as Melba Moore, Antwon Fisher, Dr. John Carlos, Sheila Raye Charles, Joseph C. Phillips, Sheila E and the Escovedo family, Denise "Vanity" Matthews and many others. She has authored three books, "Two Continents One Hope, Interception, and the forthcoming women's empowerment book, Ari'el Rising."

As a speaker, she has been described as "passionate, compelling, authoritative, and captivating." As an activist, she has organized panel discussions on race relations, anti-bullying forums, and founded Generation BEFY Network (Black, Educated, Focused, Yielded) and the ROAR Network (Reach Out And Recover), in addition to Ari'el Rising.

Denice has worked in public and private schools for the past twenty years in various capacities, including behavior modification, instructional assistant, technology, and as a substitute teacher. She is an ambassador with the Africa Alive Education Foundation, a group whose mission include providing food, clean water, supplies, and education services to families around South Africa and those most affected by the AIDS pandemic. Her personal motto, "change is the only force powerful enough to break the backbone of inevitability," is one that she teaches and lives by daily.

Do you wish to rise? Begin by descending.
You plan a tower that will pierce the clouds?
Lay first the foundation of humility.

-Saint Augustine

CPSIA information can be obtained at www.ICGtesting.com
Printed in the USA
BVOW10s0326131114

374694BV00006B/9/P